T0306035

'We learn best through real stories, and this book offers us 40 riveting examples of actual ethical coaching dilemmas. What would you do if you were the coach? Sneak behind the scenes with the expert coaches as they navigate through very tricky waters. The answers may not be as simple as you think!'

Brian O. Underhill, *PhD, PCC, Founder and CEO,*
CoachSource, LLC

'This new book provides a wealth of material through a case study approach, exploring many of the contemporary ethical dilemmas faced by coaches today from AI to race and from gender to managing multiple stakeholders. This text will be an essential addition to every coach's library.'

Prof. Jonathan Passmore, *Henley Business School, UK*

'What I loved about this book is that, at the same time as clearly having serious, theoretical or research-based underpinnings, these case studies are immensely readable and the lessons to be learned from them are clearly spelled out. I love a good case study and here we are spoiled for choice. Their strength is the way that they bring theory to life. We can talk about ethics in coaching and supervision at a conceptual level until the cows come home but the learning really begins when our CEO client walks into the coaching space at 10am and we can smell whisky on their breath. What do we actually do? The case studies that make up this very helpful book explore both straight-forward and very complex issues and cover one-to-one coaching, team coaching, and supervision in both internal and external coaching scenarios. The sheer breadth of ethical challenges presented is ultra-stimulating and a great way of helping the reader to examine and explore their own prejudices, biases, beliefs, and values and how they affect the decisions we take in and outside the coaching/supervision room. The later chapters explore the ethical challenges that the digital age has brought with it – managing digital records, avoiding data breaches, the role of AI, etc. – and handling challenges around diversity in its many forms. Very thoughtful stuff. This book would be a worthwhile addition to any coach's bookshelf.'

Katharine St John-Brooks, *Author of* Internal Coaching:
The Inside Story

'This book represents an important contribution in the exploration of ethics in coaching. The introductory chapter explores how learning in coach education and development is significantly enhanced using case studies. Chapter 2 provides a thorough summary of how case studies have been used as a learning tool in well-established fields of study and offers the coach practitioner an in-depth understanding of case formulation, why it matters, and how the task is approached. The authors caution us there is no one right way, and they offer the reader several frameworks that allow a coach to maximise in-depth learning from a case study whether in the midst of a coach education experience, coach supervision, or self-directed learning.'

Pam McLean, *Co-founder, CKO, Hudson Institute of Coaching*

'Ethics in coaching is core to the sustainability of the coaching profession and the sustainable practice of a coach. This ethical case studies book is practical, useful, and essential reading for coaches and coaching buyers. The book may invite coaches to reflect upon their previous and ongoing practice and help them to raise awareness and take charge of their development and refine their coaching practice.'

Dr Badri Bajaj, *Coaching thought leader, President – ICF Delhi NCR Charter Chapter 2019–2021 and 2021–2023*

'Kurt Lewin famously noted that nothing is so practical as a good theory. A very close second to that would be good quality case studies to learn from experience, and this book hits it out of the park in this regard.'

Aaron Jarden, *Associate Professor, Centre for Wellbeing Science, University of Melbourne, Australia*

Ethical Case Studies for Coach Development and Practice

Providing both a depth and breadth of examples of ethical dilemmas which coaches may face as part of their practice, this book is the first comprehensive handbook of case studies in the field, supporting coaches in developing their ethical awareness and competence.

The world of coaching has become increasingly complex over the past two decades. While the professional bodies have all released codes of conduct or ethical guidelines, these at best deal with general principles and serve as a point of reference for reflection. *Ethical Case Studies for Coach Development and Practice* is an essential accompaniment for coaches. Written by seasoned practitioners, this companion coaching case study book offers a more personal perspective on ethics in practice. Its simple structured layout and focus on ethical dilemmas make it an attractive course supplementary text and resource for practitioners. Divided into two sections, the guide explores the following themes: ethical development, coach education, one-to-one coaching, individual and group supervision, team coaching, external coaching assignments, internal coaching, digital and AI coaching, power in coaching, and the promotion of coaching.

This book is a vital resource for coaches at all levels of experience in their professional coach journey, and for those with more experience in the development of ethical thinking and practice such as supervisors, consultants in leadership development, human resource professionals, and students on coaching postgraduate programmes and in private coach education.

Wendy-Ann Smith is a coaching psychologist, researcher, and educator. She is the Director at her coaching boutique Eclorev, co-founder of the Coaching Ethics Forum, founding editor of the *Journal of Coaching Ethics*, and is a Visiting Fellow, Centre of Positive Psychology, Buckinghamshire New University, UK. Her recent publications are *Positive Psychology Coaching in the Workplace* and *The Ethical Coaches' Handbook: A Guide to Developing Ethical Maturity in Practice*.

Eva Hirsch Pontes is an independent coach and a pioneer in coaching supervision in Latin America. In her previous career in the corporate world, she worked for over 25 years as an executive in the shipping industry, holding several key positions including director and board member.

Dumisani Magadlela is an executive team coach from South Africa. Dumi is co-principal at The Coaching Centre (TCC) and is core faculty at the Global Team Coaching Institute (GTCI). At the time of writing, Dumi was chair of the International Coaching Federation (ICF)'s Global Enterprise Board.

David Clutterbuck is one of the last survivors of the original pioneers of modern coaching and mentoring. Author or co-author of more than 75 books, he co-founded the European Mentoring and Coaching Council and leads a global network of coach educators, Coaching and Mentoring International.

Ethical Case Studies for Coach Development and Practice

A Coach's Companion

Edited by Wendy-Ann Smith,
Eva Hirsch Pontes,
Dumisani Magadlela, and
David Clutterbuck

Routledge
Taylor & Francis Group

LONDON AND NEW YORK

Designed cover image: © Getty Images

First published 2024
by Routledge
4 Park Square, Milton Park, Abingdon, Oxon OX14 4RN

and by Routledge
605 Third Avenue, New York, NY 10158

Routledge is an imprint of the Taylor & Francis Group, an informa business

British Library Cataloguing-in-Publication Data
A catalogue record for this book is available from the British Library

ISBN: 978-1-032-51963-0 (hbk)
ISBN: 978-1-032-51962-3 (pbk)
ISBN: 978-1-003-40465-1 (ebk)

DOI: 10.4324/b23351

Typeset in Times New Roman
by Deanta Global Publishing Services, Chennai, India

Contents

Acknowledgements

When novices become masters.

There is something sweet and gratifying about working with colleagues, where you see them transition from gingerly treading into a new professional mode of working to watching them fly in their competency and confidence – becoming masters at the task at hand. This has been my experience working with Eva and Dumi during this project. Thank you to you both for a delightful collaboration. Finally, thank you to David for his continued support in new endeavours that will have a lasting legacy for the field of coaching.

Finally much gratitude to the numerous coaches and coach supervisors who have collaborated with us to bring these ethical coaching case studies to the coaching community.

Wendy-Ann Smith

When I received Wendy-Ann and David's invitation to collaborate with them and Dumi to co-edit this book, I felt thrilled, honoured, humbled, and challenged. My immediate positive response was inspired by my granddaughter Julia, who reminds me every day of the wonder of venturing out into the world with curiosity and the sheer joy of learning. My gratitude to them all for their encouragement and mentoring.

Eva Hirsch Pontes

Deep appreciation for the collaboration, with trust, confidence, and consistent encouragement to step up and show up with tight turn-arounds. Great learning that will come in handy for future projects.

Grateful.

Dumisani Magadlela

When a group of people from different countries and cultures come together with a shared purpose to create something new, it's always an adventure. Thanks to the whole team and the many contributors for joining us on this adventure into coaching ethics.

David Clutterbuck

Editors

Wendy-Ann Smith, Eclorev Coaching and Consulting, France. Wendy-Ann is a coaching psychologist, researcher and educator. She is the Director at her coaching boutique Eclorev, co-founder of the Coaching Ethics Forum, founding editor of the *Journal of Coaching Ethics*, Visiting Fellow, Centre for Positive Psychology, Buckinghamshire New University, UK, and Ethics group discussion lead at the Institute of Coaching. Her recent publications are *Positive Psychology Coaching in the Workplace* (2021) and *The Ethical Coaches' Handbook: A Guide to Developing Ethical Maturity in Practice* (2023); she has also authored various chapters on coaching psychology, positive psychology, and ethics in practice. Wendy-Ann regularly coaches a small number of one-to-one clients. She designs and delivers lectures, training, and workshops internationally in a variety of settings including universities. Her interest is supporting the development of coaches through coaching psychology, positive psychology, and increasing ethical awareness in practice. In her other time she enjoys her cat, photography, painting, and exploring.

Eva Hirsch Pontes, Phoenix Coach, Brazil. Eva is a licensed psychologist and earned her coach certification through the Hudson Institute of Coaching, California. Eva holds an MCC credential from ICF and is an accredited supervisor with EMCC (ESIA). Eva works as an executive and team coach, coach supervisor, conflict mediator, and invited faculty at several business schools in Brazil. Eva has also been actively involved in volunteer activities for ICF: she integrated the first board of ICF/Chapter Brazil, and later held a seat on the advisory board of that chapter. She also served on the local ethics committee and worked as ICF an assessor for over 12 years. Before becoming a coach in 2006, Eva worked for 25+ years as an executive in the shipping industry, holding several key positions including director and board member.

Dumisani Magadlela is founder and managing executive of Afrika Coaching, a private coaching and consulting firm operating from Johannesburg, South Africa. He is Vice Principal at The Coaching Centre (TCC), a leading coach-training school based in South Africa. He is an executive coach, team coach, Ubuntu coach, and has been a coach trainer for over 16 years. Dumi's areas of coaching interest include integral practice, Ubuntu coaching, gestalt practice, and conscious human connection. He is also faculty at Stellenbosch University Business School's MPhil in Management Coaching programme, and is core faculty at the Global Team Coaching Institute (GTCI), and Clutterbuck Coaching and Mentoring International (CCMI). At the time of writing this, Dumi was the global chair of the International Coaching Federation's (ICF) Global Enterprise Board, the largest body of coaches world-wide.

David Clutterbuck, Coaching and Mentoring International, United Kingdom. David is one of the original pioneers of coaching and mentoring and co-founder of the European Mentoring and Coaching Council. Visiting professor of coaching and mentoring at several universities, he is author or co-author of more than 75 books, including *Coaching the Team at Work*. He was lead coach in the ethical coach project in Ethiopia and facilitates ethical mentoring programmes within the UK National Health Service. He is practice lead at Coaching and Mentoring International.

Contributors

Caroline Adams Miller, Caroline Miller Coaching LLC, United States of America. Caroline is an executive coach who has been a PCC credentialed by the International Coach Federation for more than 20 years. As one of the first graduates of the Master of Applied Positive Psychology degree programme at the University of Pennsylvania, Caroline is known as one of the pioneers who integrated the science of flourishing and its connection to the science of goal setting into the coaching profession. Her global bestselling books, including *Creating Your Best Life* and *Getting Grit*, are textbooks in many coaching programmes, and she has keynoted at numerous coaching conferences, taught in business schools including the Wharton Executive Education programme, and worked with CEOs and senior leaders in organisations all over the world.

Carrie Arnold, PhD, MCC, Faculty at Fielding Graduate University, United States of America. Carrie is an educator, speaker, private practice coach, consultant, facilitator, and author. She wrote *Silenced and Sidelined: How Women Leaders Find Their Voices and Break Barriers*. Her post-doc research is also on voice and silencing and how women recover from voice oppression. Since 2011, she has owned and operated her own consulting business, The Willow Group. She obtained her coach education at Georgetown University and her supervision education at the Coaching Supervision Academy. She is an International Coaching Federation Master Certified Coach who works primarily with federal government, healthcare, and education clients. She holds a BA in psychology, an MA in organisational management, and a PhD in human development.

Inga Arianna Bielinska, United States of America. Inga is an International Coaching Federation Master Certified Coach, ACTC team coach, mentor coach, and ESIA coach supervisor. She works globally with clients who undergo change, struggle with managing remote and culturally diverse teams, find communication challenging, or wish to progress to executive positions. During her career, she gained experience as a managing partner, business owner, consultant, and a board member in non-profit organisations, which allows her to bring hands-on, credible experience to her work. Inga has been working in different countries that can contribute to her understanding of cultural diversity and its role in managing people, collaborating, and communicating with internal or external stakeholders. Currently she lives in Silicon Valley, California, where she globally supports engineers and leaders in dealing with the challenges of fast-paced VUCA reality. She has published two books for leaders in Polish and regularly writes articles for American issues of *Forbes* and *Newsweek*.

Anne Calleja, The Leading Business Limited, United Kingdom. Anne is managing director of The Leading Business with over 25 years' experience as an executive coach and master coach supervisor and is accredited with the Association for Coaching (AC). She is an honorary member of APECS. Anne is also an accredited and registered (BACP UKCP) psychotherapist, clinical supervisor; she supervises cross-professionally. Anne is actively involved in the engagement and development of those interested in strategy for coaching supervision for the AC. She blends proven business acumen with psychotherapeutic approaches to provide a unique approach to executive coaching, personal coaching, senior team development, change management, and high-level strategic direction. Anne holds an MSc in management science and is clinically trained with diplomas in psychotherapy; her early career was in psychology, management development, and learning.

Ingela Camba Ludlow is an independent coach, Mexico. Ingela has made the mind and human relations her life project. She is a coach supervisor, systemic team coach, and executive coach. Since 2020 she has been faculty in the largest virtual systemic team coaching training programme with WBECS. She is currently doing a doctorate in contemporary psychoanalysis with a specialty in neuropsychoanalysis. This time, the object of study will be the pandemic and the social effects of confinement. She is author of the book *Humor in Psychoanalysis and Coaching Supervision: From Life to Interventions* published by Routledge in 2022, aimed at helping professionals and the public in general to find in humour a way to relate to the world and face the adversities of life. Based in Mexico she also writes regularly in national newspapers and has appeared in radio and TV.

Francine Campone, EdD, MCC, F. Campone Coaching and Consulting, United States of America. Francine is editor (Americas) for the *International Coaching Psychology Review* and a member of EMCC, ICF, and the Global Supervisors' Network. Francine is the lead editor for *Coaching Supervision: Voices from the Americas* (2022) and co-edited *Innovations in Leadership Coaching Research and Practice*. Her research publications include a case study on the coaching/psychotherapy boundary; the impact of life events on coaches and their coaching; and book chapters on adult learning theories in coaching, reflective learning for coaches, coaching in the adult workplace, and trends in coaching-related research. As principal for F. Campone Coaching and Consulting, Francine offers coach supervision, mentoring, and coach training.

Michael Cavanagh, Deputy Director, Coaching Psychology Unit, University of Sydney, Australia. Michael is an internationally recognised academic, practitioner, and consultant in the fields of leadership and coaching psychology. Michael's work focuses on preparing leaders, teams, and coaches to work in complex settings. As an academic he is the deputy director of the Coaching Psychology Unit at the University of Sydney, where he and Tony Grant established the world's first master's degree in coaching psychology. He is also a visiting professor at Middlesex University (UK). He has coached leaders and managers at all levels from a diverse range of industries. Along with numerous publications in the peer-reviewed press, Michael is the principal author of the Standards Australia *Handbook of Organisational Coaching*. He is also the Australian editor of the *International Coaching Psychology Review*. Michael's passion is assisting leaders, organisations, and individuals to understand and address complex challenges in ways that increase the sustainability of the organisation, its people, and the planet.

Jonathan Drury, United Kingdom. Jonathan is a professional dialogue facilitator, consultant, trainer and therapeutic coach specialising in autism, neurodiversity and regenerative approaches to combat systemic trauma. He is the co-founder of Dialogica and creator of Mindfulness for Autism® and the Autism Dialogue Approach®.

Ramón Estrada, Spain, is an international Founder CEO coach and entrepreneur, and believes a company's success is rooted in leaders undertaking deep inner work. His entrepreneurial journey includes launching seven companies, with one notably recognized for innovation and growth. Ramón, an MBA from IESE Business School, further refined his expertise through Harvard and Berkeley's private equity and venture capital programs. Certified as an ontological coach, leadership, and executive coach, his credentials span prestigious institutions like Newfield Network, Berkeley, and the HeartMath Institute. A fellow of the Institute of Coaching and the RSA, Ramón is steadfast in his commitment to advocating for ethical leadership and pioneering change, values reflected in his vibrant coaching career and influential writings. Born in Mexico City, he resides in Barcelona, contributing to the global conversation on ethical business practices and leadership from Spain.

Rosie Evans-Krimme, CoachHub, Germany. Rosie is a coach and behavioural scientist, specialised in digital coaching. She is co-author of the 5P model of coaching industry development and regularly writes and speaks about digital coaching, coaching ethics, mental health and wellbeing. Rosie leads the Innovation Lab and Behavioural Science team at CoachHub.

Alexandra J.S. Fouracres, University of East London and Capgemini Invent, Denmark. Alexandra is a cybersecurity manager in addition to working as a coaching psychologist and academic. Her career spans over 20 years of leadership experience in financial services, fraud prevention, and currently cybersecurity. Alexandra holds an MSc in applied positive psychology and coaching psychology from the University of East London. She is a published researcher and author of *Cybersecurity for Coaches and Therapists: A Practical Guide for Protecting Client Data*, published by Routledge.

Andrea Giraldez-Hayes, PhD, University of East London, United Kingdom. Andrea is an experienced chartered psychologist, coach, supervisor, and consultant. She is the director of the MSc in Applied Positive Psychology and Coaching Psychology at the University of East London's School of Psychology. Andrea also works with a range of clients in the public and private sectors and offers regular supervision sessions to coaching psychologists. She is a renowned public speaker at conferences in Europe and Latin America, has co/authored many books and chapters, and has published in peer-reviewed journals. Her main research interests are the boundaries between coaching and therapy and the use of arts and creativity in positive psychology, coaching psychology, and supervision. She is currently the chair of the British Psychological Society's Coaching Psychology Training Committee.

Sam Isaacson, Coachtech Ltd., United Kingdom. Sam is an enthusiastic coach, coach supervisor, and adviser on coaching technology and internal coaching. He is chair of England's Coaching Professional apprenticeship trailblazer group, incorporating more than a hundred employers of coaches and several big professional bodies. Achieving approval from the UK Secretary of State for Education in 2020, this qualification is now one of England's most popular. A thought leader on the cutting edge of coaching technology, he was one of the first in the world to offer coaching in virtual reality, he actively works with the professional bodies in their work around digital coaching platforms and artificial intelligence, and he has written books and a large number of articles on the topic. In 2022 he was recognised by evoach as a CoachingTech Pioneer. He lives in London with his wife and four sons, and also writes interactive fiction books.

Yannick Jacob, Cambridge University and International Centre for Coaching Supervision, School of Positive Transformation, Germany. Yannick is a coach, coach trainer, and supervisor with master's degrees in existential coaching and applied positive psychology. He is part of the teaching faculties at Cambridge University and the International Centre for Coaching Supervision, and he's the course director of the School of Positive Transformation's Accredited Certificate in Integrative Coaching [bit.ly/CoachingCertificate], for which he gathered many of the world's most influential coaches. Formerly programme leader of the MSc Coaching Psychology at the University of East London, Yannick now presents at conferences internationally and his book, *An Introduction to Existential Coaching*, was published by Routledge. Yannick is the founder and host of Yannick's Coaching Lab which gives novice and seasoned coaches the opportunity to witness experienced coaches live in action, and he is the host of Animas Center for Coaching's popular *Coaching Uncaged* podcast, as well as his own podcasts *Talking about Coaching* and *Talking about Coaching and Psychedelics*.

Rob Kemp, Barefoot Coaching, United Kingdom. After a corporate career in the life sciences sector, Rob emerged as an independent full-time coach some two decades ago. After early coach training, Rob went on to complete an MSc (Sheffield Hallam) and then a doctorate in coaching and mentoring (Oxford Brookes, DCM). Rob is head of Accredited Coach Training with Barefoot Coaching.

David A. Lane, Professional Development Foundation, United Kingdom. As well as contributing to research and the professional development of coaching, David has coached in a wide range of organisations including major consultancies, multinationals, and public sector and government bodies. He runs work-based master's and doctorate degrees for experienced coaches. He was chair of the British Psychological Society Register of Psychologists Specialising in Psychotherapy and convened the EFPA group on psychotherapy. David has served on committees of the BPS, CIPD, WABC, and EMCC. His contributions to counselling psychology led to the senior award of the BPS for "Outstanding Scientific Contribution." He was honoured by the British Psychological Society for Distinguished Contribution to Professional Psychology, by Surrey University for Life-Time Achievement, and by Coaching at Work similarly. He is a fellow of APECS.

Pamela A. Larde, PhD, Institute of Coaching, Anderson University, United States of America. Pamela a professor of leadership at Anderson University, coach, author, and business owner, is committed to engaging in the work of advancing the reach and commitment of the coaching profession to serve and build up heart-centred leaders around the world. Her coach training academy is among the first black female-owned ICF ACTP accredited coaching schools in the world. She is also the Director of Education at the Institute of Coaching. Her research focuses on race and gender dynamics, self-motivation, joy, resilience, and posttraumatic growth.

Jo Leymarie, Walden, France. Jo is a certified professional coach (PCC) with ICF. Jo has significant experience supporting managers and teams during transformations, whether these be internal restructuring programmes or market-led disruptions. She is passionate about building cohesive and productive teams and about motivation and humanism in the workplace. Her approach is based around interpersonal relations, team, and system dynamics. Her core subjects include leadership and personal alignment, organisational change, and agility. She has worked with a large variety of organisations and industries on the creation and roll-out of collective intelligence programmes for high potential, multi-cultural coaching for international managers, and team mergers following restructuring. She also works with clients on an individual basis to further their professional development at key moments in their careers. Jo has 25 years of business experience setting up and managing profit centres for international companies in both service and technology Industries.

Mongezi C. Makhalima, Africa Centre for Work-Based Learning, South Africa. Mongezi is an organisation development specialist, organisational learning expert, author, TEDx speaker, and executive coach with 30 years' experience of working with organisations and leadership in corporates and NGOs. He's recently been named one of the Top 50 Global Leadership Coaches as well as a Top 40 Global Culture Change Champion. He is currently the chairperson of the Africa Board for Coaching, Consulting and Coaching Psychology (ABCCCP), and also sits as non-executive director on several boards in the NGO, film, and music sectors. Mongezi serves as a faculty member in the Faculty of Commerce, Law and Management of the University of the Witwatersrand as well as the Wits Business School, teaching master's and advanced programmes in leadership and coaching. Mongezi has presented and written widely on the subject of coaching, mentoring, and leadership and works with clients globally and locally.

Alissa M. Manolescu, Idealis, United States of America. Alissa is an organisational psychologist and executive coach who partners with organisations to create business impact through leadership assessment, coaching, and development solutions. In her role as Director of Leadership Development at Idealis, she leads the design, development and implementation of strategies to transform leaders, teams, and organizations for clients across industries and sectors. She is an advocate for workplace diversity, equity and inclusion (DE&I) in STEM, having presented at national psychology conferences and published on the topic. Alissa holds an MA degree in industrial-organisational psychology from the University of Georgia, and an executive coaching diploma from the Goizueta Business School at Emory University.

F.K. Tia Moin, University of Reading, United Kingdom. Tia is an organisational and coaching psychologist with over 20 years of international consulting experience developing leaders and professionals. As an elected committee member of the Division of Coaching Psychology – British Psychological Society, she is closely involved in developing and shaping the profession of coaching psychology and prides herself on professional, ethical, and evidence-based psychological practice. She is currently researching coaching for diversity and inclusion through the University of Reading, UK.

Haesun Moon, PhD, University of Toronto, Institute of Coaching at Harvard Medical School Affiliate, Canadian Centre for Brief Coaching, Canada.

Haesun is a communication scientist, an educator, and the author of *Coaching A to Z: The Extraordinary Use of Ordinary Words* and several collaborative books, including *Thriving Women, Thriving World* and *Foundations of Brief Coaching*, a short handbook for professional coaches. Haesun received her PhD in adult education and community development from the University of Toronto. She believes that conversations can change the world, and she defines this process as hosting dialogic conditions in which people participate to imagineer and perform their preferred change. Her academic and professional research in coaching dialogues and pedagogy from the University of Toronto led to development of a simple coaching model, Dialogic Orientation Quadrant (DOQ). Haesun currently teaches brief coaching at the University of Toronto and serves as executive director at the Canadian Centre for Brief Coaching.

Kim Morgan, Barefoot Coaching Ltd and Visiting Research Fellow University of Chester, United Kingdom. Kim is the Founder and CEO of Barefoot Coaching Ltd. She designed and launched the Barefoot ICF Accredited/Postgraduate Certificate Coach Training Course in 2001. Under Kim's leadership Barefoot Coaching has established an international reputation as one of the most trusted and respected providers of coach training. Kim's vision remains the same, to make the world a brighter place through exceptional coaching, by providing world-class training for coaches who want to make a difference, and by delivering coaching to individuals and organisations looking for real and lasting change. Kim's passion to spread the word about coaching has resulted in two best-selling books, *The Coach's Casebook* (2015) and *The Coach's Survival Guide* (2019). Kim writes a monthly coaching column in *Psychologies Magazine* and is a sought-after conference speaker on all things coaching related.

Colm Murphy, Praesta Ireland, Ireland. Colm is a master-accredited executive and team coach at Praesta Ireland with over 20 years' experience of designing and delivering coaching and leadership development programmes to global audiences across the public and private sectors. He is a co-editor of *The Team Coaching Casebook* (Open University Press). He completed his doctoral research on "The Contribution of Team Coaching to Team Effectiveness." Colm is a faculty member of Global Team Coaching Institute and University College Dublin's Executive Development.

Monica Murray, caratt, Canada. Monica Murray is an ICF Associate Certified Coach (ACC) with a career spanning over 25 years in a variety of roles and industries including big four public accounting firms, publicly traded global companies, start-ups, and not for profits. From finance to HR to CEO, she's also built and run her own companies developing her entrepreneurial mindset. Monica's current company, caratt, works with organisations coaching their leaders as they transition into new roles. A passionate advocate for diversity and gender equality, Monica spends her time on various boards and committees supporting these initiatives. When not at work, you will find Monica sailing with her husband getting some fresh sea air. She lives in Vancouver, BC, Canada.

David Matthew Prior, MCC, BCC, ACTC, Getacoach.com, United States of America. David brings 20+ years of organisational coaching experience working with global executive and senior leadership across a diversity of industries including financial services, insurance, communications, public relations, music, fashion, consumer goods, technology, consulting firms, mining, biotech, shipping, health care, and world agencies. His approach to leadership development is focused on performance with integrity to align the business, organisation, teams, and leadership to simultaneously hold an authentic public and private stance in work and life; where the two meet is where the integral leader lives. It is this space that leaders and their teams inhabit that requires truth-telling, safety, structure, and communication mastery. David has had the honour of structuring and teaching in the organisational coaching programme at Columbia University, guiding and coaching more than 1,000 senior leaders in more than 30 countries, training 5,000+ executive coaches, and creating results for more than 100 organisations.

Sasha E. Radin, PhD, Sasha Radin Coaching, United States of America. Sasha is a transformational coach who uses a deep, intuitive, and integrated approach that draws on mind, body, and emotional intelligence to coach leaders in different sectors. Sasha also has over two decades of global experience in the international security and humanitarian sectors. Her work with the US Army, the US Navy, the International Committee for the Red Cross, academic institutions, and non-governmental organisations has taken her around the world. She continues as a consultant, providing advice on building digital publications and using her subject-matter expertise in international law and security. Sasha holds a PhD from Melbourne University Law School, an LLM from the University of Amsterdam, and a BA from Harvard University and is a certified transformational coach through the Association for Coaching.

Annalise Roache, Auckland University of Technology and The Coaching Toolbox, New Zealand. Annalise is a positive psychology practitioner, credentialed coach, mentor, educator, and wellbeing researcher. She works with emerging leaders, managers, business owners, coaches, and individuals in personal and workplace settings. Favouring an evidence-based, solution-focused approach informed by the fields of coaching psychology and positive psychology, she develops psycho-educational short courses and online wellbeing content to promote knowledge sharing and active practice to support personal transformation. Annalise is co-president of the New Zealand Association of Positive Psychology and author of *The Ethical Guidelines for Positive Psychology Practice* (2019; 2021). She holds a master of science (MAPPCP, Applied Positive Psychology and Coaching Psychology) from the University of East London. Annalise is a doctoral candidate at Auckland University of Technology. Her research focuses on lay conceptions of wellbeing and how these compare to academic theory and models to bridge the gap and ensure effective policy, programme, and intervention design and delivery.

Charline S. Russo, PhD, EdD, University of Pennsylvania, United States of America. Charline is a member of the University of Pennsylvania Organizational Dynamics Coaching and Consulting faculty. She was awarded the 2018 University Award for Distinguished Teaching in Professional Graduate Programs. She is Chair of the Board and President of the Graduate School Alliance for Education in Coaching (GSAEC) that focuses on strengthening and promoting graduate-level coach education and research globally. She has held executive positions in pharmaceutical and biotechnology companies building Global Learning Centers of Excellence for R&D. Charline founded CampoMarzio Group, a consulting firm that fosters trusted, collaborative relationships with organisations and leaders to create, drive, and sustain major transformations through tailored consulting and coaching services. Charline received her BA in history and psychology and MBA from Rutgers University and her MA and EdD in organisational leadership from Columbia University. Her publications include coaching case studies and *Cohort Programming and Learning for Adults: Improving Educational Experiences for Adult Learners*, co-authored with I.M. Saltiel.

Silvina M. Spiegel, Genesis Coaching, Brazil. Silvina is a multi-cultural ontological and executive coach, supervisor-mentor coach, certified team coach, and coach trainer, with coaching experience in Spanish, Portuguese, Hebrew, and English. She is also a Coaching Clinic® certified trainer, a Co-development® facilitator, and a Symbolon Reflection Method® Coaching Expert and a Blanchard® Leadership Coach. Silvina represented Latin America in the ICF NALAC (North America, Latin America and the Caribbean) forum. Their mission was to integrate the collaboration between the regions on matters such as DEIJ&B and volunteer engagement and succession. She was the Brazilian representative 2020–22 for the Latin America Forum and served as ICF Brazil Chapter vice president in 2020. Silvina is passionate about human interaction and development. She works as an independent coach and facilitator for several world-leading consulting companies, training and coaching executives from all over the world, supporting them in the attainment of their goals. She has held a PCC credential issued by the International Coaching Federation since 2015 and is currently working towards her MCC. She has also authored on ethics in coaching.

Marie Stopforth, The Performance Equation, United Kingdom. Marie is a British Psychological Society (BPS) chartered coaching psychologist and sport and exercise psychologist. She was instrumental in supporting the Division of Coaching Psychology to gain divisional status in 2021, and worked as the chief assessor for coaching psychology within the BPS. Marie originally trained as a sport and exercise psychologist, and worked in academia for around 15 years before becoming a self-employed coaching psychologist in 2019. She now works with individuals, teams, and organisations to improve performance and wellbeing through coaching. She is also a coach supervisor, and delivers training in coaching psychology through the School of Coaching Psychology. Marie is passionate about the intersection between performance and wellbeing. She holds a PhD in group dynamics in sport from the University of Chichester, UK.

Eve Turner, Fellow at University of Southampton, Faculty at Professional Development Foundation Global Faculty Advisors, United Kingdom. Eve Turner is a coach and supervisor, researcher, and author, working globally. Her interests include ethics, contracting, and coaching/supervision and social issues especially climate and ecological change. Eve has authored or co-authored several books, chapters, and articles including *The Ethical Coaches' Handbook: A Guide to Developing Ethical Maturity in Practice* (2023), *Ecological and Climate-Conscious Coaching: A Companion Guide to Evolving Coaching Practice* (2023), *Systemic Coaching* (2020), and *The Heart of Coaching Supervision: Working with Reflection and Self-Care* (2019). She is immediate past chair of The Association of Professional Executive Coaching and Supervision and volunteers extensively including for several professional bodies. Eve co-founded the Climate Coaching Alliance (CCA) which now has more than 2,300 members worldwide, and founded the first Global Supervisors' Network in 2016. Eve's previous roles included senior leadership in broadcasting in the BBC and working in music.

Lorraine S. Webb, President of LS Webb Coaching and HR Consulting, United States of America. Lorraine brings strategic insight and openness to her executive coaching practice. With more than 25 years of human resources experience in the utility, pharmaceutical, and manufacturing industries, Lorraine has grown to be a trusted coach and advisor providing counsel to C-suite executives and senior management. As a hallmark of her career, she built a robust coaching culture that resulted in her organisation being cited as an "Employer of Choice." Lorraine is passionately committed to helping people identify those behaviours that will lead to their success. Prior to launching her executive coaching practice, Lorraine served as the vice president of human resources and organisational development. She spearheaded the effort to develop a strong talent bench which included creating leadership development programmes, including coaching, for both emerging and senior leaders.

Carol Whitaker, Whitaker Consulting, United Kingdom. Carol is an AC Accredited Master Coach Supervisor and has over 15 years' experience supervising both 1 to 1 and groups including Oxford Brookes university students doing their MA in Coaching and Mentoring Practice, ILM7 Executive Coaching PG Cert, and their internal Coaching programmes. Her portfolio covers coaching, team/group coaching and coach supervision, mentoring and facilitation. Her early career was in Human Resources; she has experience at Board level, various NED roles, and an MBA. She has co-authored two 5* rated books: *Coaching Supervision: A Practical Guide for Supervisees* (2016) and *Peer Supervision in Coaching & Mentoring: A Versatile Guide for Reflective Practice* (2018), both published by Routledge. She has also published a Peer Supervision chapter in *Coaching & Mentoring Supervision: Theory and Practice* 2nd Edition (2021).

Part One

Working with case studies for coach ethical development

Chapter 1

Ethics case studies for coach education and development

Wendy-Ann Smith and David Clutterbuck

Introduction

Trust and integrity are the foundations of the relational process of all helping professions, supporting the perception of credibility. Coach credibility has been determined to be a strong active element of coaching efficacy (de Haan, 2021). Ethics underpin trust, credibility and integrity. Ethics are a combination of interweaving morals, values, beliefs, intuition and principles that help guide (Carroll et al., 2013; Iordanou et al., 2016; Smith et al., 2023) and encourage an approach to decision-making that invites a spirit of inquiry to understand circumstances so that the rule-of-law, functional and fairness legitimacy is upheld (Breakey, 2020). Ethics help to protect individuals, institutions and society and should be the guiding principle for every perspective of coaching. This chapter will explore how ethics can be learned, the preconditions and mechanisms underpinning adult ethical development, awareness and decision-making, professional development practices and ethics in coach education. A case is made for the use of 'real life' and pre-defined examples – case studies – as a tool in coach education and supervision to facilitate ethical competency, capability and capacity and bridge the gap from '*Knowing to Doing*'. Completing this chapter are considerations for the coach educator, a case study and reflective questions.

Ethical development

Can ethics be learned?

James Rest found that young adults (in their 20s and 30s) experience major changes to their capacity to problem-solve to deal with ethical dilemmas, and that this was linked to how they perceive society and their role in society (Velasquez and colleagues, 1987). The degree of change is directly linked to their formal education on ethics and morality, and other influences such as parents, broader family members, teachers, religious organisations, childhood and adolescent groups, Scouts and Girl Guides and their equivalents in various cultures. If you do not learn to be ethical pre-adult, is it too late? Can adults learn how to be ethical? Some may argue 'No' (e.g. Kristol, 1987; Irving, 1989). However, many across the ages argue 'Yes'.

DOI: 10.4324/b23351-2

Philosophers[1] such as Socrates argued that ethics consists of knowing what we ought to do, and such knowledge can be taught.

Stages of ethical development

Kohlberg and colleagues (1975, 1983) suggest moral and ethical development doesn't form all at once, but in general levels of development. The levels are not fixed but rather one transitions in and out of each as one develops and matures with greater self-understanding. The levels are as follows.

Preconventional: Right and wrong, reward and punishment or the avoidance of unpleasant experiences are learned from what authority figures say and do. For example, if you do not do your homework, you will not be able to go out and play.

Conventional: Right and wrong are defined by the adoption and internalisation of wider group and societal norms and laws. For example, family, friends, religion, corporate culture or even gang culture.

Postconventional: Here, group loyalties and norms are less influential. The individual gains the ability to understand and work with principles, informed by personal morals and values.

How do we support growth through the stages of increasing ethical acuity? Kohlberg (1983) argues for a three-pronged approach: **socialisation, moral dilemma discussions and community** – essentially, a mix of exposure, modelling and discussions. Kohlberg and many others have since evidenced the importance of education where morality and ethics are challenged, discussed and revisited. They conclude that this is how progression through the levels occurs, in an upward trajectory of sophisticated knowing, understanding and decision-making.

Professional development: Ethical maturity

Professional development is a process of engaging in a range of activities (e.g. workshops, reading, training, conferences and supervision, etc.) as a way to learn, develop and refine skills and proficiency. Lane (2017, p. 651) notes that the literature highlights development as a "gradual progression from rule following to pattern recognition and increasing confidence to step outside protocol". For example Dreyfus and Dreyfus (2008, cited in Lane, 2017, p. 651) suggest there are five stages of skill acquisition:

Novice – essentially rule learning and following; Advanced Beginner – using more sophisticated rules and able to recognise contextual elements but tending

---

1 Can ethics be taught? https://www.scu.edu/ethics/ethics-resources/ethical-decision-making/can-ethics-be-taught/.

to treat all aspects of a task equally; Competent – able to set plans conceptually and within context and use standardised procedures within a decision hierarchy; Proficient – sees client's Issues holistically and can combine analytical decision making with intuition; and Expert – no longer rule dependent and able to use novel decision making processes.

(2008, cited in Lane, 2017, p. 651)

However, fixed-stage development frameworks have come under increasing criticism. Bachkirova (2017) suggests that the education of coaches should focus on capabilities rather than methodical competency approaches, due to the complexity and non-linear causal process and outcome of coaching. Some suggest extending the concept of having capabilities to include an individual's capacity (e.g. Hawkins, 2011). In analysing real cases, a coach increases their ability to be aware of 'critical moments of choice'. Van Nieuwerburgh (2020, p. 180) reflects on how to 'be' in those scenarios, which develops ethical fitness and thus contributes to building capacity.

Rajasinghe and colleagues (2022) studied the narratives of experienced coaches, and found coaches often let go of the 'rule book' and questioned much about themselves and their coaching and engaged in autonomous self-directed intentional cyclic learning, reflection and practice, as such increasing their capacity to 'be' in the moment and refine and trust their professional intuition.

We propose that ethical maturity is a process of growing competency, capability and capacity deriving from the ongoing cultivation of ethical sensitivity, awareness, acuity and intuition in professional practice. Ethics is an essential – perhaps the most important – part of coach education.

Coach education

Coaching

Coaching a relational creative dialogic process to enhance wellbeing, learning and development – multidisciplinary in nature – draws on knowledge and skills from various domains of helping and disciplines of knowledge (see Figure 1.1), each influenced by varied ethical codes, for example, educational ethics, clinical psychology/counselling ethics, medical ethics, journalistic ethics, business ethics, and arriving at varied levels of ethical development.

Adult education

Adult educational needs are different to those of children. The latter are still developing their capacity to understand, reason and make moral decisions (Piaget, 1954). Adults, however, have greater levels of psychological abilities (i.e. cognitive, affect, interpersonal and intrapersonal) to make sense of the world and handle complexity (e.g. Kegan, 1980) and so require different learning conditions.

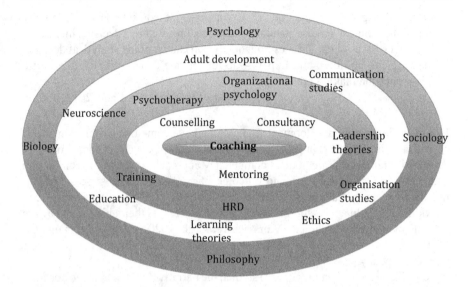

Figure 1.1 Cross-disciplinary influences of coaching. Title adapted: Positioning coaching amongst other disciplines of knowledge (Bachkirova, 2017, p. 29). Permission kindly granted by Tatiana Bachkirova.

Experience is a powerful learning condition for adults. Knowles (1980) proposes six needs for adult learning: (1) the need to know why they are learning something; (2) the need to learn experientially; (3) the need to be involved in the planning and evaluation of their learning, (4) the need to be interested in learning new things of relevance, (5) the need to have relevant problems to work on rather than theory, and (6) the need to be self-motivated.

Additionally, Kolb (1984) maintains that learning is optimal when one progresses through four learning stages.

1) Concrete experience (feeling) – new experiences and situations are understood and/or reinterpreted.
2) Reflective observation (watching) – the capacity to reflect on understanding of the experience.
3) Abstract conceptualisation (thinking) – thinking about what can be learned from the experience.
4) Active experimentation (doing) – one applies the new learning.

The four stages are repeated as new experiences emerge. The cyclic process ensures that new learning is understood and applied. Within Kolb's above stages model are two distinct dimensions, representing two dialectically opposed adaptive orientations:

1) Concrete experience vs. abstract conceptualization
2) Active experimentation vs. reflective observation.

These dimensions are independent but mutually enhancing, each being in opposition to the other (Lane, Kahn, & Chapman, 2018, p. 370). Such opposition creates tension, with learning the result of resolving the tension; therefore learning is a process of meaning making, fostering development, providing optimal learning conditions to develop ethicality.

Adults who actively make sense of their objective and subjective experiences, and anticipate consequences, increase their capacity for moral and ethical development (Dewey, 1986), cultivating enhanced sensitivity, increased awareness and the capacity for well-reasoned decision-making.

It follows logically that the cultivation of ethical sensitivity, awareness and decision-making are fundamental to the development of professional ethicality.

Ethical sensitivity and acuity

Ethical development/maturity is firstly about understanding the importance of ethics across all life domains and particularly the personal and professional. It's also about acquiring sensitivity to moments of ethical choice/s, an attunement to such moments and the capacity for appropriate self-awareness: emotions, intuition, beliefs, values, motivation, responsibility, fears, use of power, etc. (see Carroll & Shaw, 2013, pp. 150–151 for discussion). It also encompasses critical and systemic thinking, the capacity to discern right and wrong or the best action (ethical decision-making) and the courage to act on those decisions.

For the field of coaching, ethical development requires a deep understanding that ethics is the guiding principle for every perspective of coaching: coaching bodies, coach education organisations, coaching supervisors and practitioners. Critical reflective practice is the method ethically mature coaches should regularly employ and embody.

Ethical awareness

One cannot make right what one does not see or know. Developing awareness requires in the first instance critical reflection on one's own values, principles and interactions with others. Ethicality requires the ability to understand and recognise ethical issues in the moment and what may arise. One also needs to be conscious of the influence and effect of action (Brennan & Wildflower, 2014) at all levels of the system.

Corrie and Lane (2015, cited in Garvey et al., 2023, p. 270) argue that there are six main elements of ethical awareness as follows:

1) Ethical sensitivity – self-awareness and an awareness of the consequences and impacts of behaviour.
2) Ethical discernment – is the ability to reflect with emotional awareness, solve problems and make ethically based decisions.
3) Ethical implementation – is an awareness of what supports one or blocks one from implementing ethical decisions.
4) Ethical peace – is being able to live with a decision by drawing on one's support networks and being able to learn from the process of ethical choice, let go of the decision and knowing one's limits.
5) Ethical conversation – is about being able to defend a position by going 'public' with it and showing that the decision is linked to key ethical principles.
6) Ethical growth and development of character – the MacIntyre 'qualities of the person' that are developed through learning. This has a progressive and developmental aspect to it as one develops and extends ethical understanding and alertness over time.

More recently, Rajasinghe and colleagues (2022) investigated narratives of development of experienced coaches. They identified six awareness states: awareness in the moment; intuitive awareness; reflective awareness; awareness of boundaries; and general and systemic awareness that influences their coaching and so their ethical awareness. Some coaches described a feeling or tension within themselves or the coaching, the tension alerting them to a potential ethical issue providing them with points of critical decision-making.

Ethical decision-making

Ethical decisions to the novice may appear simplistic. As one matures, nuances and complexity become more apparent. Bommer and colleagues (1987) showcase the various elements at play in decision-making that end in either an ethical or unethical decision (see Figure 1.2).

A number of ethical decision-making frameworks have been created and updated. We refer you to Chapters 2 and 5 in *The Ethical Coaches' Handbook* (Smith et al., 2023) for an overview and discussion. A useful starting point for reflections on the ethical decision-making process is Breakey (2020, p. 122), who claims that thefollowing seven-stage process has consistently been found to be fundamental for ethical decision-making. Important to the process is that each stage is completed before progressing to the next.

1) Ensuring awareness of ethical issue/s at stake in the decision.
2) Gathering knowledge of the relevant facts and laws, and situational awareness.
3) Developing a full range of feasible options.
4) Making a correct ethical judgment about the justified course of action.
5) Crafting a practical, actionable plan to implement that course of action.
6) Implementing the plan proficiently.
7) Debriefing – and preparing for next time.

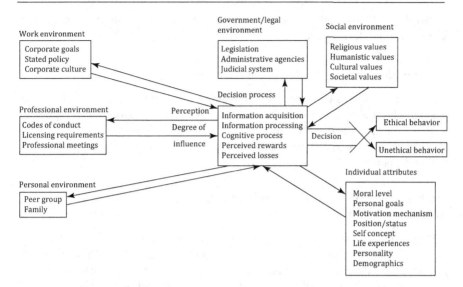

Figure 1.2 A behavioural model of ethical/unethical decision making (Bommer et al., 1987). Permission kindly granted by Michael Bommer.

John Bruhn at Scottsdale, a management consultant with an ethics specialty, states "The thing … courses … do is create awareness. They're not going to change behavior, because ethics is learned by modeling, not by reading a bunch of books over a weekend" (cited in Ethics India, accessed February 11, 2023). This position fits with Breakey's (2020) and others' assertion that *teaching* ethics is possible. Breakey argues that teaching frameworks in educational settings is easy enough for stages 1 to 5 above. However, inherent in stage 6 are psychological factors, such as the need for courage and motivation, that are unteachable. What factors impede action? There is a long tradition of ethical learning that stems from the earliest literature (e.g. Homer's *Odyssey*; Fenelon's *Telemachus*; and more recently Löfström, Ammert & Edling, 2021) that emphasises reflection on experience as core practice.

Carroll and Shaw have identified eight reasons we fail to act on what we should.

1) "personal cost
2) conflicting values
3) personal versus professional consistency
4) collusive stances
5) competing commitments
6) damage to the brain
7) sub-personalities (mini-selves) in conflict (zombie systems)
8) will power and procrastination."

(Carroll & Shaw, 2013, p. 225)

Breakey (2020) explains that a weakness in educating ethics is converting knowledge and decisions to action.

How can the 'Knowing to Doing' gap be bridged?

Increase courage and confidence to motivate action using real life scenarios/case studies. The use of case studies in professional education is not new. Medicine, nursing, business, law, psychology and other fields regularly use case studies. However little formal rigorous attention has been given to developing ethicality within the coaching space using case studies.

Using 'real life' experiences/case studies in coach education

Life experiences and professional practice bring with them uncertainty about what is a 'right' action. Ethical dilemmas often contain 'zones of ethical acceptability' hidden within the *grey* areas (Fatien & Clutterbuck, 2023). These can often only be identified through formalised, principled and well-thought-out decision-making followed by best choice action (Giraldez-Hayes & Smith, 2022). Case studies are stories or scenarios often based on 'real life' or invented stories in a narrative form. They are the equivalent of the biblical concept of a parable. They can make available for examination nuances of life such as the influence of culture, race, gender and disability that may otherwise be unavailable in 'real' life to aid understanding.

Case studies provide a basis for active learning through participation to develop skills such as critical thinking via the analysis of complex scenarios with multiple perspectives; engaging in discussions with colleagues/peers; learning decision-making processes; and role playing for increased confidence and courage to move from '*Knowing to Doing*'.

Fundamental practices to support the move from 'Knowing to Doing' ethical practice include reflection, case formulation, supervision and an intentional focus on the wellbeing of the coach and the client and the professionalisation of coaching.

Ethical reflection

Reflection is a process of taking time to ponder, to be curious, to ask questions of oneself as well as the situation under examination. It helps bring the unconscious into the conscious, facilitating new insights, along with learning about the self, life experiences and professional practice. Voller (2009, p. 21) describes reflection as

> Purposeful focusing on thoughts, feelings, sensations and behaviour in order to make meaning from those fragments of experience. The outcome of this reflection is to create new understanding, which in turn may lead to: increasing choices, making changes or reducing confusion.

The practice of reflection – by both coach and client – is fundamental to coaching practice and the development of awareness, insight and decision-making.

Reflection is a skill to be developed to increase ethical sensitivity and effective professional practice (Kovacs & Corrie, 2022).

Building reflective practice

Reflection requires questioning with a critical lens that prioritises ethics, enabling coaches to anticipate issues, to understand past issues and to learn from positive and negative experiences.

When to reflect?

Make time for reflection a priority of coaching practice. Some examples are before, during and after coaching, and in the moment.

See Table 1.1 for sample reflective questions proposed by Kovacs and Corrie (2022) to promote deep reflection.

Aids for reflection are as numerous and varied as your imagination can conjure. Of note are keeping a reflective diary and note-taking on sessions with a focus on themes, disappointments and successes (Kovacs & Corrie, 2022). Recording sessions is another method; however much caution, consideration and clarity of purpose, storage and confidentiality must be well understood. See Carroll (2009) for a deep exploration of the reflective practice processes in the helping professions.

Understanding the coaching case

In helping professions, such as psychology, case formulation is a fundamental process that provides a rich source of information, especially when the case is complex. Case formulation helps us to understand and identify the many interacting parts of issues arising for the client. It is much less common, yet equally valuable, within coaching, both alone and within supervision. It is a vital skill that should be included in coach education. Chapter 2 provides an in-depth discussion of case formulation with practice examples.

Supervision

While not mandatory for all – some coaching bodies require it (e.g., the coaching psychology division of the British Psychological Society) – supervision for coaches and coach supervisors is critical to coaching practice and in developing ethical maturity and facilitating the becoming of reflective practitioners. Supervision provides the opportunity and space for critical reflexivity, learning and planning the way forward for the coach and coach supervisor (Carroll, 2009; Hewson & Carroll, 2016). Supervision will at times resemble teaching, counselling, consulting or mentoring (Loganbill et al., 1982), all playing a critical role in facilitating the coach's maturity towards more independent practice.

An in-depth exploration of coach supervision can be read in Chapter 8 in Smith, Boniwell and Green (2021) and Chapter 9 in Smith et al. (2023).

Table 1.1 Questions to support the development of reflective practice

Reflection-on-practice:

- What worked well? What does working well mean in this context?
- What was not as effective? What does not effective mean in this context?
- What do my responses to the questions above reveal about the hypotheses I hold about the client and their situation?
- What would I do differently next time?

In building capability for reflection-in-action, it can be helpful to listen to recordings of sessions. This provides an opportunity to re-live the session and consider:

- What did I miss, or what was I not considering, in the moment?
- What was going through my mind and what did that lead to?
- What was my line of enquiry?
- What hypotheses was I holding in mind and how did I go about testing these?
- What could I have done differently and in what way might that have changed the conversation?

In building capability for reflection-on-action, some questions to hold in mind include:

- What is the pattern here? What might this pattern mean?
- How does this interaction make me feel and what might that mean?
- How are my emotions, beliefs or assumptions influencing my ability to work with the client at this point?
- What hypotheses am I forming and how can I test these?

For developing the ability for greater self-reflection:

- What does this situation or case tell me about my values and assumptions?
- What different assumptions or beliefs would help me act differently next time?
- What would be the potential impact on the client?
- Am I applying the theories in which I am trained or just going with the flow and my gut feel? What are the implications of this?
- How did my beliefs and assumptions interact with the social context in this situation?
- What impact did this have on the coaching and the client?

Source: Kovacs & Corrie, 2022, p. 93.

Prioritising the wellbeing of clients, of coaches and of the reputation of coaching

On the whole, humans have the best of intentions. However, they are not infallible. As much as their intentions may be honourable, without ethical awareness and courage for appropriate action their integrity is in question. Ethics help to protect society, the institutions we are affiliated with, the profession, clients and personal and professional relationships. Ethicality requires conscious thought for the right/best or least harmful action as opposed to unconscious or by chance right action or inappropriate – harmful – action. Behaviour is influenced by numerous factors, both external to ourselves and internal. External influences can be political, social and institutional. Internal influences are our beliefs, values and capacities to think, reflect and hold views different to our own. Ethics requires an approach to decision-making that asks "'What is the best thing to do in this case?', the practitioner [coach] will often ask, 'What can I live with? What is an outcome that is not intolerable or unreasonable?'" (Breakey, 2020, p. 120). While the aforementioned questions are useful, they look to find solutions to decrease harm.

A relatively new paradigm of ethical practice, known as Positive Ethical Practice, invites coaches to ask "What will provide the most benefit to the client?" (see Chapter 16 in Smith et al., 2023 for a deep dive into the topic). Expanding the influence of a wellbeing/virtuous approach, Arthur, Kristjánsson, Thompson and Fazel (2023, p. 8) propose that "care, integrity, fairness and diligence" are the foundations to ethical practice for the greater good or 'flourishing' of organisations and society. It follows that coaching grounded in wellbeing or Positive Ethical Practice has an important place in protecting the coach, coaching client and broader domains of coaching (for example, academia, research, education, coach accrediting bodies, associations and administrative personnel) and the reputation of the field of coaching.

The coach educator

This volume of case studies is designed to provide a breadth and depth of coaching scenarios for examination in coach education settings. The aforementioned text discusses many elements involved in developing ethical maturity (stages of ethical development, needs for adult learning, etc.). However, there is a paucity of agreement between educators of the required skills and principles the learner should develop. Arthur and colleagues propose that ethics education programmes should include three components: (1) knowledge and expertise; (2) good character; and (3) good practice (Arthur, Kristjánsson, Thompson & Fazel, 2023). There is, however, a challenge for educators of ethics to support students to progress from 'Knowing to Doing'. We suggest coach teachers and supervisors check on their own ethicality and role model ethical behaviour. How? By verbalising their thoughts and rationales for their decisions and behaviour in the learning space they are effectively providing an important mode of confidence and motivation building for action.

Case studies provide the basis to develop good character and practice.

Teaching NSW[2] proposes a five-stage process to students learning with case studies:

1. clarification/information seeking (*what?*) and [identifying all parties, understanding what is fact and what are assumptions and biases]
2. analysis/… (*why?*) [case formulation to understand and identify challenges and ethical points]
3. conclusion/recommendation (*what now?*) [having a clear rationale for decisions and identifying possible consequences]

---

2 Teaching NSW: How to Teach Effectively with Case Studies, accessed June 8, 2023 https://www.teaching.unsw.edu.au/case-studies.

4.   implementation (*how?*) [scripting responses and role plays] and
5.   application/reflection (*so what? what does it mean to you?*) [what is the learning about the self and practice]

Rather than outline how case studies should be used, we invite you to reflect and find your own ways to use case studies to enhance ethicality as a way of being. The questions can be found following the case study below. The central character in the study is a coach educator with multiple circumstances that are influencing their work with a number of challenges and ethical implications.

Case study

A coach unwell or overworked

Liam is CEO of a coach training school. He has been training coaches and coaching leaders for 20 years. He describes his coach education and one-to-one and team coaching as being part of a suite of coaching-related activities that complete his working week. He finds the mix of activities very fulfilling. He has also been regularly teaching coaching as an adjunct at the postgraduate level in a number of universities.

Over the past year he decided to shift gears and increase his one-to-one client hours to just over half a normal working week, while maintaining his educator hours, which average approximately ten hours per week.

Three months ago, Liam began studying a two-year part-time postgraduate diploma course that required him to be in attendance two nights per week with a minimum of ten hours of home study.

As the weeks wore on, he found himself tired around lunch time. This was unusual for him. He has until recently led an active life outside of work, going on long bike rides with his wife on Sundays. He worked out at the gym twice a week and practised yoga every other day.

Coach education

Liam regularly seeks feedback from his students. He was well known to be warm, attentive, intelligent and politely and gently challenging. However the feedback from the last cohort of students was alarming. The students reported Liam's feedback to be short and sharp, without clarity on how to go about making changes. They also reported Liam didn't appear to be interested in their progress and the classes were very large. A number of students felt the course was just a money-making scheme with little value to skill or personal development beyond the lectures.

Liam's brother-in-law also attended the last course. The students reported feeling uncomfortable and excluded by what they felt was favouritism and focus on the family member.

The coaching

Recently, Liam realised he was feeling impatient, less interested in the clients' stories and wanting the coaching sessions to end. He was distracted and wanted to think about his studies. One day upon returning home, he said to his wife Fari,

> Work was horrendously boring today. Not one of the clients seems to be moving from where they were last time we met. I was getting really annoyed. It was difficult to hold my frustration back. The whole day was very tedious.

Fari responded,

> Liam, you said the same thing at the end of last week. And you have been complaining of headaches lately. Remember you haven't wanted to ride the last couple of weeks. Maybe you should see a doctor? What do you think is going on?

Liam thought about Fari's response. He realised he had stopped post-session note taking recently and that more than one client has made a comment about not feeling understood. One coaching client even asked if Liam was enjoying his coaching nowadays.

Liam pondered what has changed and what to do about it. He was fearful of losing business. He had worked hard to earn his reputation and build the business. He didn't want to lose any of it.

Reflective questions for both the educator and student of coaching:

- Having read the conditions and needs for adults to learn and cultivate a reflective way of being, how would you use case studies such as those in this chapter and volume to foster reflection?
- Using this case study in an educational setting, what might the learning objectives be?
- What might the challenges be when using case studies in education settings?
- How can the coach educator role model an ethical way of being?
- What are the critical points of challenge for the coach educator?
- Identify all parties who could be affected by challenges and ethical points of concern.
- What are ethical considerations for the coach educator? Do they align with any point within a coaching code of ethics? What guidance is provided in the code? What tools would you use to support your decision-making?
- What options are available to the coach in both the coaching setting and the education setting to manage the challenges arising?

Conclusion

Like coaching, ethics are complex, relational and contextual, which makes educating for ethical development challenging. Paradoxically, an understanding of complexity is a prerequisite for ethical awareness, while ethical awareness in coaching may be required to appreciate the scope and role of complexity.

The conditions for ethical development – socialisation, moral dilemma discussions and community – as identified by Kohlberg (1983) can be well created within coach education settings using case studies, group discussions and role playing by both the educator and peers. Ethical maturity requires acquiring ethical sensitivity through engaging in a rigorous process of parsing a scenario, identifying possible courses of action and making well-thought-out decisions underpinned by a focus on the wellbeing of the coach, the client, their system and the field of coaching.

Coach education has to date generally failed to address the development of coach ethicality in professional practice, in a comprehensive ongoing manner. The inclusion of ethical case studies within coach education, supported by reflective practice and regular supervision, provides a pragmatic way forward.

References

Arthur, J., Kristjánsson, K., Thompson, A., & Fazel, A. (2023). *The Jubilee Centre Framework for Virtue-Based Professional Ethics*. Accessed May 20, 2023. Framework _Virtue_Based_Prof_Ethics.pdf

Bommer, M., Gratto, C., Gravander, J., & Tuttle, M. (1987). A behavioral model of ethical and unethical decision making. *Journal of Business Ethics*, 6, 265–280.

Breakey, H. (2020). Incorporating philosophical theory, ethical decision-making models, and multidimensional legitimacy into practical ethics education. In *Educating for Ethical Survival* (pp. 117–126). Emerald Publishing Limited.

Brennan, D., & Wildflower, L. (2014). Ethics in coaching. In E. Cox, T. Bachkirova, & D. Clutterbuck (eds.), *The Complete Handbook of Coaching*, 2nd edn (pp. 430–444). London: Sage.

Carroll, M. (2009). From mindless to mindful practice: On learning reflection in supervision. *Psychotherapy in Australia*, 15(4), 38–49.

Carroll, M., & Shaw, E. (2013). *Ethical Maturity in the Helping Professions: Making Difficult Life and Work Decisions*. London: Jessica Kingsley Publishers.

Corrie, S., & Lane, D. (2015).*CBT Supervision*. In R. Garvey, & A. Giraldez-Hayes (eds.), *Chapter: Ethics in Education and the Development of Coaches* (pp. 270). London & New York: Routledge.

de Haan, E. (2021). *What Works in Executive Coaching: Understanding Outcomes through Quantitative Research and Practice-Based Evidence*. Routledge.

Dewey, J. (1986, September). Experience and education. In *The Educational Forum* (Vol. 50, No. 3, pp. 241–252). Taylor & Francis Group.

Fatien, P. & Clutterbuck, D. (2023). What is ethics, and how does it apply to coaching?. In W. A. Smith, J. Passmore, E. Turner, Y.-L. Lai, & D. Clutterbuck (eds.), *The Ethical Coaches' Handbook: A Guide to Developing Ethical Maturity in Practice* (pp. 22–35). Routledge. https://doi .org /10 .4324 /9781003277729

Garvey, B., & Giraldez-Hayes, A. (2023). Ethics in education and the development of coaches. In W. A. Smith, J. Passmore, E. Turner, Y.-L. Lai, & D. Clutterbuck (eds.), *The Ethical Coaches' Handbook: A Guide to Developing Ethical Maturity in Practice* (pp. 267–278). Routledge. https://doi.org/10.4324/9781003277729

Giraldez-Hayes, A., & Smith, W. A. (2022). 3 Coaching psychology as a profession: Ethical and practice-related issues. In M. Shams (ed.), *Psychology in Coaching Practice: A Guide for Professionals* (p. 28).

Hawkins, P. (2011). Expanding emotional, ethical and cognitive capacity in supervision. In J. Passmore (ed.), *Supervision in Coaching: Supervision, Ethics and Continuous Professional Development*. London: Kogan Page.

Hewson, D., & Carroll, M. (2016). *Reflective Supervision Toolkit*. Hazelbrook, NSW: MoshPit.

Iordanou, C., Hawley, R., & Iordanou, I. (2016). Values and ethics in coaching. In *Values and Ethics in Coaching* (pp. 1–224). London: Sage.

Kegan, R. (1980). Making meaning: The constructive-developmental approach to persons and practice. *The Personnel and Guidance Journal*, 58(5), 373–380.

Knowles, M. (1980). *The Modern Practice of Adult Education: From Pedagogy to Andragogy*. Englewood Cliffs, NJ: Prentice Hall.

Kohlberg, L. (1975). The cognitive-developmental approach to moral education. *The Phi Delta Kappan*, 56(10), 670–677.

Kohlberg, L., Levine, C., & Hewer, A. (1983). Moral stages: A current formulation and a response to critics. *Contributions to Human Development*, 10, 174.

Kolb, D. A. (1984). The process of experiential learning. In *Experiential Learning: Experience as the Source of Learning and Development* (pp. 20–38). Englewood Cliffs: Prentice Hall

Kovacs, L., & Corrie, S. (2022). Building reflective capability to enhance coaching practice. In D. Tee & J. Passmore (eds.), *Coaching Practiced* (pp. 55–64). Chichester: Wiley.

Kristol, I. (1987). "Ethics anyone" or "Morals?". *The Wall Street Journal*, September 15, 1987.

Lane, D. A. (2017). Trends in development of coaches (education and training): Is it valid, is it rigorous and is it relevant? In T. Bachkirova, D. Drake, & G. Spence (eds.), *The SAGE Handbook of Coaching* (pp. 647–661). London: SAGE.

Lane, D., Kahn, M. S., & Chapman, L. (2018). Adult learning as an approach to coaching. In S. Palmer & A. Whybrow (eds.), *Handbook of Coaching Psychology A Guide for Practitioners* (2nd ed., pp. 369–380). Routledge. https://doi.org/10.4324/9781315820217

Löfström, J., Ammert, N., Edling, S. *et al.* (2021). Advances in ethics education in the history classroom: After intersections of moral and historical consciousness. *International Journal of Ethics Education*, 6, 239–252. https://doi.org/10.1007/s40889-020-00116-w

Loganbill, C., Hardy, E., & Delworth, U. (1982). Supervision: A conceptual model. *The Counseling Psychologist*, 10(1), 3–42.

Piaget, J. (1954). *The Construction of Reality in the Child*. (M. Cook, Trans.). Basic Books.

Rajasinghe, D., Garvey, R., Smith, W. A., Burt, S., Clutterbuck, D., Barosa-Pereira, A., & Csiga, Z. (2022). On becoming a coach: Narratives of learning and development. *The Coaching Psychologist*, 18(2).

Smith, W. A., Boniwell, I., & Green, S. (eds.). (2021). *Positive Psychology Coaching in the Workplace*. Switzerland: Springer International Publishing.

Smith, W. A., Passmore, J., Turner, E., Lai, Y.-L., & Clutterbuck, D. (eds.). (2023). *The Ethical Coaches' Handbook: A Guide to Developing Ethical Maturity in Practice* (1st ed.). Routledge. https://doi.org/10.4324/9781003277729

Tatiana Bachkirova, T. (2017). Developing a knowledge base of coaching: Questions to explore. In T. Bachkirova, D. Drake, & G. Spence (eds.), *The SAGE Handbook of Coaching* (pp. 23–41). SAGE.

Van Nieuwerburgh, C. (2020). An introduction to coaching skills: A practical guide. In *An Introduction to Coaching Skills* (pp. 1–240). London: Sage.

Velasquez, M., Andre, C., Shanks, T., & Meyer, M. J. (1987). Can ethics be taught. *Issues in Ethics*, 1(1), 101–102.

Voller, H. (2010). Developing the understanding of reflective practice in counselling and psychotherapy. *D. Prof, University of Middlesex*. Cited in Michael, Carroll (2009). From mindless to mindful practice: On learning reflection in supervision. *Psychotherapy in Australia*, 15(4), 38–49.

Chapter 2

Case formulation

A tool for working with coaching case studies

*David A. Lane, Michael Cavanagh,
and Wendy-Ann Smith*

Introduction

The role of case study in developing ideas and as a teaching tool is well established in a number of professional areas of practice. In medicine the case study has long provided the starting point for new ideas as usually cases have generated possible insights that later can lead to confirmatory evidence gathering and a new diagnosis (Crowe et al., 2011).

In business the case study has been a staple of teaching at universities globally. It has enabled in-depth study that can lead to new ways of dealing with issues presented. Nohria (2021) as Dean of Harvard Business School argues that working with case studies enhances discernment, recognition of bias, judgement, collaboration, curiosity and self-confidence.

In psychology the case study has provided many of the early ideas which later initiated new theoretical perspectives (Jarrett, 2015).

Case study has provided a core research tool across many fields with important contributions to understanding emerging from the detailed analysis that it provides.

However, a case by itself adds little without a framework to understand key factors impacting and through this the construction of an explanatory account. In a number of fields different concepts have been applied to the creation of these accounts.

For example, within medicine it is useful to consider the difference between a diagnosis and a formulation (sometimes called a case conceptualisation). A particular set of symptoms in a case study may lead to a definition that a person has a specific condition – e.g., a diagnosis of erythrocystosis. However, this in itself does not convey much information. A formulation would include the understanding of this for the coaching client (referred to as client in this chapter), how it may or may not impact on their future, how they may or may not address it, its impact on their sense of self and what that might mean for future actions by them or their medical team. Thus a formulation incorporates the person in a way that a diagnosis of a condition does not. A person is not a condition, not a cancer patient but a person living with cancer.

DOI: 10.4324/b23351-3

In the completely different context of arts practice, how authors, actors and directors make sense of character in pursuit of the performative act of the encounter with the audience also has something to contribute. While not defined as formulation the process has parallels. Approaches included by Corrie and Lane (2010) explore examples from narrative work by David Drake, understanding a play by Simon Callow, authoring a text by Bryan Rostron, the role of stories in our life by Sheelagh Strawbridge, acting by Timothy West and Prunella Scales and conceptions of identity, positionality and professional development for creative practitioners by Alan Durrant. These bring together understanding of how case and character formulation operate in both psychology and arts practice. An application of the work of the actor, director and theorist of performance Stanislavski (1863–1938) to the field of counselling (Lane & Corrie, 2012) provides a frame that could easily reflect how coaches explore the work with their clients. This includes three key processes.

1. *The super objective* – finding and agreeing super objectives for the work. In coaching this would include the initial conversation to try to agree the purpose of the work they will do together.
2. *Interior and exterior work* – undertaking interior and exterior work to prepare to develop an appropriate stance and attitude to the work. In coaching this would include exploring the sense of self and the context for the work to develop an understanding of the perspectives that impact on the work or need to be challenged to create a stance to the work likely to be beneficial.
3. *The through line of action* – undertaking the endeavour of moving from work on self through the performance with our clients in the context of the encounter with our clients – the through line of action. In coaching this would include the process through which client and coach work together to reach an outcome.

It would be entirely possible to explore the cases in this book through asking how did the coach and coaching client arrive at the 'super objective'; what 'interior and exterior work' did they undertake; and what was the 'through line of action' seen in the encounter?

In psychology case formulation has been the central feature of the work of clinical psychologists (BPS, Good Practice Guidelines, 2011) and latterly has become core in other fields of psychological practice (Lane, Watts & Corrie, 2016). Its use in coaching (Corrie, Kovacs & Lane, 2021) and coaching psychology (Lane & Corrie, 2009) has increased in recent years. It is this later approach – case formulation – that forms the basis for the framework used in this chapter.

What is case formulation and why does it matter?

A formulation has been described by Corrie and Lane (2010, 2021) as a psychologically informed explanation of the client's story and presenting concerns that have implications for change. What does this mean within our areas of interest as coaches? When we work with a client in coaching we are trying to make sense of their story. Every client brings their own account of their world, their own reflective narrative. However, as coaches we have our own account of the world both personally and professionally. In the encounter between client and coach, the coach is trying to make sense of the challenges faced while bringing those perspectives to the engagement. We construct a shared relational narrative of the work we do together (what Lane, 1990, called a shared concern). Thus, the attempt to make sense of this through formulation is not just like two friends discussing an issue; the client has come to the coach with at least some sense that they have expertise to share of potential benefit. If a client thought they were able to simply use their own resources to address their goals, challenges and/or concerns, they would not need a coach. The client's story will include assumptions, details about the context and beliefs and emotions about possibilities for change. The coach is trying to create a space within which the client's story can be fully told and the client can have the comfort of knowing that they have been fully heard.

However, the coach is not simply hearing the story, even though that is the essential starting point, but rather is trying to make sense of the account using their perspectives on the situation presented. A case formulation is both the sense made of the account as stated (noun) and the ongoing and emerging process of formulating an understanding (verb). The benefit is not just for the client but also for the coach. According to Corrie and Kovacs (2019) formulation can:

a) Support the coaching
b) Support the coach
c) Enable the relationship
d) Enhance the quality of practice

Cavanagh (2006) has described this process in his Three Reflective Spaces model of the coaching interaction. This model outlines the dynamic, ongoing process of accessing, sharing and processing case-relevant information in order that the coach and client can come to a shared understanding of the issue being brought by the client. For this new understanding to be effective, it must make sense of the issue in a way that enables the possibility of effective change. It must also be informed by, and tested against, the realities of the world external to the coaching conversation. In this process the formulation is an emergent and ongoing outcome of the dynamic conversation between the client, the coach and the external systems within which this plays out (see also Cavanagh &Spence, 2012).

There are, therefore, two questions this chapter has to answer.

1. How may we approach the task of formulating?
2. How does a formulation enable an enhanced reading of the case studies in this book?

How may we approach the task of formulating?

There is no one way to do this

For example, Worrell (2010) discusses the way in which those who work existentially would not direct the client's attention to any ideas felt to be important or seek an educational role by introducing ideas. Rather there is an attempt to form a descriptively focussed exploration of the client's reflective narrative that stays with the experience in the way it is being disclosed. This takes the form of a phenomenological investigation which he argues has relevance to our understanding of formulation. This involves three stages:

1. The epoche – this involves the attempt to suspend assumptions and expectations in order to create openness to the disclosures.
2. Description – this is concerned with describing, not explaining, the phenomenon. Any analysis tries to stay close to the experience to open up the interpretations.
3. Equalisation – this attempts to broaden out as far as possible a context for understanding the meaning of this experience for the client.

It is this emphasis on staying close to the descriptive clarification of client concerns that Worrell argues has much to bring to our understanding of formulation. In attempting to explore case studies, formulation in this sense would focus on how the coach suspended assumptions, the closeness of the description to the client's experience and how the attempt is made to understand the context within which the meaning and significance of the experience for the client is explored.

Drake provides a narrative approach to case formulation with four elements (2010, p. 247). If cases were either conducted or read using this frame the emphasis would be to understand:

> Person: An emphasis on (a) self-knowledge for both coach and client; (b) creating an empathic container for awareness; (c) multiple sources of expertise and knowledge; and (d) attention to what they think is going on.
>
> Story: An emphasis on (a) foundation knowledge about narrative structure and psychology; (b) searching for openings for change; (c) the impact of the past, present and future; and (d) attribution of what they think caused it.
>
> Elements: An emphasis on (a) professional knowledge about work with the narrative material; (b) new opportunities that emerge from the interplay of the elements; (c) insights gained from assessing various streams of causality; and (d) action based on what they think they should do about it and why.
>
> Field: An emphasis on (a) contextual knowledge as found in the space between and around the coach and client; (b) a structure for new stories and behaviours; (c) a holistic view on what is possible now; and (d) anticipation of what they think will happen as a result.

In approaching any case study, it would be possible to ask how person, story, elements and field are represented.

Chapman (2012) presents a framework that draws on the work of Kolb and Wilbur, and more recently (Chapman, 2023) he has included approaches from neuroscience in what he terms an Integrated Experiential Learning Process. Lane, Chapman and Kahn (2019) examine the role of the team and provide a framework based around roles. Stout Rostron (2019, 2021) presents multiple models but in particular draws upon diverse cultural perspectives. There are, therefore, many approaches that could be used to explore case studies. Bachkirova, Clutterbuck and Cox (2018) provide an approach similar to the one proposed below. Although offered as a personal model of coaching practice it could also form a basis for exploring case studies. Their framework used this way would ask three questions:

1. How do practitioners see human nature and the world and in particular what is important to them? (The philosophy that underpins their coaching practice.)
2. What is the coaching for and what is the coach trying to achieve? (The main purpose of the coaching.)
3. What tools, methods and procedures are used that are appropriate for this purpose and coherent with this philosophy? (A coherent process.)

In part the approach to formulation is influenced by the view we take of evidence and ethical practice (Lane & Corrie, 2023). Case studies in coaching are often presented and understood through the prism of a particular theoretical position (Cox, Bachkirova & Clutterbuck, 2018). Case formulation might be similarly focussed such as in cognitive behavioural or narrative coaching.

Numerous authors have argued for the introduction of case formulation to coaching and supervision and for it to be included in coach education as a practice undertaken by the coach – alone or in supervision – in aid of helping the coach obtain deeper understanding of what is happening in the coaching and for the client (e.g., Cavanagh, Stern & Lane, 2016; Corrie & Lane, 2009; Drake, 2014; Grant, 2011; Lane, Watts & Corrie, 2016; Watts, Bor & Florance, 2021). Rather than presenting a theoretically focussed approach to case formulation and hence to the reading of case studies a framework is presented in this chapter which stays neutral on which if any theories might be considered useful. It arises from multiple studies over many years which sought to understand what happens in professional relationships and subsequently in coaching encounters. Originating in work within school systems (Lane, 1975, 1978, 1990) and later therapy (Bruch & Bond, 1998; Bruch, 2015) it was concerned with five areas named as DEFINE.

1. **Definition** of the shared concern and objectives that formed the basis of the work to be undertaken.
2. **Exploration** of factors influencing the current situation, predisposing factors (historical, developmental, cultural) and contextual factors that impacted on the concerns and objectives.
3. **Formulation** of the range of factors to generate a coherent understanding shared by the participants creating a potential for change.

4. **Intervention** plan and action based on the formulation to generate change.
5. **Evaluation** of outcomes, modifications of the intervention as needed and optimisation of gains for the future.

Given that coaching often operates in complex areas across multiple disciplines this approach to formulation was restructured (although still used when appropriate, see Lane, Chapman & Kahn, 2014) following a number of large-scale studies (over 900 organisations) on employability (Rajan & Lane, 2000) which indicated that coaching was fast becoming the intervention of choice. Corrie and Lane (2010) in providing a guide to formulation through the stories people tell also explored how the narrative of the work unfolds. They provided three processes for understanding narrative. One such approach considers areas such as whose priorities drive the story, the setting for the story, principal players, the unfolding plot, initiating events, goals and outcomes. Further revisions are in progress related to how we position ourselves in the world as persons, people and practitioners (Lane, Corrie & Kovacs, 2023).

Various studies of the future of coaching have concluded by considering how client and coach come to an understanding of the purpose of the work they do together, what perspectives on the issues they each bring to the endeavour and what process guides the interactions in the encounter (Cavanagh & Lane, 2012; Lane & Corrie, 2006; Lane, Stelter & Stout-Rostron, 2018). The coherence of the process was examined and a proposed way of formulating and reading case studies follows.

How does a formulation enable an enhanced reading of case studies?

Initially, this chapter outlines the formulation framework and the questions it generates. This will be presented as a precursor to considering the reading of cases in this book and 'real life' cases.

Purpose – where are we going and why?

The shared journey in any coaching endeavour begins as you define the purpose of the work you will do together. How that endeavour was initiated, by whom and to what end is part of the discussion. You each bring your own ideas on its purpose, but you will also seek to find a shared concern that it makes sense to explore. The oft-quoted adage, "a problem cannot be solved with the same level of thinking that created it", is important here. Our purposes are not independent of our perspectives – the way we make sense of the world. They co-define and serve each other. The way we understand the world will determine what is a problem to be solved and the pathway to that solution. What seems to be a useful goal in the short term may lead to negative outcomes over longer time frames. The purposes that are deemed relevant and primary will depend on the world view or meaning-making capacities of the participants. Hence, if we are to understand our shared purpose, it is important to reflect on the level of thinking we are bringing to the conversation (see Cavanagh, 2013 on the relationship between purpose and perspective-taking capacity).

Questions such as the following are important in this reflection:

- What is our purpose in working together?
- Where do we really want to go, and will our stated purpose get us there?
- What does this purpose enable, and what does it constrain?
- Does our purpose enable useful outcomes over different time frames?
- Is our purpose genuinely shared by all relevant stakeholders?

Thus, in reading a case study, essentially four areas need to be defined.

1. What are the questions/challenges/concerns/objectives we wish to explore together?
   a) Is this an open enquiry which may lead to an unknown destination?
   b) Do the questions raised need a fixed point of resolution, that is, a problem to be solved or a solution achieved recognised as appropriate by key stakeholders?
   c) Is it possible in this case to define in advance what an acceptable resolution would look like?
   d) Has the definition of the purpose of the work negotiated between coach and client been agreed with key stakeholders?
   e) How will changes in, or new, objectives/questions/concerns/challenges be incorporated in the coaching as they emerge throughout the coaching conversation?
2. What are our expectations about the work and those of key stakeholders?
   a) Is the intention of participants and key stakeholders known and transparent?
   b) Are those who could impact on any outcome identified?
   c) Are there anticipated outcomes or results and how do these relate to the objectives of key players?
   d) What will be different as a consequence of achieving these outputs or results?
3. What role do we each want to play in this encounter?
   a) Who should (or does) play a role in identifying key objectives, data or hypotheses?
   b) What role does each party or key stakeholder want to play?
   c) What investment of time, energy and resource will each party make and how willing are they to commit?
   d) How will each party be initiated into the journey to ensure a sense of partnership and ownership?
4. What is the context for the purpose and the way in which it has come to be defined?
   a) What does the client need to enable them to tell their story?

b)   Have coach and client been able to identify a shared concern that is appropriate to the boundaries of the contract and is best served by them working together?

c)   Have they identified and understood the position of other stakeholders who might benefit from or be unnerved by the intervention?

d)   What makes this a meaningful encounter for coach, client and other stakeholders?

Perspective – what will inform our journey?

In reviewing a coaching case you will be faced with two common approaches. The first applies where a coach has a particular perspective, say as a cognitive behavioural, gestalt, solution-focussed or positive psychology style of coach. In this the practitioner looks at particular aspects of the client's concerns and seeks to unlock the puzzle by privileging certain aspects of the client's story over others. This does not mean they cannot listen carefully or do excellent work, but it does mean they have to be careful to work with clients where their preferred approach has value and refer on clients for whom their perspective may not be best fitted or supported by an evidence base.

In the second approach the coach seeks to hear the client's story first and then explores the perspectives that might best work with them at this point in time. The coach and client seek to understand the goals/challenges/issues through multiple lenses as they work to construct, deconstruct and reconstruct the meaning of the encounter.

The key to formulating effectively within either of these two approaches is to maintain a balance between curiosity about different ways of understanding the client's unique experience and meaning making, and insights and understandings derived from experience, theory and research. Hence, attention should be paid to how theory and the evidence base are used in the coaching engagement, and how responsive is the coaching conversation to the client's unique story and circumstances. Bruch and Bond (1998) in relation to the therapy alliance (but this could also describe the coaching relationship) refer to the importance of the client's construction of the world in which they work together to construct a shared model. This enables them to consider experiments with behaviour they can try out and thus the formulation becomes personalised to that client in those circumstances.

There are four areas to consider in relation to perspectives.

1.   What perspectives inform the journey between coach and client?
   a)   What perspectives are informing the coach's understanding of the case?
   b)   What perspectives is the client bringing to understand the situation?
   c)   How does the coach or client position themselves in the world and how is that influencing understanding?
   d)   What is the coach doing to ensure that the client is able to openly explore their beliefs, knowledge and competencies within the encounter?

2. What beliefs about models of practice are visible in the encounter?
    a) What beliefs about self and other inform the understanding of the puzzles we face as clients or the service we offer as practitioners?
    b) What perspectives based in personal theories of behaviour and change are informing the encounter?
    c) What perspectives based in interpersonal theories and change are informing the encounter?
    d) What perspectives based in systemic theories and change are informing the encounter?
3. What beliefs relating to the nature of evidence are visible in the encounter?
    a) What seems to count as evidence in the way the work is interpreted or undertaken?
        I.   Through the use of data which has a clear scientific basis.
        II. Through the use of a 'what works' perspective such as a protocol or manual.
        III. Through deliberative action specific to the context and reflection.
        IV. Through critical engagement with dominant discourses to challenge assumptions and power structures.

4. Who in the encounter decides what counts as evidence?
    a) Who will benefit most or least by the decision on what counts as evidence?
    b) What impact does the approach taken to evidence have on the client or coach where it conflicts with cultural expectations?
    c) Who has the power to decide?
    d) What political, economic, social and environmental concerns are driving the choices made?

Process – how will we get there?

Once a purpose for the work is understood and the encounter has begun to explore influential perspectives it is possible to decide on the process by which coach and client work together. For some, using a single theoretical model, the approach will reflect that, and it will have to be outlined to the client to gain their buy in to proceed. For others, exploring the narrative more broadly, a framework for managing the story-telling process will need to be agreed. There are six common discourses in coaching practice likely to influence the process chosen.

1. A formulation derived from diagnostic classification – for example, the client has undertaken various psychometric tests, 360 feedback or an assessment centre which provides a classification that impacts decisions on the work.
2. A formulation based on scientist-practitioner models in which coach and client work together to identify hypotheses that can be tested to arrive at useful and accurate explanations.
3. A formulation based on a given theoretical position (either single or integrative) that will guide the encounter.

4. A strategic formulation based on a future orientation and the strengths people bring to the encounter.
5. A formulation as a means of social control based on actions and processes defined by those in power in an organisation which states that a given way of working is mandated and only pre-defined objectives are considered legitimate. This may sometimes include a requirement that any coach must be trained in a particular way.
6. A narrative formulation that explores the way the story is told and what is included or excluded from the account.

There are four areas to consider in relation to process when reviewing a case.

1. What process was used to ensure that the purpose was met given any constraints available in the work?
2. How did the coach and client structure the work?
3. What factors seemed to mediate the choices made?
4. What changed over the course of the work in terms of the definition of purpose, the perspectives employed or the process used?

In addition, we are focussed on ensuring coherence between the process used to ensure consistency with the purpose of the work and the perspectives that inform it. Awareness of how purpose, perspective and process emerge in the encounter and how the participants use the information gathered to develop their sense of the purpose of the work, factors that have to be taken into account to understand the issues and the process necessary to create a shared concern, formulation and intervention plan provide the basis for case study analysis. This is a key consideration for analysing case studies.

Reading case studies – three brief case examples from this book

In reading a case study the focus could be on any of the three areas above, *Purpose*, *Perspective* and *Process*, depending on the issues in the case. For example, a senior manager has referred a middle manager as a possible client for coaching citing a recent 360 feedback exercise asking to identify developmental potentials to be addressed. In this example the case study might be read in terms of how the purpose of the work is defined, by whom, for whose benefit and how the views of the identified coaching client are incorporated into the defined purpose. The aim is to identify the areas that the case study is trying to address and ask the appropriate questions of it to fully grasp how the parties to the encounter are trying to formulate their understanding of the work and how it needs to proceed given the factors that are taken into account. A formulation can be seen as a narrative of the journey intended.

A starting point for reading a case study is to ask:
What is the story for the case study I am reading?

What is included, what is missing, with what consequences for making sense of the case?

Case studies are, by nature, summaries that select and put forward only part of the information available – that part deemed important by the author. When reading a case, questions will emerge which cannot be answered as there is no one to ask. However, by reflecting on the areas of interest, you can consider how, if you were seeking to formulate this case, you might explore the narrative. As you explore case studies and your own 'real life' cases the focus might be on how the purpose was developed, the perspectives that were or were not apparent and what process for working was seen. The examples from this book below simply provide a guide to questions you might consider. They are not definitive and in reading you make take a different view – that is absolutely appropriate.

Case example A: from Chapter 4 Case Study 7

This is an interesting supervision example in which the supervisor brings to a supervision group a coaching case in which the client was referred by a manager following 360 and other feedback. In reading this case the way the purpose of the work came to be defined is of particular interest.

The questions above related to Purpose are worth considering. For example, does the feedback indicate that there needs to be a fixed point of resolution, a problem to be solved? Has it been defined in advance what an acceptable resolution would look like? What work has been done to agree the purpose between coach and client and other key stakeholders? Who are the key stakeholders in this example? What role does each party or key stakeholder want to play? Have coach and client been able to identify a shared concern that is appropriate to the boundaries? Given it is not clear if this is best served by a therapeutic or coaching intervention, is the client best served by them working together?

These are just some of the questions that might arise as you reflect on this case. In reviewing the other areas covered in the Purpose section above what questions would occur to you if you were part of the supervision group supporting the coach? In learning from this case study reflection on how you as a coach or supervisor would respond and what areas you would seek to explore provides a way to try out ideas.

Key learnings from this case could arise from placing yourself in the role of client, coach, supervisor, member of the supervisory group, manager or colleague and asking from that point of view what you would like to explore and how you would feel in any of those roles.

Case example B: from Chapter 7 Case Study 22

This example looks at coaching within the context of a major organisational change programme. It provides an interesting example to consider the relationship between how the purpose was defined, by whom and with what perceived benefit for whom and the process by which change was initiated within the organisation.

This would cover relationships between those coached, managers, internal coaches and the external consultants and the pivotal position of human resources.

The Process section above suggests that once a purpose for the work is understood and the encounter has begun to explore influential perspectives it is possible to decide on the process by which coach and client work together.

The question arises: how was the Purpose defined, by whom and what perspectives (beliefs, theories, world views) were influencing the decisions? How was a process to undertake the work agreed and how coherent were those elements?

From the Process section, key questions would include understanding what factors seemed to mediate the choices made in the case? Subsequently, what changed over the course of the work and how did this impact on the definition of purpose, the perspectives employed or the process used?

Key learnings in this case would include how you would seek to define the multiple potentially conflicting views on the purpose of the work, how you would seek to understand the different beliefs and world views operating in the organisation and what approaches you would seek to employ to manage the project to ensure a coherent process?

Case example C: from Chapter 9 Case Study 32

This complex and challenging case tests both the coach and client who find themselves in the middle of an increasingly bitter power play. A starting point for reflecting on this case could be to consider the overall narrative. What stories seem to be in play from the different parties?

In the process section above a narrative formulation was identified. This explores the way the story is told and what is included or excluded from the account. In reading the case identifying the stories and the relationship between them could provide a way to make sense of the challenges faced. The approach from Stanislavski or Drake or the narrative areas identified by Corrie and Lane above might be used to explore the case. Thus, considerations could include whose priorities drive the story, the setting for the story, principal players, the unfolding plot, initiating events, goals and outcomes?

Core questions from Purpose could include how the expectations in the case were addressed, the role each party wanted to play and how they identified and understood the position of other stakeholders who might benefit from or be unnerved by the intervention?

Questions 3 and 4 from the perspectives section might be particularly potent, including who has the power to decide and what political concerns are driving the decisions made?

From the process section reflection on the factors that seemed to mediate the choices made and what changed over the course of the work could be very illuminating.

Key learnings from this case could emerge from constructing the narrative and then subjecting it to analysis to identify the discourses operating in the environment.

There is an ethical and potentially problematic discourse around the role that client and coach choose to play and the less than transparent positions they took in relation to the work and their colleagues which mirrored the lack of transparency and conflict in roles from their co-workers.

Conclusion

Understanding coaching cases is fundamental to best coaching practice. How that is done is complex and dependent on the theoretical frame of reference from which the coaching is viewed.

There are a number of ways to develop an understanding of cases presented in the book. The chapter outlines several from different authors. Any one of these would aid interpretation. Discourses common within coaching have been explored and it might be valuable as a starting point for reflecting on cases to consider which of these is personally or professionally resonant. This could lead to further reflections on the implications of this discourse for practice, what is left in and what is left out.

Whatever approach to case conceptualisation one uses, a number of evaluative criteria can help us to assess the adequacy of our formulations:

1. Is the formulation clearly understandable to both coach and client?
2. Has the formulation been created collaboratively with the client (as opposed to being done to the client)?
3. Does the formulation open up the possibility of effective change?
4. Is the formulation process an active ongoing process in which conclusions are held tentatively? In other words, is the formulation open to change based on new information/disconfirming evidence?
5. Does the formulation identify patterns within the client or in the way the client and other stakeholders are interacting? In other words, does it help participants to understand the emergence of new/allied issues?

The theoretically neutral three-step enquiry of purpose, perspective and process, presented, undertaken by the coach alone or in supervision and/or with the coaching client serves to bring a nuanced understanding to the coaching point of exploration. Detailed analysis of case studies and our own case work provides a way to enhance practice and provides a template for possible areas for continuing professional development. It may also raise questions related to how we look after our clients and ourselves in the complex world in which coaches seek to provide a service.

References

Bachkirova, T., Cox, E., and Clutterbuck, D. (2018). Conclusion. In Cox, E., Tatiana, B., and Clutterbuck, D., *The Complete Handbook of Coaching* (3rd Edition). London: Sage.
British Psychological Society. (2011). *Good Practice Guidelines on the Use of Psychological Formulation*. Leicester: British Psychological Society.

Bruch, M. (2015). *Beyond Diagnosis Case Formulation in Cognitive Behavioural Therapy*. Chichester: Wiley Blackwell.

Bruch, M., and Bond, F. W. (1998). *Beyond Diagnosis: Case Formulation Approaches in CBT*. Chichester: Wiley.

Cavanagh, M. (2006). Coaching from a systemic perspective: A complex adaptive conversation. In Stober, D., and Grant, A. M. (eds.), *Evidence Based Coaching Handbook*. New York: Wiley, pp. 313–354.

Cavanagh, M. J. (2013). The coaching engagement in the twenty-first century: New paradigms for complex times. In David, S., Clutterbuck, D., and Megginson, D. (eds.), *Beyond Goals*. Gower Publishing, Farnham Surrey, UK, pp. 151–183.

Cavanagh, M., and Lane, D. A. (2012). Coaching psychology coming of age: The challenges we face in the messy world of complexity. *International Coaching Psychology Review*, 7(1), 75–90.

Cavanagh, M., and Spence, G. (2012). Mindfulness in coaching: Philosophy, psychology or just a useful skill? In Passmore, J., Peterson, D., and Freire, T. (eds.), *The Wiley-Blackwell Handbook of Psychology of Coaching and Mentoring*. London: Wiley Blackwell, pp. 112–134.

Cavanagh, M., Stern, S., and Lane, D. A. (2016). Supervision in coaching psychology: A systemic developmental psychological perspective. In Lane, D. A., Watts, M., and Corrie, S. (eds.), *Supervision in the Psychological Professions Building Your Own Personalized Model*. London: Open University Press.

Chapman, L. (2012). *Integrated Experiential Coaching Becoming an Executive Coach*. London: Karnac. more recently (2023).

Chapman, L. (2023). *The Evidence Based Practitioner Coach Understanding the Integrated Experiential Learning Process*. London: Routledge.

Corrie, S., and Kovacs, L. C. (2019). The functions of formulation in coaching psychology. *The Coaching Psychologist*, 15(1), 66–75.

Corrie, S., and Lane, D. A. (2009). The scientist-practitioner model as a framework for coaching psychology. *The Coaching Psychologist*, 5(2), 61–67.

Corrie, S., and Lane, D. A. (2010). *Constructing Stories Telling Tales A Guide to Formulation in Applied Psychology*. London: Karnac.

Corrie, S., and Lane, D. A. (2021). *First Steps in Cognitive Behavioural Therapy*. London: Sage.

Corrie, S., Kovacs, L. C., and Lane, D. A. (2021). Making sense of the client's story: The role of formulation in coaching. In Watts, M., Bor, R., and Florance, I. (eds.), *The Trainee Coach Handbook*. London: Sage.

Cox, E., Tatiana, B., and Clutterbuck, D. (2018). *The Complete Handbook of Coaching* (3rd Edition). London: Sage.

Crowe, S., Cresswell, K., and Robertson, A. (2011). The case study approach. *BMC Medical Research Methodology*, 11, 100. https://bmcmedresmethodol.biomedcentral.com/articles/10.1186/1471-2288-11-100

Drake, D. B. (2010). What story are you in? Four elements of a narrative approach to formulation in coaching. In Corrie, S., and Lane, D. A. (eds.), *Constructing Stories Telling Tales A Guide to Formulation in Applied Psychology*. London: Karnac.

Drake, D. B. (2014). Three windows of development: A post-professional perspective on supervision. *International Coaching Psychology Review*, 9(1), 38–50.

Grant, A. M. (2011). Developing an agenda for teaching coaching psychology. *International Coaching Psychology Review*, 6(1), 84–99.

Jarrett, C. (2015). Psychology's 10 greatest case studies. *BPS Updates*. https://www.bps.org. uk/research-digest/psychologys-10-greatest-case-studies-digested Accessed 29.03.2023.

Lane, D. A. (1975). *Analysis of a Complex Case*. London: Islington Educational Guidance Centre.

Lane, D. A. (1978). *The Impossible Child*. London: ILEA.

Lane, D. A. (1990). *The Impossible Child*. Stoke on Trent: Trentham.

Lane, D. A., and Corrie, S. (2006). *The Modern Scientist-Practitioner a Guide to Practice in Psychology*. Hove: Routledge.

Lane, D. A., and Corrie, S. (2009). Does coaching psychology need the concept of formulation? *International Coaching Psychology Review*, 4(2), 195–208.

Lane, D. A., and Corrie, S. (2012). *Making Successful Decisions in Counselling and Psychotherapy A Practical Guide*. Maidenhead: Open University Press.

Lane, D. A., and Corrie, S. (2023). What might be an evidence base for coaching - Ethical issues. In Smith, W. A., Passmore, J., Turner, E., Lai, Y., and Clutterbuck, D. (eds.), *The Ethical Coaches Handbook A Guide to Developing Ethical Maturity in Practice*. Abingdon: Routledge.

Lane, D. A., Corrie, S., and Kovacs, L. (2023). *Handbook of Formulation in Coaching*. (2024).

Lane, D. A., Kahn, S., and Chapman, L. (2019). Adult learning as an approach to coaching. In Palmer, S., and Whybrow, A. (eds.), *Handbook of Coaching Psychology A Guide for Practitioners*, 2nd Edition. Abingdon: Routledge.

Lane, D. A., Stelter, R., and Stout-Rostron, S. (2018). The future of coaching as a profession. In Cox, E., Tatiana, B., and Clutterbuck, D. (eds.), *The Complete Handbook of Coaching* (3rd Edition). London: Sage.

Lane, D. A., Watts, M., and Corrie, S. (2016). *Supervision in the Psychological Professions Building Your Own Personalized Model*. London: Open University Press.

Nohria, N. (2021). What the case study method really teachers. https://hbr.org/2021/12/what -the-case-study-method-really-teaches. Accessed 29.03.2023.

Rajan, A., and Lane, D. A. (2000). *Employability: Bridging the Gap Between Rhetoric and Reality*. Tonbridge: Centre for Research in Employment and Technology in Europe.

Stout Rostron, S. (2019). *Business Coaching International: Transforming Individuals and Organisations*. Abingdon: Routledge.

Stout Rostron, S. (2021). *Transformational Coaching to Lead Culturally Diverse Teams*. Abingdon: Routledge.

Watts, M., Bor, R., and Florance, I. (2021). *The Trainee Coach Handbook*. London: Sage.

Worrell, M. (2010). Existential formulations of therapeutic practice. In Corrie, S., and Lane, D. A. (eds.), *Constructing Stories Telling Tales A Guide to Formulation in Applied Psychology*. London: Karnac.

Part Two

Case studies

Chapter 3

One-to-one coaching

Chapter 3, in its focus on a one-to-one coaching dyad, highlights the complexities arising in a relatively 'simple system'. Such concerns arising include power, diversity and inclusion, death, boundaries, and client wellbeing.

DOI: 10.4324/b23351-5

Case study 1

Coaching the "boss from hell"

Haesun Moon

Overview

This case study highlights the challenges faced by a coach in a situation where the client expects them to 'fix' the organization's leadership and employees. The misaligned definitions and expectations of coaching, as well as the implicit power dynamics between the client and coach, create ethical implications around confidentiality, transparency, and power dynamics.

Reflective questions for discussion include how a coach can navigate situations where stakeholders' understandings of coaching are in opposition, how to handle a situation where the coach has biases towards or against the client, and how to respond to multiple stakeholders wanting the coach to take a side.

These multiple points of tension eventually resolved in a useful and productive way in the actual case, and this case study presents one of the moments that the coach experienced at the beginning of the project.

Case study

Background

The following case took place as part of an organizational review that a coach (Helena Cho) was invited to conduct. The organization in question was a highly visible part of the broader public sector, and was subject to regular public scrutiny due to its responsibility for public policies. Every six months, enterprise-wide engagement surveys were conducted for all 20,000 employees, and each division received their results compared to other divisions and the overall enterprise. This particular branch was comprised of five teams of legal counsels who had recently participated in the survey. When the results were received a few weeks later, the branch's leadership team reached out for leadership coaching, an employee 'pulse check,' and a review of other workplace processes and culture. One of the deputy chiefs of the branch was responsible for procuring an external vendor for the project, and she strongly felt that the root issue was with their chief.

"Can you please tell us what's wrong with our leadership?" was the not-so-subtle opening line of a desperate deputy chief, Tina, on the phone with Helena. The

DOI: 10.4324/b23351-6

storyline was not uncommon – a semi-annual employee engagement survey came back biting the leadership with the lowest satisfaction score in the entire organization. What was uncommon was their request: "please come and find what's wrong with us leaders." Tina almost sighed through the next line, "the problem is the chief. He's got no idea how bad he is, and you just gotta coach him to realize that himself."

"Ok, let me get this straight," Helena looked up from her notes as if Tina could see her through the phone, "so, your employees scored your leadership team the lowest in the organization." Tina quickly added, "it's not the whole leadership team. It's really all Pedro." She paused briefly, "and to top it off, our division was featured on the front page of the newspaper this Monday."

Surprised, Helena asked, "Oh, wow, for what?"

Tina lowered her voice as if she was spilling a secret, "ready for this? The headline was Bosses from Hell."

"Oh my goodness, haha, okay," Helena chuckled nervously, "why don't you send me some background documents and we'll go from there?" Tina and Helena quickly drew up a tentative plan to conduct a few focus groups, team interviews, and one-on-one coaching with the leadership team including our dear Pedro, aka the Boss from Hell.

The assignment

The following week Helena was invited to their leadership meeting on-site. There were six of them waiting – three deputy chiefs, one of them being the newest hire with a rumor of being parachuted in by the chief, manager of operations, manager of administration, and Pedro, the chief. As Helena entered the boardroom, Pedro stood up to greet her in his formal suit with a silk pocket square.

"Welcome, Dr. Cho, how do you do?"

"Ah, you must be Pedro. How's it going? Please call me Helena."

Pedro was soft-spoken, Helena's first surprise, and he gestured her to an empty chair across the table. There were a few copies of charts and reports – perhaps the engagement survey results – spread out on the table.

As Helena settled in the seat, Tina introduced her to the group. "So, I suggested that Helena come and meet us in person before we start the listening sessions with our teams here." They nodded at her as she smiled back.

"Listening session? Is that what we call it?" Pedro asked as he took out a fountain pen, getting ready to write in his black leatherbound notebook. The nods stopped and everyone looked at him. "We'll get a tangible action plan after all that listening to fix this, right?" He tapped his pen on one of the charts as he looked around the room before he set his gaze on Helena. "In six months, there's another engagement survey, and the scores need to be better than this."

It felt like a time-out room with an angry parent scolding, and no one spoke up – Helena's second surprise. So, she said, "so, Pedro, you want to see the score go up in the next survey."

"Absolutely. This is not acceptable. This is embarrassing!"

"For us to move in that direction, we might need to do a few things including talking to your teams." As Helena was subtly presenting the plan, he interrupted, "yes, please find out who is saying all this." Helena continued, "and it might mean that you will participate in coaching." He raised his eyebrows with his finger pointing to his chest, "me?" Helena nodded, "yes, to get a better sense of your vision of your team, is that okay?"

Perhaps surprised or hesitant, Pedro quickly replied, "of course, whatever it takes."

That's how it began – a six-month coaching engagement with a group of 80 lawyers in one of the largest agencies in the public service sector.

The coaching

Before meeting with Pedro for his first coaching session, Helena got to meet the team first. Some of them came to a focus group while most of them chose to meet privately as they feared retribution, they said. Many of them sat silent when asked "so, what do you appreciate, even a little bit, about Pedro as a leader?" Some even joked, "at least he dresses nicely," while some others got visibly irritated at that question. Helena was able to gather more answers when she asked "what would you like for your leader to do differently?" But almost all of them asked her for reassurance, "you're not gonna tell him that I said this, right?"

On the day of Pedro's first coaching session, he emailed in the morning requesting a last-minute change that they meet at her office, not his. He walked in right on time, and Helena ushered him to a coaching room.

"So, you've been talking to my team?" he asked, taking off his coat.

"Yes," Helena answered with a smile.

"Who did you talk to so far?" came next as he settled into his armchair.

"Quite a few," was what he got as Helena took out her pen to take notes.

"I already know who told you what, but I want to hear from you. What are they saying that I need to know?" Clearly irritated, he leaned forward with a frown on his face.

"Well..." Helena hesitated, looking for her next words.

Key challenges

- Expectation that the coach's work is to 'fix' someone or something.
- Misaligned definitions and expectations of what coaching is and what a coach does.
- The coach's emotional context interacting with a client with potentially unreasonable or questionable demands.
- Education and role clarification bordering on implicit power dynamics.
- Leadership using coaching as camouflage for pushing through an agenda or even as a corrective tool.

EXAMPLE ETHICAL IMPLICATIONS

- **Concerns around confidentiality** – the coach is being asked by the client to share the information gathered during the focus groups and one-on-one sessions.
- **Power dynamics** – there are power dynamics (and pressure) between the client and coach, within the leadership team, and among the employees.
- **Transparency** – the coaching process, the role of coaching, and the coach's boundaries are not clarified, leading to potential conflicts of interest.

REFLECTIVE QUESTIONS FOR DISCUSSION

1. How might a coach navigate a situation where multiple stakeholders' (sponsor, client, other stakeholders) understanding of coaching is very different, even opposing each other?
2. How might a coach handle a situation where they may have a strong opinion or bias toward or against their coaching client?
3. How might a coach respond to multiple stakeholders wanting the coach to take a side or persuade them to be on their side?

Case study 2

Just because a coach can coach, should they coach?

Annalise Roache

Overview

Coaching is built on the bedrock of trust, where the client's agenda is prominent, and the coach serves the client's needs and development. Adding to the foundation of trust is the principle of beneficence, "acting in the best interests of the client ... it directs attention to working strictly within one's limits of competence and providing services on the basis of adequate training or experience" (Jarden et al., 2021, p. 13). In this case study, the reader will be asked to explore how trust and beneficence extend beyond professional expertise and training to personal beliefs. Van Nieuwenburgh (2014) refers to "ethical moments of choice" (p. 172), which coaches face throughout any engagement. A point of decision about which path to take. In this case study, we explore such a choice. Can a coach, and should a coach, detach from deeply held personal beliefs that do not align with the client's? Can a coach provide safe, dignity-enhancing quality service when they do not understand their client's worldview? We extend this quandary to explore the challenges of using third-party providers to deliver coaching services and ask if enough is done to safeguard that accurate information is provided during the matching process. The reader will be asked to reflect on a profoundly challenging 'ethical moment of choice': just because a coach can coach, should they coach?

Case study

Background

Ruru Tech is a recent entrant into the digital technology industry and is expanding globally at a fast rate. To support the increasing operational needs and attract and retain high-quality personnel, Ruru has elected to invest in two flagship initiatives: firstly, a comprehensive emerging leadership development programme and secondly, a commitment to inclusion and diversity including the pursuit of LGBT+ and Rainbow accreditation in countries with such programmes in place. The initiatives are being rolled out through Ruru's People Management Division, which has enlisted the assistance of a third-party training and coaching provider, Flotsam Group, to deliver and coordinate the emerging leaders' programme across their global network.

DOI: 10.4324/b23351-7

Flotsam Group is an international training organisation that uses a hybrid mix of employees and contracted associates for instructional design, training delivery and coaching resources.

Elliot is a credentialed coach who has worked in private practice for a decade as a leadership and career coach. Before training as a coach, Elliot held several senior leadership roles in a global organisation. He is a lay preacher and active church member. His faith is an ever-present guide in his personal and professional life; however, this is not explicitly stated on his coaching biography or website, as this is not common practice. He is a long-standing associate working with Flotsam. He has provided coaching to support many of their global programmes. Elliot recently secured a place on the coaching panel for the Ruru Tech programme. The project involves working with several emerging leaders over the coming years; it is a lucrative and exciting opportunity.

Jax is an aspiring leader who has been with Ruru Tech for five years working in Research and Development and is on track for promotion in the coming months. Jax is thrilled to have been selected for the next intake of the emerging leaders' programme and sees this as a real commitment from Ruru for future opportunities within the company. Jax volunteers at a local LGBTQI+ youth service providing mentoring outside of work. Along with Andie, whom Jax has been with for ten years, they are planning their upcoming wedding. When Jax receives the coaching profiles, Elliot's positive psychology training stands out. Jax believes this could be an excellent way to learn valuable tools and techniques that could be applied in all parts of life.

Barnaby is a trained mentor, supervisor and credentialed coach who has had regular supervision sessions with Elliot for several years. The pair initially met through their church, establishing a professional relationship.

The assignment

Flotsam includes one-to-one coaching support for each participant during the term of the one-year emerging leaders' programme.

Before the programme started, participants were sent a link to the Flotsam website to review the Coaching Panel, which provides an overview of the coaches and outlines their professional experience, credentials, education and a brief statement about their personal interests. Ruru and Flotsam are committed to supporting the whole person's wellbeing and development. As such, they expect coaching topics to cover both the professional and personal, stipulating that a coaching client will work towards two leadership goals and one personal goal.

The coaching

Jax and Elliot connect via Flotsam's automated booking system for an initial phone call and chemistry check. The call is brief and centred on Elliot explaining how coaching works. They explore Jax's intentions for the programme with a focus on understanding how coaching will support Jax's progress and highlighting any concerns or hesitation which may impede progress during the opening stages of the programme. They agree to meet at the first in-person emerging leaders' session, where they will confirm a regular meeting schedule and dive into goal setting.

During the first meeting, Jax immediately notices that Elliot is wearing a crucifix around his neck; this raises alarm bells for Jax, who is aware that not all people with strong religious views support the Rainbow Community. At the same time, Elliot glances at Jax's nametag and notices the words in brackets (they/them). Looking around the room, Elliot sees that all of the Ruru staff have words listed on their nametags, and as people stand up to introduce themselves to the group, they state their name followed by he/him or she/her or they/them, etc. Unsure of what this means, Elliot feels a degree of unease mounting.

As they sit down to have their first official coaching session, Elliot asks Jax, "can I ask you about the words listed after your name?" to which Jax responds, "yes, these are my pronouns, and I would appreciate you using them." Elliot is perplexed, not sure what it means for someone to be a "them or they," and asks Jax, "what does it mean? Are you not a man or a woman, he or she?" Jax responds, "I am neither, I am non-binary." Feeling unsure of how to react, Elliot shrugs, smiles and asks if Jax would like to get underway with their first coaching session. Jax is taken aback and, without thinking, nods in agreement.

The first session focuses on setting goals, with Jax identifying a leadership programme goal, a work goal and a personal goal focused on managing stress with the pressures of organising a wedding. Elliot and Jax leave the session with good clarity around the expected goals. However, underlying uncertainty exists about whether they are a good coaching match.

Later that same week, Elliot has a coaching supervision session with Barnaby, where he outlines his concerns about this new coaching connection and his hesitations about someone being non-binary, especially when marriage is being discussed. Barnaby asks Elliot, "how are you feeling about this engagement?," to which Elliot responds, "I am torn; on the one hand, I do not understand who this client is, and on the other hand, I am committed through my training to put aside my personal beliefs and to focus on the client's needs and agenda." Barnaby asks, "is that something you believe you can truly do in this case?" Elliot says, "I would like to think so."

Key challenges

- The coach has the skills and experience to coach the client but needs to make an ethical choice.
- The coaching client is faced with an ethical decision about the safety and suitability of working with the coach.
- Unconscious biases may be at play for the supervisor, coach and coaching client in this relationship.
- Coach and client wonder whether this is an ethically appropriate coaching match.

- The sponsor and training provider may be unaware of any ethical challenges.
- Ethical choices are left to the individual to enact.

EXAMPLE ETHICAL IMPLICATIONS

- **Shift in value and trustworthiness** – the coaching client became aware of differences in values and beliefs which called into question if the coach was the best fit.
- **Recognise personal limitations and potential biases** – the coach sought professional support to explore their ability to provide coaching.
- **Avoid discrimination by maintaining fairness and equity and justice** – the coach maintains fairness and equity in the provision of services.
- **Respect for people's rights and dignity** – the coach seeks clarity and knowledge by asking questions about the use of pronouns.
- **Responsible caring** – the coach must recognise the boundaries of their expertise (including a deficiency of knowledge) and protect their clients' welfare.
- **Autonomy** – the coach respects the client's right to be self-governing and self-directing regarding the provision of services.

REFLECTIVE QUESTIONS FOR DISCUSSION

1. What 'ethical moments of choice' can you identify in this case study?
2. How can the systems be set up to match the coaching client and coach in order to serve the desired purpose?
3. Do you believe a coach can genuinely separate their personal beliefs from their practice, and even if they can, should they?

References

Jarden, A., Rashid, T., Roache, A., & Lomas, T. (2021). Ethical guidelines for positive psychology practice (version 2.0: English). *International Journal of Wellbeing, 11*(3), 1–38.

van Nieuwerburgh, C. (2014). *An Introduction to Coaching Skills: A Practical Guide* (1st ed.). Sage Publications Ltd.

Death of a parent

Coaching or therapy?

Yannick Jacob

Overview

The coaching client approached the coach for a six-session engagement focused on navigating away from a toxic work environment. Two weeks ahead of commencing the coaching, the coaching client informed the coach via email that her mother had passed away. With the coaching client adamant to start the coaching relationship, with an awareness that bereavement can throw a spanner into the works of coaching, and left with lots of assumptions as to the actual state of mind of the coaching client, the coach had to decide whether to go ahead with meeting the client, whether coaching would be the right intervention, and how to navigate the ethical questions that emerged in the process.

A carefully considered email response acknowledging the coach's concerns, and attempting to ensure that coach and coaching client continue to co-create the space, was followed by an initial chemistry call in order to ascertain the resourcefulness of the coachee, as well as the extent to which coach and coachee were willing and able to engage in coaching at this time. Bracketing assumptions about what death means to people and to what extent it may be in the way of engaging in coaching was key in this scenario.

Case study

Background

Sitra contacted the coach, "Jack," following a friend's recommendation. She stated that her work environment was "toxic" and that it was time "to have the courage to make a change, leave my job, and move into a different sector."

Shortly after deciding to seek help from Jack, Sitra learned that her mother's health was deteriorating. She saw synchronicity in the timing of these events, and a profound awareness of the brevity of life instilled in her a sense of urgency to make changes sooner rather than later.

Sitra felt drawn to Jack's approach, grounded in existential philosophy and positive psychology, due to its emphasis on endings as an inevitable part of living. She felt it would allow her to explore some big questions surrounding the

DOI: 10.4324/b23351-8

approaching death of her mother. She felt that the positive psychology angle would help her build on her strengths and resources and look positively into the future.

Sadly, two weeks ahead of their consultation, Sitra's mother died. In the email describing the events, Sitra expressed she was eager to go ahead with the coaching as planned.

In the face of this profound loss, Jack questioned whether coaching would be the right fit at this moment. While Sitra never asked for help processing the loss of her parent, it was likely to play an important role in the coaching conversation. Jack knew that loss and grief can affect people in paralyzing ways, while others are well resourced to navigate their life and career well in the face of significant endings.

Jack noticed several assumptions that he was careful to 'park' ahead of answering Sitra's email, such as:

- Sitra and her mother were very close.
- Sitra seemed resourced, 'together', and processing this loss relatively well. She was responding to emails in a timely manner and without noticeable changes in tone. While she did sound sad, she seemed to be able to distinguish between processing her loss and thinking about her future.
- Her mentioning 'synchronicity' pointed to a spiritual framework that gave her strength.
- Nonetheless, it would be too early to engage in coaching. Some form of therapy or counselling would likely be more suitable.

Jack hence responded as follows:

Dear Sitra,

I'm very sorry to hear about your mum. I know you knew this day would come sooner rather than later, but still…

I am very mindful that this is all really fresh and, as you say, a big change in your life. I hear you when you say you're ready to do some work on navigating 2023, but I still wanted to check in with you to make sure that coaching will be the right fit for what you're going through at the moment.

While the existential approach to coaching is much more comfortable with conversations about endings and death than more traditional approaches to coaching, it can't and won't replace more bereavement-oriented services such as counselling or therapy. Coaching clients tend to be reasonably resourced and generally able to cope with life. So if you're feeling in a hole at the moment, you may want, or need, some time to just process what's been happening. In that case I think you'd probably be in much better hands with someone who just holds space for you to do that, without feeling the need to plan or navigate the year ahead. We could always tackle the more career and change-oriented topics at a later date.

I have the utmost respect for the impact that losing a loved one so close to you can have on people, so that's why I want to check in with you as to how you really are.

We could always meet as planned for a conversation and then decide together whether working together will be the right fit at this time. Given the significant change of your mother having passed away, I wanted to give you the option to call things off, or to move them to a later date. If, on the other hand, you feel in a decent enough space to engage in coaching and think ahead, then I would be delighted to hold this space for you and journey alongside you as you're entering a significant year.

Let me know your thoughts.

With love and condolences

Jack

A few days later Sitra replied:

Dear Jack,

Firstly, thank you for your thoughtful, empathetic, and professional feedback. I truly appreciate it.

I didn't reply straight away because I took very seriously what you wrote, and I needed to reflect on it.

I came to the decision to embrace the journey and to engage in coaching under your supervision if you agree of course. I feel that my strong desire, motivation, and commitment to enter a transformational process (workwise) got even stronger since the loss of my mother. However, I leave the final decision to you.

Yours sincerely,

Sitra

Jack and Sitra hence decided to meet for a conversation to ascertain whether to enter a coaching relationship at this time.

The assignment

Sitra expressed a profound desire to take her life to the next step by transitioning into a different career. Having reached her mid-50s, she wanted to live her life "with purpose, passion, and grace".

The chemistry session

The chemistry session was key in this engagement, and confirmed that Sitra was indeed very resourced and had been processing the passing of her mother in a healthy way. Her family and friends supported her well, and she made appropriate time to grieve and take care of her mental health.

Jack did not start the session by exploring her grief, but instead let Sitra lead the session as much as possible. When the conversation inevitably acknowledged the profound impact of her recent loss, Jack paid careful attention to *how* Sitra talked about her feelings while noticing body language, tonality, and other signs at the periphery of communication that might be in contrast to how resourceful Sitra presented herself.

It was clear that Sitra was affected by her loss. Yet, she was not only willing and able to engage in a coaching conversation about her future, but motivated by the perceived synchronicity of the events. Her mindset was positive, and she described feeling "gratitude and kindness towards the universe" in relation to how things had played out.

Jack and Sitra decided to enter a six-session coaching relationship with an understanding that, if Sitra's state of mind were to change during its course, or if Jack were to get a sense that Sitra may be in better hands with another practitioner, they would both be honest about whether to stop, pause, or refer.

Key challenges

- Whether to take on a client who presents with recent, significant loss and grief.
- How to handle the communication with the coaching client about the coach's concerns around the timing of coaching engagement following the passing of her mother.
- Coach needed to monitor signs of the coaching client's readiness for the process.
- Coach needed to be both willing and able to safely hold space and work with the coaching client.

EXAMPLE ETHICAL IMPLICATIONS

- **Responsibility to client and to practice** – when coaching someone who is grieving, it's important to be aware of their vulnerability and the increased responsibility taken on by the coach.
- **Managing boundaries** – the coach needed to be aware of and contract for boundaries as he was about to enter the gray area between coaching and therapy.
- **Duty of care and clarity** – coach was careful with taking the client's written word (which is limited in its scope as a means of communication) at face value as not to create a space that may be inappropriate or harmful to the client.
- **Monitoring biases and assumptions** – personal stories and experiences can have a profound effect on the coach–coaching client relationship. Projections and transference may affect the client involuntarily.

REFLECTIVE QUESTIONS FOR DISCUSSION

1. How far are you willing *and* able to go with a coaching client? *Can* you, and do you *want* to hold the space that you enter when you and your coaching client open certain doors together?
2. What relevant training, education, qualification, and personal experiences have you acquired that contribute to your willingness and ability to work with your coaching client's material?
3. How might your personal experiences, relationships with, and/or transference related to your coaching client's scenario affect your ability to hold space for your coaching client?

Protecting boundaries

One coach, two clients

Charline S. Russo

Overview

Coaching multiple members in an organization can be challenging. Having discussions with the clients, clarifying boundaries, confidentiality and maintaining trust do not always mitigate critical points of tension for the coach. Ethical dilemmas and conflicting agendas can still challenge the coach and the coaching process. Some challenges can present themselves in the moment, requiring immediate decisions. An executive coach has been asked to coach the CEO and CHRO (who is also the point of contact for the coach and the organization) of a start-up biotech company. The critical points of tension for the coach in this case were the coaching conversations concerning the disconnect between the CEO and CHRO on the timing of the COO transition and how to maintain boundaries, confidentiality and trust while not withholding critical information that could seriously affect the company. Consideration of what might have happened if the coach wasn't coaching both of them is one of the many "what ifs…" which contribute to the difficult ethical dilemmas. How can a coach demonstrate how to look out for clients without breaching the coach–client contract?

Case study

Background

The Scipio Consulting Group (SCG) was invited to meet with Marta Caspari, Chief Human Resources Officer (CHRO) of Othrys Pharma, a start-up biotech company that has grown from three employees two years ago to 287 employees today. The focus of the meeting was to discuss potential coaching and organizational development initiatives. Dr. Allison Thalia and Dr. Jason Pater, two of the SCG principals, met with her and discussed Othrys Pharma and how coaching and organizational development might be appropriate at this time. They shared their approach to coaching and organizational development. They also shared information about the members of the team, their capabilities and their previous work in coaching and consulting.

DOI: 10.4324/b23351-9

Shortly after this meeting, Marta contacted Allison and said that Othrys Pharma wanted to partner with the SCG. It was agreed that Marta would be the point of contact, the primary client, for Othrys Pharma.

The assignment

Soon after meeting with Allison, Marta asked her to meet with Dr. Simon Macherenko, MD, the CEO of Othrys Pharma, and a founding member, for a potential executive coaching engagement. Simon and Allison met and discussed coaching and the conditions of an engagement including confidentiality, boundaries and standards. After this meeting, Simon engaged Allison as his executive coach.

Simon and Allison were working together for two months when, during a point of contact meeting with Marta, the possibility of engaging Allison as an executive coach for her was raised. Allison offered other members of SCG for consideration, but Marta said that she wanted to work with Allison. She said that she and Simon discussed this and that they both agreed that if Allison was willing to coach them both, they trusted her and felt comfortable with her as their coach.

Allison thought about this and discussed it with her colleague, Jason. They agreed that she would have a meeting with Simon and Marta, reviewing the conditions of the coaching engagements. Simon and Marta agreed to the meeting which was scheduled that week. They discussed their expectations of boundaries, confidentiality, standards and how potential conflicts would be managed and agreed to the two executive coaching engagements with Allison who would be an executive coach to each one. They planned to share their coaching conversations just as they share other important information in their roles as CEO and CHRO.

The coaching

A few weeks into the coaching engagement, Marta shared in a coaching session that she had an important and crucial meeting with the president and chief operating officer (COO), Sarena Reddy, one of the founding members of Othrys Pharma. Sarena was known as a very smart, strategic, powerful micromanager at Othrys. She intimidated her direct reports and colleagues as well. The purpose of the meeting with Sarena was to discuss Sarena's transition to a new role of chief strategy officer, effective next month. They talked about how she would conduct what she expected to be a difficult meeting with challenges from Sarena and how important it was that Simon created and supported this new role for Sarena. The meeting would be held at Sarena's home for privacy and to make her more comfortable with what would surely be difficult news. Allison and Marta role played a few scenarios and Marta felt ready for this critical conversation.

Two days later, during a coaching conversation, Simon discussed his challenges in managing Sarena. She was becoming more difficult in the executive leadership team, disregarding organizational structure, trying to run everyone's departments. Newly hired executives were threatening to leave and recruiting executives for the expanding company was becoming more difficult. Biotech is a small world!

He said that he was planning to change her role to chief strategy officer after Othrys submitted its first FDA filing in nine months. As Allison listened to Simon, alarms went off in her head. Marta is meeting with Sarena, later this week, to discuss her transition to the new role, effective next month. She understood that she had Simon's support and was moving ahead confidently with this knowledge. Simon just told Allison that he plans this move in nine months.

Allison knew that maintaining confidentiality and boundaries is one of the cornerstones of the coaching relationship. However, if Marta moved forward with announcing Sarena's transition next month while Simon was planning for the transition in nine months, the potential damage to Othrys could be catastrophic. Allison also knew that she could not violate confidentiality ... and she knew that she could not ignore this information because of its potential impact on the success of Othrys Pharma. She also remembered that they both agreed that they would share their coaching conversations. However, Allison did not know if they had actually shared any coaching conversations. She did not agree to share their conversations.

The timing of Marta's meeting with Sarena required quick action. Allison was listening to Simon while processing several scenarios. This was the conversation:

Allison: How do you plan to announce this transition to Sarena?
Simon: After our FDA filing in nine months, I will have a meeting with her and tell her that her new role will be Chief Strategic Officer.
Allison: Have you discussed this plan with anyone else yet?
Simon: Yes, I have spoken with Marta so that she can plan the transition in an effective way.
Allison: Have you and Marta created a plan?
Simon: Well, we have talked about the need for Sarena's new role, how important it is for her to be on board and for the organization to be prepared. We will speak with Sarena after the FDA filing.
Allison: You have shared some previous missteps with Marta. Are you sure that you are aligned on this plan?
Simon: I'm not sure. I think I will check in with her today and review our plan.
Allison: That's a good idea.

Key challenges

- The coaching conversation concerning the disconnect between the CEO and CHRO on timing of the COO transition.
- How to maintain boundaries, confidentiality and trust while not withholding critical information that could seriously affect the company.

EXAMPLE ETHICAL IMPLICATIONS

- **Boundaries in the coaching engagement** – although there was 'agreement' about boundaries, confidentiality and trust, the agreement was not checked during the engagement to determine alignment and clarity between the coach and each client and the clients as well.
- **Boundary in the relationship with the organizational client** – the boundary between the organizational point of contact/primary client was not checked at regular intervals, potentially confusing roles and relationships (i.e., what role is the CHRO in when meeting the coach—organizational representative, coaching client?).
- **Confidentiality** – the coach and each client discussed confidentiality. When specific issues arose, they did not check in and make sure that their original understanding was still aligned and consistent with their coaching conversations.

REFLECTIVE QUESTIONS

1. What ethical challenges did the coach face?
2. Did the coach handle the challenges appropriately? What other strategies might she have used?
3. How might the coach handle future challenges in these coaching engagements?

Case study 5

Focusing on the whole person

Co-creating successful coaching outcomes in organizations

Alissa M. Manolescu and Sasha E. Radin

Overview

Many coaches working in corporate contexts will be guided to focus on organizational objectives and, sometimes, to address a performance problem for a particular person. There is often an expectation that the coach will produce results for the contracting (and presumably funding) party in line with their organizational goals.

If this happens, is there a bias towards focusing on the problem as perceived by the organization, rather than on the person being coached? Can organizational goals be met if the whole person is not attended to? What if the organization is in part responsible for the very problem they brought the coach in to solve?

Industry experts maintain that clients' intrinsic aspirations can induce meaningful change (Boyatzis et al., 2013). Boniwell, Smith and Green (2021) argue that focusing on individual wellbeing is fundamental to organizational health. At the same time, Roche and Passmore emphasize that coaching must "address the systems that are the source of the problem" (2021, p. 15).

The authors propose that focusing on the whole person first – including the systems that shape them – allows space for the goals and desires to emerge from within the coaching client that, in turn, enable overarching organizational outcomes to be realized.

Case study

Background

Jill (coaching client) is an executive relatively new in her role and to the organization (~6 months in). She is an African-American female in her 40s.

Angela (coach) is an external coach brought in by Jill's boss, Kevin.

Kevin (sponsor), a white male in his 50s, is the CEO. According to him, Jill isn't meeting expectations. Like many organizations, this business is going through a major transformation. Kevin brought Jill on to lead this transition given her track record of successfully leading her previous company through a restructuring.

DOI: 10.4324/b23351-10

The assignment

Angela is brought in to help improve Jill's performance. The CEO, Kevin, still sees potential for Jill and thinks a coach can help Jill improve her strategic planning and decision-making abilities – skills he deems key to the team re-gaining confidence in her ability to lead through change and uncertainty. He also believes improving her executive presence will contribute to her ability to influence the team more effectively. As part of the coaching engagement, Angela is contracted to conduct a 360 assessment for Jill to obtain feedback to aid in her development.

Angela has already sat down with Kevin to get a clearer picture of what he is looking for and discuss his role throughout the coaching period. In her conversation with him she suggests having a number of three-way conversations throughout and advocates for maximum transparency between himself and Jill. Of course, what is said between herself and Jill will remain confidential. Angela also reminds Kevin that Jill's 360 results are for Jill only, but that she would be encouraged to share as much as she is comfortable with Kevin. He agrees.

The coaching

In Angela's first meeting with Jill, Angela spends much of the session listening to Jill share what the past six months at her new organization have been like for her. She asks what's most important for Jill to get out of their time together. They then discuss Kevin's agenda for the coaching and how Jill sees that.

Jill: It's been hard to build connections here; I underestimated how hard it would be to start over. It's a boys club here – I'm not making excuses, but I definitely feel like I'm an outsider, that there are discussions that are had and consensus reached before I even get into the room. I need to improve my ability to influence the team.

Angela asks Jill how she's engaged in Kevin's support in building influence. Jill shares that "Kevin suggested she improve her executive presence; to have influence, people need to see her as the leader."

Jill tells a story about a leadership team meeting, during which the team's reactions to her comments made her feel she wasn't "part of the club."

Jill: I told them I thought there was a lot of risk we weren't accounting for, that we weren't ready to move forward … After an uncomfortable silence they made it clear that I'm new and don't get how they do things here. I ended up agreeing to their recommendations against my better judgment. I'm angry at myself for caving in.

Angela asks, "How did your discomfort influence your actions in that situation?"

Jill is visibly upset. "It's not just that situation, but yeah, I've been second-guessing myself more. In that moment when I feel like an outsider I think – 'maybe they do know better.'"

Angela takes a breath, and says, "It seems like that is really striking a nerve in you. What is coming up for you now?"

Jill: I realize that I am making myself small, the opposite of what a leader does. It's hard to see that.

Angela pauses, taking another breath and says, "That's painful." She pauses again. "What would the opposite of that look like for you?"

Jill: I would be confident in myself, irrespective of the push back from others. It's really about my confidence, isn't it?

Angela reflects that she hears two threads they could work on: (1) Jill's own inner work on self-doubt and confidence and (2) how she navigates a corporate culture that sees her as an outsider. Jill smiles and agrees.

Angela then suggests bringing in Kevin's agenda, and asks Jill how she sees it.

Jill: If you had asked me that at the start, I would have felt really defensive. I know that I am a good strategic thinker and am capable of making tough decisions. Now, I still feel a little reactive. But I also see that working on my confidence and self-doubt may actually be good for both me and the company.

Angela expresses curiosity about Jill's reaction. Jill acknowledges there are opportunities for her own development, but also points out that there are cultural barriers in the organization that she is up against as one of the few women, and the only woman of color, in leadership.

Jill: I feel like a successful outcome will take more than just me shifting.
Angela: Yes, I hear you. Would this be something you would be open to bringing up in our meeting with Kevin?

Jill hesitates, but is up for trying. They proceed to discuss what Jill might say to Kevin and how she would say it.

Follow-up session

Several weeks later, Angela sits down with Kevin and Jill to discuss the feedback from Jill's 360 assessment.

As Jill is summarizing the feedback she received from her colleagues, Angela notices she does not mention her perspective or the experiences she described in their initial conversation.

Angela turns to Jill: "I'm curious if you'd be open to sharing with Kevin what you shared with me in our first meeting? How do you experience your colleagues and the environment on the team? How does that impact you?"

Jill shrugs. "Ah. I guess you're talking about how I'm not really part of the club – like there are these side conversations happening and I'm missing context and important information to drive decisions for our business."

Angela: You said something I'd like to dig into – that you're not part of the club. Is it fair to say you don't feel included as a member of the team?

Jill nods.

Angela: Jill, do you feel seen by Kevin? Does he make you feel like you belong here?

Jill turns her head and looks down. She is silent for a full ten seconds. She seems to gather herself and sits up straighter. "Sometimes I do. Other times I don't."
Kevin is quiet, and his face registers what appears to be shock.

Angela: That is very brave of you to share, Jill. You know, research shows that when employees don't feel a sense of belonging, their performance suffers – so it's no surprise that it could also affect your performance.

Later that afternoon, Kevin calls Angela directly.

Kevin: I've been thinking all day about that debrief. At first I felt kind of defensive and angry – then I realized I'm accountable here. I'm angry at myself, partly, for missing what was happening – I had no idea, but I should have. What can I start doing differently?

Key challenges

- Angela needs to make Jill feel comfortable enough to trust her and speak freely. This is a particular challenge for a coach hired by another stakeholder (the organization).
- Angela must figure out how to create space for Jill to truly figure out what she needs to work on, while still addressing Kevin's agenda.
- Angela must navigate the tension between what is in Jill's locus of control (e.g., her behavior) and the wider sociocultural factors and organizational environment that impact the very problem Jill presents.

EXAMPLE ETHICAL IMPLICATIONS

- **Preserving the confidentiality of the coach/coaching client relationship** – the coach establishes the confidentiality boundaries with the sponsor from the start.

- **Cultivating safety and presence** – the coach acknowledges the coaching client's perceptions and experiences as valid.
- **Focusing on the coaching client's vision and goals** – the coach is present with what is emerging for the client, rather than limiting the conversation to her sponsor's specific goals.
- **Addressing broader context and systems** – the coach navigates issues of race, gender and power dynamics in the coaching engagement.
- **Contracting (or setting other formal agreements)** – the coach works with all stakeholders at the outset of coaching to establish clear expectations and roles, as well as addressing potential for conflicting stakeholder interests.

REFLECTIVE QUESTIONS FOR DISCUSSION

1. How can a coach best navigate the coaching client's wellbeing and needs while attending to organizational coaching priorities?
2. Does starting with the coaching client's goals and leaving space for what emerges actually result in a better outcome for the organization?
3. As coaches in organizations, we often serve as advisors to the sponsor or organization, even if not formally contracted as such. What are the ethical implications of focusing only on the individual coaching client vs. addressing the systems-level (including sociocultural, organizational, etc.) factors that may be impacting the coaching client?

References

Boniwell, I., Smith, W. A., & Green, S. (2021). PPC in the workplace: The business case. In Smith, W. A., Boniwell, I., & Green, S. (eds.), *Positive Psychology Coaching in the Workplace*. Cham: Springer. https://doi.org/10.1007/978-3-030-79952-6_1

Boyatzis, R. E., Smith, M. L., & Beveridge, A. J. (2013). Coaching with compassion. *The Journal of Applied Behavioral Science*, 49(2), 153–178.

Roche, C., & Passmore, J. (2021). *Racial Justice, Equity and Belonging in Coaching*. Henley-on-Thames: Henley Business School.

Chapter 4

Supervision

Supervision, the bedrock of professional growth and ethical practice, brings with it its own challenges both for the supervisor and within the supervision. Chapter 4 delves into complex scenarios such as mental health, roles, bereavement, the educator and the supervisor, and values.

DOI: 10.4324/b23351-11

Collusion brought to coach supervision

Eve Turner

Overview

A coach comes to supervision with concerns about a new external assignment. These include boundary management, issues with contracting, clarity of outcomes, risks to confidentiality, bullying and racism, the latter two being among the coach's 'hot spots.'

The coaching client, a team leader ostensibly trying to improve poor performance in her team, is being accused of bullying. She herself feels she is being bullied and subject to racism from her team, and feels unsupported by the organisation. While the organisation's outcomes relate to the coaching client changing her approach to the team, the coach's concerns are around the client's well-being and mental health.

The coach has organisational knowledge he is unwillingly privy to that may affect the client's career. He believes she is unaware of this information and its possible influence on her future. The coach reflects he is being drawn into seeing the situation from the client's perspective and is in danger of collusion and not building a collective picture. The coach also has concerns about risking trust and is uncomfortable knowing he has 'secret' information that could impact negatively on the client. He also fears he may jeopardise a long-term professional relationship with the client's line manager.

Case study

The background

Raj is a coach, working with public sector organisations in several countries, including central and local government departments, universities, other higher education institutions and health services. Raj is concerned about an assignment he is working on. The current coaching client, Imani, is a team leader in her department. She feels that her attempts to give constructive feedback to some team members to improve their performance are being met with accusations of bullying. In turn, Imani, who is black, believes that she is being subject to bullying and to racism herself by the same team, and Raj has concerns about her well-being and self-care.

DOI: 10.4324/b23351-12

The sponsor of the coaching, Jean, took part in an initial three-way meeting. Since then, Jean, who is also the line manager, has tried to have 'off the record' conversations with Raj, and give him additional information, at times information which Imani is unaware of.

Imani believes the allegations against her may be an unspoken criterion used as part of a process to take her down a performance route with dismissal possible. She feels particularly vulnerable as there are rumours staffing cuts will be announced soon. Raj is feeling drawn to take Imani's side, against the poor, unsupportive and ineffectual management, as he sees it.

Jean is also the person who brings Raj into the wider organisation for coaching assignments; he has had a few dozen in recent years. In the initial assignment one-to-one briefing with Raj, Jean had mentioned areas such as possible redundancies that may include Imani, but did not then mention these in the three-way meeting. This leaves Raj unwillingly privy to knowledge Imani does not have, although given the rumours she is fearful.

Raj has been coming to Ash for supervision for a long time. They have a trusting, supportive relationship where mutual challenge is safe. Raj is normally very self-aware and keen on working to the highest ethical standards. Raj is aware that he has 'hot spots' that include bullying and racism.

The assignment

The key organisational objectives for the coaching are given as:

1. Imani needs to be less abrasive in her department, and to develop a less blunt approach to some of her team.
2. She is encouraged to communicate better, with more nuance, and to listen more.
3. Imani is being urged to develop ways of dealing with different situations from a more 'mindful' place – and be adaptable and draw on different approaches as a team leader.

The coaching supervision

As the coach, Raj addressed the intention of coaching with some trepidation. He already felt "wrong-footed," because he believed that the coaching context was not overt and transparent, so unethical to him. There is an organisational picture not wholly known to the Imani. Raj feels the organisation is trying to get him 'on side' by giving him 'confidential' information. Raj told Ash, "I am feeling very worried. The line manager has had no recent conversations with Imani and has an agenda that she is unaware of."

From Raj's conversation with Imani, he believes that her mental health and well-being are at stake, as she deals with what she describes as "malicious allegations." At one point Raj wondered, "Is she having a breakdown?" So, while he has agreed to an assignment where there is pressure on Imani to change, he now worries more about her personal state. He says, "I want to help Imani feel more resourceful, but I am not sure how to do this and help her meet the organisational outcomes."

Raj is also pondering how to make his concerns known to the organisation. This is partly because in the initial three-way conversation, giving feedback, or the continuing involvement of the organisation, through the sponsor, was not discussed and therefore no approach has been agreed. So he has no agreed route (Raj, Imani and Jean) to bring in the organisation as the situation becomes more complex. And he also has concerns now that any disclosures could breach the trust he has built with Imani.

Imani's coaching intention is that she gets support, someone who will stand by her, at a time when she is experiencing the organisation as unsupportive and uncaring. The outcomes agreed in the three-way conversation are, in her eyes, secondary. Imani has told him,

> I trust you, Raj. You are the only person on my side. You can see that my intention of addressing poor performance in the team has been met with these false accusations of me bullying them. They don't appreciate that my leadership style, because of my background, is different from theirs and they want me to conform to their notions of what is "right."

In the background is Raj's awareness that a significant part of his coaching portfolio relies on the strong relationship he has built up with Jean. Meanwhile Jean's intention, mentioned in the initial briefing, includes wanting Raj to "make Imani see that it is how you talk to people that counts. She is talking at them and is telling them off."

Ash's intention, as supervisor, is to support Raj to see the whole system, so he can be better able to help Imani and Jean see the system too. Ash helped him step back and see the perspective of all parties and not get drawn into believing that there might be 'one truth' about the situation.

Raj has also become overwhelmed by the situation, in parallel with Imani, and by rediscovering his resourcefulness, and recalling many previously successful approaches he has used, he can decide what to draw from.

The key challenges

- Lack of clarity in outcomes and issues around boundary management.
- Raj being 'sucked into' the client's world and losing perspective, and not seeing the 'whole system.' Each party may see themselves as acting ethically and Raj is not standing back to consider what might change in the system to create a collective ethical perspective.
- Raj's own experience of racism and bullying, which have made these two of his 'hot' spots.
- The coach feeling his relationships with Imani and Jean could both suffer through his actions.

- Imani seeing the organisation as the 'enemy' and therefore not engaging in the outcomes.
- The organisation believing there is no progress.

EXAMPLE ETHICAL IMPLICATIONS

- **Boundaries of the coaching engagement** – these were not clear, nor was a process agreed to revisit these regularly throughout the coaching assignment.
- **Confidentiality** – the agreement on the sharing of information among all parties was unclear.
- **Lack of transparency** – Imani lacked knowledge that others had, relevant to the assignment.
- **Trust** – Raj was being drawn to take one perspective as truth, that of Imani. This risked trust and the relationship with the organisation.
- **Multiple relationships** – Raj had different relationship 'hats' with the line manager and sponsor of this assignment.

REFLECTIVE QUESTIONS FOR DISCUSSION

1. How can a coach deal with wearing multiple hats in working as an external coach in an organisation?
2. What ethical issues are raised for a coach when accusations of racism are made?
3. Each of the parties may see themselves as acting ethically, and the others acting unethically. What could change in the system to create a collectively ethical perspective?

Case study 7

When mental health shows up in cross-professional group supervision

Listening to different perspectives

Anne Calleja and Carol Whitaker

Overview

The case is a cross-professional supervision group of four coaches and two thera-peutic coaches, co-supervised by two accredited supervisors – one an executive coach and supervisor and the other a clinical psychotherapist, supervisor, and lead-ership coach. Co-facilitated supervision offers the opportunity for supervisors to complement each other's style, explore the learning from working with difference, and role model trust and vulnerability (Whitaker & Lucas, 2012). The supervisors work together to role model the value of working with different perspectives and backgrounds.

This case study demonstrates how cross-professional supervision can add value and provide a pathway for exploration that meets the coach where they are, and helps them support a coaching client who arrives with mental health issues.

The case is an exploration of the human response and how to 'contain' a safe space, by not going beyond the coach's competency and capability. Different and wider systemic perspectives and contracting with the complex relationships between coach and coaching client/s, coach and supervisor, and coach and organi-zation are considered.

Case study

Background

In this method of group supervision one of the coaches presents a case to one of the co-supervisors and peers listen and observe. Once the story is told, the other co-supervisor joins the original supervisor and they discuss and reflect on the case together. They position themselves face to face in a 'gold-fish bowl' avoiding eye contact with both the presenting coach and peer coaches, thus allowing both the coach and peers to digest the conversation and reflect on their learning.

In this study the clinical supervisor is Maggie, the coach supervisor is Pam there are five peer coaches in attendance, and coach Clare who shares her story.

DOI: 10.4324/b23351-13

The assignment

The goal is to support the coach, offer options, raise their awareness and confidence, and exchange knowledge, experience, and different perspectives.

Another aim is to give developmental feedback to the coach and share learning with the whole group.

Coaching supervision

Clare has brought a client case to the group. Maggie (lead supervisor) asks Clare to "bring her client 'into the room'" by describing how the client presents themselves and to set the scene. Clare says "Latisha is female, in her 50s, Head of Finance, a trusted employee and a high achiever. She presents as 'fidgety' with lack of eye contact. Smartly dressed."

A 360-feedback appraisal revealed that Latisha is technically proficient, yet staff find her challenging to work with. The feedback includes the fact that she works long hours, has high expectations, does not listen, and finds it difficult to delegate, connect, and work in a team.

Latisha's employer is very supportive and engaged Clare to coach Latisha to develop interpersonal relationships and trust to delegate to the team.

In the first meeting, Latisha presented as being very upset with her 360 feedback. She asked for help in building trusting relationships. Latisha recognized she lacks trust in others to do a job to her standards and knows she comes across "with a clipped accent" and "high attention to detail." She thinks through everything before speaking, for fear of being judged/getting 'it wrong.' She also expressed that she "had difficulty in dealing with several things at once; and that her focus of attention and thinking were disturbed by noise in the open plan office, so she wears headphones to help her concentrate." She recognized that her staff found her aloof particularly when under pressure (e.g., at accounting month end). Latisha also shared that she "felt she had failed in her personal relationships with two marriages ending in divorce, having had a controlling father, and feeling that no one seemed to understand her." Latisha was born in South Africa, where her family, daughters, and grandchildren still live. She feels very alone, and what gets her 'out of bed' is to go to work and have a sense of achievement. The feedback left her feeling isolated and hopeless. She desperately wanted to find out how she could build meaningful relationships. Latisha had researched ADHD online and identified with many of the symptoms. She asks the coach whether she should seek a diagnosis for ADHD.

Clare says she feels stuck, out of her depth, and frustrated.

Maggie asks Clare: "Describe Latisha's demeanor and the impact it had on you – what you noticed, felt and thought." Clare shares: "Latisha came across quite 'aggressively'." Clare feels frustrated that Latisha talks 'non-stop' and that her competence is being challenged. Latisha 'laughed' that her father was very strict; she was expected to be perfect, or she got a good telling off. Latisha says to Clare: "I can't do this" and asks, "What do you think?" and "What can you as a coach do about this?" She seems to expect Clare to fix the issue for her. Clare says she feels under pressure and that Latisha is casting doubt on her ability to help.

Maggie reflects to Clare,

Thank you for sharing what seems to be a very challenging and complex case. I sense this has caused you to question your own competency. I can hear your frustration with not being "allowed" to contribute in the way you would prefer, and your internal conflict of meeting the expectations of the employer, the emotions of Latisha and her wanting you to resolve the situation

Maggie then says to Clare, "Take a breath." Pause. "Check, inside, what are you noticing now? Take note of this." There is silence as they pause.

Maggie asks Clare, "How would you like the supervisors and peer group to offer any feedback?"

Clare suggests using the 'gold-fish bowl' approach that the group has used before as she would like time to process what is happening within her.

The two supervisors introduce the 'gold-fish bowl' process. They ask the group to listen, observe, and notice what happens within them as they experience the case.

The supervisors discuss (in front of the group and Clare) what they have heard. Clare therefore has the space to self-reflect, listen, and not feel pressured to contribute to the conversation.

Pam (second supervisor) asks, "I wonder about the impact of Latisha's need to be in charge/perfect. What effect has this had on Clare? Is there any transference?"

Maggie replies, "It would seem that Latisha's need to 'be perfect', the tone of voice described has triggered a strong response in Clare? Clare could consider this and share her reflection and learning with the group later?"

Pam asks Maggie, "In your role as a psychotherapist what's your view on the question raised about ADHD?"

Maggie responds, "In this complex case, it's important to recognize the key issues: Latisha's emotional response, reason for raising ADHD, role of the coach and focus for the coaching."

Pam says,

From an organization perspective, do we know the context in which the 360 was delivered by the employer? Was there any three-way meeting between Latisha, the line manager and Clare? It seems Latisha is very upset and surprised by the 360 feedback.

Pam observes,

Latisha seems to be specific and practical, e.g., asking Clare to help. A focus could be to agree goals based on the 360 feedback and discuss how Latisha can be confident and share the 360 feedback with her team, gain their support, and deliver a development plan.

Maggie says,

> In this way it would help Clare build on her strengths rather than cast doubt on her coaching ability, through reflecting with Latisha. This validates Latisha's emotional response, recognizes team relationships, and clarifies Clare's role as a coach. This would help identify priorities, what the coach can/can't do, discuss options for ADHD referral and employer expectations.

At the end of the discussion, Maggie and Pam ask Clare, "What are you noticing now? Are you comfortable sharing your reflections?"

Clare says,

> Yes. It has been very useful to observe and listen and not to have to respond in the moment. It gave me time to reflect on some actions I could take. It also helped to clarify my role as a coach in this context and where to focus my attention, whilst considering options for my next coaching session with Latisha. I now feel more settled and confident going forward.

The supervisors then ask the group members to give one word of appreciation to Clare and one piece of their own insight.

Key challenges

- The client's stream of dialogue made it difficult for the coach to contain the conversation, give feedback on her observations, and ask questions. This led to the coach doubting her own competency.
- The client questioned whether ADHD was the reason for the team feedback and assumed the coach's ability to diagnose ADHD. She was seeking answers rather than a developmental conversation.
- There was tension between holding the client's emotional response and providing space to explore the 360 feedback.
- The coach felt she had to deliver solutions that she felt belonged to the line manager.

EXAMPLE ETHICAL IMPLICATIONS

- **Competency** of a coach when a mental health issue arises in coaching.
- **Boundary** between coaching and counselling, specifically diagnosing or treating/working with mental health issues.
- **Contracting**, confidentiality, and re-contracting.
- **Duty of care** – the coach's self-care and duty of care to the client and any safeguarding policy. Where does the responsibility lie for a coaching client's mental health and wellbeing?

REFLECTIVE QUESTIONS FOR DISCUSSION

1. How can a coach ensure they practice within their competency in a session?
2. How does the coach resource him/herself and be reflexive in the moment?
3. As a supervisor how do you respond or recognize when a coach brings a client's potential mental health issue to the supervision space?

References

Whitaker, C., & Lucas, M. (2012). Collaboration in practice with co-facilitated Group Coaching Supervision: What could you learn from hearing our story? *International Journal of Mentoring and Coaching*, X(1), 111–120.

Case study 8

How many hats?

Eva Hirsch Pontes

Overview

This case study explores the discussions held in a group coaching supervision session, when one of the coaches asked the group to support him in preparation for an upcoming alignment meeting with client and sponsor. The coach appeared to be oblivious to the multiple implicit and explicit contracts in the working relationship which led to role confusion and difficulty in establishing clear boundaries in his conversations with the sponsor. This led the coach to frame his challenge to the group as needing to step in wearing a conflict mediator hat. The group's initial exchange failed to address the issues arising. The supervisor noticed the effect – on herself and all group members – of the parallel processes that seemed to reflect not only the systemic role confusion, but also a tendency to resist holding candid and clear conversations about expectations, roles, and responsibilities.

Case study

Background

This case was brought to a group supervision session by Mark, a former human resources (HR) professional who became a coach eight years ago. More recently, he was certified in systemic constellations and conflict mediation.

Mark was hired by an institution with close to 1,000 employees, which is financed partially by the state and partly by the private sector, to produce and deliver public interest content. In the country where it is based, cases of nepotism are commonly present in this kind of organisation.

Mark was referred to Joyce, the organisation's HR director, by a common acquaintance who had previously hired Mark as his coach and highly recommended his work. In their first interaction, Mark learned that this would be the first time the organisation would sponsor a coaching engagement and would like to start simultaneously with a coaching offer to three managers. He offered to bring other coaches to the project, but Joyce stated she would rather work exclusively with Mark.

DOI: 10.4324/b23351-14

Mark was then appointed to coach three managers: a board member's nephew (Jack), Joyce's goddaughter (Mary) who worked in the HR team, and an executive (John) who managed a support area and did not have family ties within the institution.

The assignment with Jack was put on hold after Mark referred his client to a mental health professional.

This case outlines discussions that enabled Mark and the group to become aware of the dynamics which mostly contributed to potential ethical repercussions in the assignment.

The assignment

This session takes place with very experienced coaches who have been together in the same supervision group for over three years and whose level of trust allows them to feel confident that they will not be judged, no matter how sensitive the topic they bring.

As Mark presents his case, he tells the group: "I need your support to reflect on how I can better prepare for an upcoming alignment meeting with my client, his boss, and the HR Director. I know I will need to act as conflict mediator in that meeting".

The supervision session

Mark presents the case and, as he mentions the HR director's decision to work only with him, he shares with the group that, due to his previous experience and expertise in HR functions, he thinks that Joyce might see him as a potential mentor.

Mark then reports a recent follow-up meeting with Joyce on the coaching engagements with Mary and John. Other members of the HR team – who had no direct connection with the coaching process – were present in the room and would have witnessed some of Joyce's statements, such as: "Mary is not happy with the pace of the meetings; she thinks they should take place in shorter intervals and I agree" and "there are several complaints concerning John's behaviour and his lack of skills to deal with people; you are the coach, Mark, you must fix this".

Mark shares with the group his reaction to Joyce's words: "In Mary's case, I failed to understand what was stopping Mary from speaking to me directly about this". Mark also said:

I also felt Joyce was stepping in more as a godmother than as HR director. So, my initial response was quite defensive – I know – and I replied that Mary had repeatedly told me how happy she was with the process.

Mark adds:

> As for John, I told Joyce that neither his boss nor the HR Business Partner pre-
> sent in the four-ways alignment meeting had mentioned John's need to work on
> his relational skills, but rather had focused on processes he needed to conduct
> better. During that alignment meeting, I did probe the participants a few times
> to clarify which behaviours they would suggest John to focus on for a successful
> outcome of the coaching engagement, to no avail.

Mark tells the group he felt pressed to 'fix' the situation and proposed to facilitate a
new alignment meeting with Joyce, John, and his boss, to ensure Joyce's expectations could be formalised in the appropriate forum, so that the coaching agreement
would accurately reflect the sponsor's expectations.

After presenting the details of the case, Mark states: "There is clearly a lack of
alignment between John's boss and Joyce. That is why I know I will need to mediate a conflict that is likely to arise in the coming meeting".

The coaches in the group ask questions which range from different aspects
of the coaching agreements with the sponsor and individual clients, to exploring
Mark's emotions and reactions. The group does not seem to be fully sensitive to the
implications deriving from the multiple contracts in this case.

The supervisor steps in to bring the group's focus to these aspects: "it looks like
Mark is wearing several hats, each one implying specific boundaries, roles, and
responsibilities; how many hats can we identify?"

The group goes on categorising the several hats they see. Some of them are visibly compatible with Mark's expected roles, such as coach, account manager and
project manager. Other hats may originate either from Mark's own expectations
and experience or from the silent psychological contract established between him
and Joyce: HR expert, mentor, conflict mediator, and rescuer ("you must fix this").

The group goes on examining Mark's role confusion and the resulting conflicts
of interest. He and the group also explore some parallel processes as they consider
the system's intertwined relationships.

Mark thanks the group for helping him see what he was unable to realise on his
own and affirms he has gained clarity and confidence to facilitate the upcoming
alignment meeting wearing what he calls "the right hat".

Key challenges

- The key challenge for the supervisor was to help the group understand and
  explore the ethical implications arising from the existence of multiple explicit
  and implicit contracts in the working relationships. An additional challenge
  was to analyse the formal roles, responsibilities, and boundaries Mark would
  need to clearly draw for himself and all parties in this engagement.
- Another challenge for the supervisor was to choose the 'right hat' to examine the parallel processes that seemed to reflect not only the systemic role

confusion, but also a tendency to resist holding candid and clear conversations about expectations, roles, and responsibilities.

EXAMPLE ETHICAL IMPLICATIONS

- **Conflict of interests** – multiple contracts (and hats) leading to role confusion.
- **Boundaries** – the boundaries of the working relationship were not clarified with the sponsor/HR.
- **Trust** – sensitive issues were discussed in front of other members of the HR team, leading to a potential negative impact on trust between coach and client.

REFLECTIVE QUESTIONS FOR DISCUSSION

1. Were boundaries overstepped? If yes, what were they? Who overstepped them and when?
2. What could the supervisor do to help examine the ethical implications in this case?
3. What hats do you unconsciously tend to pick as coach or supervisor? How can you safeguard transitioning from one role to another?

Intersectionality and supervision through bereavement

Mongezi C. Makhalima

Overview

During COVID-19 and the related lockdowns, more than in any period prior, the issue of grief, bereavement and loss showed up persistently in supervision. This raised intersecting boundary management issues relating to individual, task, gender, role and culture. This case study presents the complexities these factors bring to the coach supervision space, specifically highlighting the issue of grief and bereavement as a task and role boundary issue within a supervision session.

Case study

Background

COVID was an emotionally challenging period of significant duration, a context that the whole world population found themselves in. During this time, Kofi, an experienced coach supervisor, spent a lot of time providing supervision to coaches and consultants. Kofi also engaged another coach to provide him with coaching.

In one particular supervision session, Kofi had a 'full house', as had become a pattern, with ten coaches and consultants. Ten became a limit Kofi had to deliberately set for these sessions, since a few weeks prior the supervision sessions had become too large and felt crowded, with more than 25 people in a virtual room. This had made it difficult to create spaciousness and attend deeply to individual needs and allow for shared holding of learning and resourcing space.

Two coaches in the supervision group presented practice-related issues, one on feelings of incompetence as a new coach and another on growing their business differently given the circumstances. One of the coaches started presenting a case that was not related to practice but more to the passing of her brother and how she felt about it. While internally it surprised Kofi that she spoke not of her coaching but of her personal experiences, he allowed for a space for the issue to go where it may.

It may have had to do with the period that the issue was so easily embraced by the group. It may also have been that all the participants were female, but the response from the group was no longer that of supervision technically, but a well held group therapy session.

DOI: 10.4324/b23351-15

One by one, each of the participants began to share their own experience of grieving and death. With lots of tears in the virtual room, there were also smiles, as each participant seemed to feel relieved to have a moment to share their own experience of grief and loss.

While on the surface Kofi may have looked like he was responding easily to the situation, he was at first taken aback slightly. However, his experience kicked in and holding the space, supporting and connecting the dots on behalf of the coach supervisees seemed to help.

As Kofi was stepping out of himself to observe the situation from a third position to himself and the group, he shared his observations about what had been going on in the session. He remarked that he was the only male with a group of female clients. He noticed that everyone in the room was African (this was not very unusual with his groups – although he did tend to have a few Caucasian clients in his supervision groups). He also observed that, while everyone was crying, his were the only dry eyes in the virtual room – not out of lack of empathy, but out of the deliberate work of psychological compartmentalisation and being both the observer and participant of the system and managing those boundaries. Immediately after sharing, Kofi noticed that those who had been waiting for their turn to speak didn't end up sharing. The session was over.

During the last quarter of 2020, little did Kofi know that this was a preparation for what was to come. Firstly, Kofi was hospitalized with severe COVID at the beginning of 2021 and ended up in the intensive care unit (ICU) for two weeks, "negotiating with God for my breath". Kofi resumed supervision practice a few weeks later, where it seemed an abundance of death and grieving experiences was the dominant theme. There were cases of coaches losing clients to death; coaches losing parents, other family members and friends; and clients losing coaches. 2021 became the year in which every supervision session would have a story of death and grieving. Kofi as the coach supervisor had to support many clients through bereavement and grief and, through his own experience of being in ICU for two weeks, he sometimes found it useful to share his experience with some clients ("and for myself, frankly", as Kofi later said, on reflection) to make sense of his own loss, grief and bereavement.

Key challenges

The key challenges presented by this case related to the intersectional nature of the function of the coach supervisor, especially in periods of crisis where boundaries become blurred.

- The classical task boundary issue between therapy and supervision.
- The role of the supervisor as one of the humans in the room, but also the distant observer of the process that sweeps in and out of multiple roles on behalf of and to the service of the clients.

- Questions about the responses of the clients to unconscious or conscious gender roles in the sessions (how would it have been different if the coach supervisor was female and the participants all male?).
- The cultural implications of grief, bereavement and loss for the coach supervisor. Some African communities have a culture, for example, of grieving publicly. Could this have been different in other cultural frameworks?

EXAMPLE ETHICAL IMPLICATIONS

- Crossing the boundary between supervision and therapy and thereby creating a new issue or leaving the client uncontained.
- There is also the possibility of greying of task boundary – for example working with the client within their professional sphere as opposed to their personal sphere.
- Interpreting phenomena within one's own cultural context and potentially missing the crux of the work to be done (off task) or potentially damaging the relationship.
- In many cases where clients of different genders are working together, and the client is vulnerable (tears, sadness, etc.), there's potential to cross appropriate physical/personal space boundaries.

REFLECTIVE QUESTIONS FOR DISCUSSION

1. What are the key differences between supervision and therapy? In what way are they similar?
2. What could a coach supervisor do to prepare themselves to deal with the intersectionalities related to working with multicultural, multiracial, cross-gender environments?
3. What are your experiences of dealing with grief, bereavement and loss in coaching or supervision sessions? What was your approach? How different would your approach be from regular supervision?

Case study 10

Dual roles

Coach educators serving as coach supervisors

Carrie Arnold

Overview

Coaching supervision within coach training programs is beginning to emerge. Ethical considerations of the dual role of the instructor, which also assumes the evaluator, and coaching supervisor, have yet to be explored. A pilot project and a comparative study with students in an advanced mastering coaching skills course throughout Spain, Mexico, Argentina, and parts of Latin America, conducted by Espinal and Rodriguez (2023), found "100% of the participants who received supervision recommended including it in training programs" (p. 306). Each participant was already serving, in some capacity, as a coach. The pilot project established that 100% of the supervisees recognized an impact on their way of being as coaches compared to their 'doing.' This acknowledgment of 'being' suggests reflective practice, identity, and coaching mindset were all deepened during the coursework. Their coaching competencies also improved because of increased confidence and awareness. These findings are significant to consider as coach training programs continue to update their educational models and determine the core curriculum. Coach supervisors must create a safe psychological space for coaching clients to reflect on their practice. However, the duality of roles may create ethical dilemmas if supervisors also serve as educators, evaluating student competencies.

Case study

Background

Clarice is a mid-career consultant working primarily in the IT industry. She has over 25 years of experience helping organizations solve technical problems, implement software, and complete system conversions. She was looking for a new challenge when a colleague suggested she become a coach, allowing her to navigate the human reaction to change and better serve her clients. Clarice enrolled in a graduate-level coaching education program, supported by her consultancy, and began the coursework. She did not clearly understand the distinctions between coaching and consulting until she was several weeks into her program.

DOI: 10.4324/b23351-16

Clarice began to internally question the premise that coaches should refrain from giving advice. She struggled with this notion and how she would integrate coaching into being a consultant, as she believed her clients expected problem-solving and answers to technical questions far more than they desired a thought partner on managing change.

Clarice shared her concerns and personal experience in a synchronous class with her cohort and two faculty instructors. One of the instructors, Dr. Jansen, normalized Clarice's concerns, as many new coaching students struggle with this concept. It is hard to let go of having answers and be in the space of uncertainty. Dr. Jansen invited her to set aside her problem-solving nature when working with her coaching practice clients and encouraged her to stay entirely in the coaching mindset. The two instructors co-facilitated the conversation and shared that becoming a coach meant trusting the process. Integration or separation in her role as a consultant and her emerging role and identity as a coach would become more evident as she progressed in the program.

Clarice worked hard in class to set aside her problem-solving expertise. However, her first two observed coaching sessions were a blend of her directing, mentoring, and problem-solving. She did not ask clear, direct, primarily open-ended questions at a pace that allowed her client to think, feel, or reflect. Clarice also struggled to partner with the client and let them choose what happened in the practice session. Dr. Jansen, serving as her mentor, provided this feedback in writing and agreed to continue mentoring her on fully adopting the competencies and mindset needed to be successful as a coach.

In month six of the education program, Dr. Jansen saw significant improvements in Clarice's coaching. Her fifth and sixth observed coaching sessions with fellow students demonstrated considerable progress, and Dr. Jansen felt confident that Clarice could pass her final coaching assessment.

The assignment

In the final month of the coach education program, Dr. Jansen, also a trained supervisor, was asked to cover a supervision session as one of the other faculty supervisors had a family emergency. Dr. Jansen agreed and, upon opening the virtual classroom, found six students, two of which were her mentees. One was Clarice.

The supervision

Dr. Jansen opened up the group supervision with a presencing exercise. She then discussed confidentiality and psychological safety and invited the supervisees to reflect on a client case. The protocol for group supervision was to have everyone briefly name an issue they were experiencing with a client. The group then decided which case to address first. Clarice shared that she had a client who was not responding well to her coaching, and she was seeking suggestions on facilitating client awareness, growth, and accountability. After each of the six supervisees briefly shared their challenges, Clarice's case was voted the first one to address.

Dr. Jansen asked her to spend another five minutes discussing more detail and to share one question she was sitting with. As she presented the case, Clarice referenced the following:

- "I told him the project would fail if he chose that path"
- "I provided several examples of ways they could bypass the system requirements"
- "For homework, I told my client he should explore some other software solutions"

Clarice then said her one big question was, "How do I help someone I think is making wrong choices?"

Dr. Jansen allowed the group to self-reflect on what was surfacing for them in Clarice's case. She also had them name one or two questions they were sitting with and, after allowing everyone to share, invited Clarice to respond to the question(s) that resonated with her the most.

Some of the reflective questions offered up in supervision included:

- What coaching competency is most needed with this client?
- What parallel process might be happening?
- Where in your body are you experiencing the phenomenon that this might be the wrong choice?
- What does it mean for you if nothing changes with this client?
- How would you describe your relationship with this client?
- What if this client does not want or need advice?

Clarice reacted to this question: "What does it mean for you if nothing changes with this client?" Clarice responded by sharing how important it was to her that clients had access to updated information, recent technology studies, and the coach's expertise.

Dr. Jansen built on the student's question by asking the following:

- "What does Clarice, the consultant, want to do if nothing changes with this client?"
- "What does Clarice, the coach, want to do if nothing changes with this client?"

Clarice struggled to answer the questions separately and continued reinforcing her values that it is important to share expertise when working with a client who does not know what to do.

Dr. Jansen closed the client case discussion with suggestions that Clarice only serves as a coach when working with this practice client. She also supervised her with suggestions on how to partner with the client at the beginning of each session. She also provided some mentoring on ways to return to the coaching mindset. Clarice accepted the feedback while admitting, "It is hard just to stand by and watch a client's project fail."

After the supervision session, Dr. Jansen received a call from a fellow student who attended the supervision with concerns that Clarice was not coaching her clients but instead extending her consulting practice with coaching clients and claiming them as coaching hours. Dr. Jansen reflected on the information and then called the program director to discuss the student and her progress in the program. Dr. Jansen voiced concerns about graduating the student based on what she saw and heard.

Key challenges

- Coaching supervision is still new in the Americas, and few coaching programs have incorporated coaching supervision. Few coach educators are certified as supervisors. Those who hold the dual role of supervisor and instructor must ensure students understand how supervision differs from mentoring. There is also the challenge of how a supervisor should respond when a student brings a client case to supervision that could disqualify them or delay them from completing a coaching education program.

EXAMPLE ETHICAL IMPLICATIONS

- **Role confusion** – information gained in a reflective supervision session informed a faculty member who also held an evaluative role in the coaching education program.
- **Boundaries between supervision and instruction** – the faculty member became aware of a student's misaligned coaching practice within supervision and through another student.
- **Supervision timing** – the student's understanding of supervision versus mentoring was not clearly formed throughout the coaching education program.
- **Competency versus confidentiality** – the faculty member was unable to maintain the confidentiality embedded in reflective supervision as it pertained to coaching competency.

REFLECTIVE QUESTIONS FOR DISCUSSION

1. What steps should Dr. Jansen have taken before, during, and after the supervision session?
2. What actions should the program director take?
3. What responsibility does a student have if they learn something they deem unethical about another student?

References

Espinal, E., & Rodriguez, A. (2023). Introducing supervision into training programs for professional coaches. In F. Campone, J. A. Digirolamo, D. Goldvarg, & L. Seto (Eds.), *Coaching Supervision: Voices from the Americas* (pp. 288–309). Taylor & Francis.

Chapter 5

Team coaching

Chapter 5 brings a focus to the complexity of team coaching. Challenges arising in contracting, leadership inheritance, coach competency and challenging confidentiality are some of the tensions explored.

DOI: 10.4324/b23351-17

Is it about ethics or values?

Ingela Camba Ludlow

Overview

Coach certifications and training equip their students to support their clients in handling conflict in values. However, fewer coaches are prepared to have conflicting values with their own clients, and this goes beyond a matter of likes and tastes, to the very axis where the identity of both and client are important. These moments tend to be mislabeled as an unfortunate event, a bad day or with the judgment that the client is not "coachable". When going through these moments, coaches may initially feel that they are inadequate, mainly due to lack of experience.

This case will review two situations through this lens, so the practitioner will have a guide to review from her/his own perspective. This is of particular importance while working in team coaching; there is an enhanced tension since team members become an audience, compared to one-on-one coaching when there are no witnesses. Thus the coach's intervention needs to be exemplary for the benefit of the overall team, not just one individual, and the coach also has to be brave enough to do it on time, because timing is of the essence.

Case study

Background

A leading motor industry company had identified the need to improve their relationship with their customers. The company consisted of several department teams, e.g., finance, operations, sales, customer service, but had not formed a leadership team that was to help guide this new organizational focus.

The assignment

The assignment was part of a 12-month plus long-term coaching engagement. The coaching contract included individual coaching for the general manager and team leaders while also conducting a team coaching process. The objective was to impact business results positively through increasing the satisfaction scores in the customer journey.

DOI: 10.4324/b23351-18

This case describes two scenarios that occurred within the longer contracted coaching engagement.

Team coaching: Situation one

Before the individual interviews with team members, the leadership team gathered and the general manager introduced the coach to the team as follows: "we have an expert to come and help us because, despite your years of training in your areas, this team is full of goofies". This was unexpected for the coach, since no initial conversation had given a hint that the leader would address their collaborators in this way. There was a very tense moment, not when he said this, but when the coach requested a pause, to question this way of addressing them.

Team coaching: Situation two

In this project, during one-on-one sessions, many individuals ventured to confide in the coach and openly shared what, in their view, was deeply hurting the overall system. However, this content could not surface during team sessions because of the lack of psychological safety in the team. The tension reached its peak when the team and the coach were working on identifying as a team what their key challenges were. Silence was the response.

Key challenges

- How to reflect on what the coach perceived as an insult and lack of respect, while at the same time maintaining the alliance with the manager, and not threatening his authority.
- How to address fear in an environment already sown with fear as part of a cultural environment built by the general manager. This had to be done without breaching any confidentiality that would prevent the individuals from trusting the coach again.
- The shift from a personal interaction to opening a group conversation. Inviting the team through a coaching conversation on how they can utilize a culturally tolerated habit to reflect on the culture they want to create for the customer and for themselves.
- Reflecting on present values versus desired values. This is related to the values expected in the organization vs. values that are being lived within the organization.
- Leveraging the importance of a working alliance or golden rules of conduct.

EXAMPLE ETHICAL IMPLICATIONS

- **Conflicts of value** – individual values come up very often in the discussions and can come between people in reaching agreements; identifying the values that are conflicting can help settle discussions.

- **Setting boundaries** – the work alliance, or golden rules, introduce a frame in which relationships and discussions take place and most of them include respect. However, some teams might be used to dynamics that have overlooked some elemental rules and the coach is required to intervene in a way that is neither derogatory nor admonishing but has gentleness and even candid curiosity.
- **Beware of competing in morality** – when caught in a confrontation of values, it is easy to start simplifying the conversation by saying who is right and implying the other is wrong, and in the end, this might be felt as a competing morality.
- **Acting responsibly** – the coach needed to find ways of constructively challenging the team leader who was perceived to be using derogatory language so he could take responsibility for his behavior.

REFLECTIVE QUESTIONS FOR DISCUSSION

1. How can awareness of fear be utilized to counteract fear and lack of trust?
2. How can you work with contracting to address the issues arising?
3. How can identifying the differences in values potentially help to address this situation more sympathetically?

Conspicuous contracting in team coaching

David Matthew Prior

Overview

This case illustrates the potential for both possibility and peril within a team coaching engagement when an experienced executive coach, extensively trained and practiced in one-to-one coaching, as well as being a veteran corporate trainer, makes the transition to coaching within a wider organizational system for a six-month contract with a team. The dilemma focuses on what occurs in the initial contracting for the work with the team and its leader, and how a multiplicity of implicit stakeholder agendas quickly become entangled within a more complex organizational web, revealing the need for a coach's careful and concentrated ethical sorting to arrive at a proper team diagnostic and intervention.

Case study

Background

Richard had been working as an experienced and certified executive and organizational coach for ten years. As part of his client portfolio, he had been coaching an executive leader in a retail organization for two years with rave reviews from the leader he was coaching and the leader's human resource business partner (HRBP), Ellen. Ellen approached Richard about being a coach for the marketing team that was undergoing stress given the company's global business imperative to accelerate the transition from brick-and-mortar shop to a digitally driven e-commerce presence.

Richard was excited and motivated to take on this assignment because it paralleled a transition he wanted to accelerate within his own profession toward more coaching work with teams. Richard quickly drafted a six-month team coaching proposal and submitted it to the consultancy that was contracting him to do the executive coaching work with the client organization. Within a few days, the consultancy emailed Richard that his proposal had been approved by the client organization and requested his invoice for the complete six-month team coaching engagement. Richard was promptly wired the full fee before beginning the work with the team.

DOI: 10.4324/b23351-19

The assignment

Richard held his first meeting with Ellen, who was delighted to have Richard on board as she had been shouldering complaints from the marketing team about being overworked, under-resourced, stressed, and in need of less conflict in the workplace. As an HRBP Ellen reassured Richard that, while she worked very closely with the team and the team leader, she was not an official member of the team. Ellen provided Richard with a personality and behavioral profile of each team member, including details about their personal lives.

Beginning to feel uncomfortable, Richard asked Ellen's permission if it would be possible for him to have a one-to-one meeting with the team leader before the retreat. Ellen indicated that the team leader was quite stretched herself, though she would attempt to find 30–45 minutes on the team leader's calendar for the two of them to meet before the retreat day.

In preparation for the offsite, Richard began qualitative interviews with the team members and conducted an online team effectiveness diagnostic assessment. During a 45-minute in-person interview with the team leader (Karyn), ten days before the retreat, Richard learned that she was quite stressed by the organizational and business demands being placed on her leadership. Karyn expressed anxiety about the potential risks of losing her team to market competitors given the stressful workplace environment, though seemed equally comforted by the fact that each team member had their own personal executive coach. As team leader, she had high expectations that the retreat would reduce anxiety about workloads and resolve troubling interpersonal conflicts among team members. Upon leaving the meeting with a sense of uneasiness, Richard ran into Ellen in the hallway who wanted to know the details about his meeting with Karyn and expressed her bubbling enthusiasm and excitement about attending the upcoming team retreat.

Following subsequent meetings with Ellen to set up the retreat day, Richard received a telephone call from her two days before the retreat informing him that Karyn would be unable to attend the retreat due to a personal situation, though she indicated that the leader was okay with having the retreat delivered just the same. Richard was beginning to feel the organizational pressure of the team coaching engagement as canceling the retreat at this late date would have systemic implications given the amount of time that had been invested in preparation, the expenses involved in having booked a venue, and the collective efforts it took to coordinate and align all of the team members' calendars. While Richard felt conflicted and time pressured in this predicament, he also appreciated the client's desire to proceed with the retreat and thus put his trust in the belief that a successful team coaching engagement would manifest as long he focused on the client's agenda.

The coaching

Arriving early on the Thursday morning of the retreat and unexpectedly accompanied by Jenny, a junior human resources assistant, Ellen introduced her assistant to Richard to let him know that Jenny was there to participate as a silent observer of the retreat activities. Following the establishment of ground rules that included confidentiality for the information shared in the retreat session, Richard facilitated the team diagnostic assessment debrief along with an activity on metaphors.

The morning was going well with psychological safety and transparent sharing by the team. After lunch, Richard initiated a workflow process activity which seemed to dampen the team's positive emotional energy from the morning, as he learned that the team had just arrived at this retreat from a heavily task-driven, strategic-mapping three-day intensive. While Richard was running his workflow process activity on a whiteboard, he noticed team members beginning to withdraw their engagement in the activity, wincing and casting side glances toward Ellen and the junior human resources assistant. During the afternoon coffee break, Ellen and Jenny privately conferred with the team members and subsequently cautioned Richard that the retreat was going downhill fast, letting him know that all the team members were unhappy. Richard shifted the remaining activities of the afternoon to facilitating a group discussion to harvest team learnings and wrapped up the day one hour early by securing individual action commitments from each team member.

Richard reached out to Karyn the next day for a telephone debrief of the retreat. During the call, he learned that Ellen had already convened a conference call with Karyn earlier that morning, having included the confidential shares of team members while reporting that the retreat had negatively impacted team morale. Karyn indicated that she would touch base with Richard the following week.

On Monday morning, Richard received an urgent call from the lead partner of the consultancy who notified him, following a private meeting that happened over the weekend between the consulting partners, Karyn and Ellen, that the team coaching engagement was to be immediately terminated, with no questions asked. Richard was directed to cease contact with all members of the team, as well as the HRBP. The partner of the consultancy requested that Richard promptly return 50% of the prepaid coaching engagement fee, though reassured him that the organization still held Richard in high esteem as an executive coach who could continue one-to-one coaching with other leaders in the organization.

Key challenges

- **Define ethical cornerstones**: Fit for purpose means that the team coach has a clear definition of and philosophical orientation toward team coaching, with the ability to provide an evidence-based rationale behind the interventions which are best suited to the varied situational yet complex organizational and business contexts.
- **Detail implicit agendas**: Working in a complex social system, it is incumbent upon the external coach to map multiple coaching agendas held by different constituencies (e.g., team members, team leader, team, HR business partner, organizational change, business imperatives, internal and external

stakeholders) so that these can be collectively surfaced and integrated within the team as the primary client agenda holder.

- **Process and reconcile emotional uneasiness**: As a team coach, there will be times within a client engagement when the practitioner will experience a range of emotions that could increase self-doubt and uncertainty about what constitutes 'right' action and ethical decision making to serve the needs of the client. Team coaches can partner with professional support to gain empathic validation, an impartial perspective, a strategic sounding board, and consultative expertise.

EXAMPLE ETHICAL IMPLICATIONS

- **Fit for purpose** – ensuring that the team coach qualifies the readiness and preparedness of all of the involved team coaching stakeholders (e.g., team coach, team leader, team members, team sponsors, team consultancy) to engage in the work at hand.
- **Power and authority** – clarifying the authorizing environment within the team coaching partnership when it comes to who makes key decisions concerning team engagement design, launch, participation, evaluation, and termination.
- **Team coach as instrument** – fine tuning the team coach's performative ability to recognize, register, and respond to emergent situational events, utilizing a repertoire of cognitive, emotional, social, and somatic capabilities.

REFLECTIVE QUESTIONS FOR DISCUSSION

1. What were some of the early warning signs in this case that could provide Richard with reflective time for improved ethical discernment and decision making?
2. What is the appropriate role that non-team members, such as the human resource business partner, should play within a team coaching engagement?
3. What specifically does Richard need to do now to create an ethical compass to guide his future team coaching practice?

Navigating an unpredictable team leadership inheritance

Dumisani Magadlela

Overview

Team coaching is relatively new compared to other human development modalities such as mentoring and therapy. Numerous studies on the impact of coaching on individuals and organizational systems have consistently shown that coaching is one of the most powerful transformational development interventions any coaching-ready individual and organization can undertake. The understanding of teams and the definition of what a team is is still a contested subject. One of the common definitions of a team is that a team is "a small number of people with complementary skills, who are committed to a common purpose, performance goals, and approach, for which they hold themselves mutually accountable" (John Katzenbach, 1994, in Clutterbuck, 2020. p.28). Team coaching involves working with the whole team to leverage the team's strengths in the team's effort to deliver on their purpose and serve the organization and their stakeholders as best they can. This case study presents a team coaching scenario encountered by a team, their team leader, and the team coach. The case explores challenging relationship dynamics and the perceptions of a team leader replacing a much-loved team leader in a team in transition.

Case study

Background

The case study below was drawn from an actual team coaching engagement within an international telecommunications and technology company operating in different countries across Africa.

The client company has offices – referred to as operations by team members – in different countries. The business has operations in over 25 African countries, with more locations identified and earmarked for growth in the future.

The case study focuses on a team coaching engagement with one of multiple teams being coached across the organization. This was a sales team of eight members spread across six countries. Team members constituted a virtual team that met

DOI: 10.4324/b23351-20

regularly. The team leader, Johan, was not based on the African continent among the team members. He was based at the company's head office in western Europe.

Johan inherited the team over a year ago when Muntu, a well-loved and charismatic leader from one of the in-country African operations, died of a heart attack.

Johan was a white male from Europe. Muntu was a black man from one of the African countries.

The focus of the case study is the fluid and constantly changing nature of relationships among all parties, especially between the team and Johan, and the team and Themba, the team coach.

The assignment

The objective of the coaching engagement was a collective one for the whole organization. Each team of managers or leaders had to select their team coach from a panel of team coaches assigned to support the whole business.

One of team coaching's focus areas in the organization was to support teams to build greater cohesion and heighten team members' awareness of their critical role in growing the brand across the region. This was the goal for this team. The team coaching engagement was introduced after the passing of Muntu, who was "respected, loved and revered by the whole team" (in the words of one of the senior team members).

The coaching

The external team coaches working across the organization were required to regularly meet with their team leaders before every virtual team coaching session. These pre-session team leader engagements formed part of the system check or dipstick to 'sense-into' the energy and dynamics of the organization and the team shortly before each team coaching session.

Johan expressed excitement in working with the dynamic team of young African business leaders keen to drive business development and craft new innovative solutions across the continent. He also expressed growing dissatisfaction with the constant reference to Muntu, the previous, late, and loved team leader. On several occasions in the team leader debriefs, he repeatedly laughed at his own joke that he found it "impossible to compete with a ghost". Themba had never met Muntu. He only heard about the 'brilliant and inspirational' leader from the new team leader who inherited the team.

The requirement for all teams before commencing their team coaching sessions was for all team members to complete a diagnostic questionnaire. The team survey was aimed at gathering systemic and team data and intelligence to assist with the team coaching engagement.

The main results of the team's diagnostic survey were generally positive and welcoming of the opportunity to work together in team coaching sessions, as opposed to what team members complained was the "constant drudgery of a series of business meetings". They welcomed the opportunity to interact with each other outside of business meetings.

While the rest of the diagnostic survey results were unequivocally positive about the team and their team dynamics, it was the anecdotal, especially narrative, aspects of the survey results that worried Johan.

After the submission and initial sharing of the diagnostic results with Johan, he expressed discomfort with some of the sentiments expressed by some members of the team about the team members' relationships.

Johan repeatedly expressed that the team coaching sessions may fuel discontent against him as a "new and external team leader" or foment collusion against him. He admitted that he had not, however, experienced or felt any signs of collusion in the team up to this point, yet. He indicated that as a leader based outside the region, he had to anticipate challenges and prepare for them before they could harm the team.

After several delays in scheduling the next team coaching session (third team coaching session), Johan requested a meeting with Themba. In the meeting, Johan indicated that he would like to pause the team coaching sessions until he was clear where the team was going. Several team members approached Themba separately to inquire about continuing the team coaching sessions.

Key challenges

- The team coach's role in supporting the new team leader and the team to find common ground.
- The team coach needed to address team members' direct approach with requests to continue with team coaching sessions after the team leader paused them.

EXAMPLE ETHICAL IMPLICATIONS

- **Conscious and unconscious bias** – the role of the coach in supporting the team leader.
- **Systemic and positional authority** – managing the team leader's perceptions of his influence in the team.
- **Trust and confidentiality** – consciously growing rapport with trust. Assuring all parties of confidentiality from the start of the team coaching engagement.

REFLECTIVE QUESTIONS FOR DISCUSSION

1. What could a team coach do to resolve this situation?
2. From a professional standpoint, what are the options available to the team coach in this situation?
3. How could the team coach handle the team members' direct and/or private conversations with the team coach?

Reference

Clutterbuck, David. 2020. *Coaching the Team at Work. The Definitive Guide to Team Coaching*. London: Nicholas Brealey Publishing.

Case study 14

Coach competency in unchartered waters

Eva Hirsch Pontes and David Clutterbuck

Overview

A coach is about to start a team coaching engagement in a subsidiary of a global corporation. The engagement was requested by the local president who feels the leadership team needs to collaborate more effectively. Prior to commencing the engagement, the coach has one-to-one interviews with every team member. During her conversation with one of the directors, his choice of words and examples leads her to suspect he might be on the autism spectrum. While he shares his colleagues' views about specific challenges they must overcome as a team, he states team coaching will also help him deal with personal difficulties in interacting with the team.

The coach has never had autistic people in the several teams she has coached and wonders if and how she needs to adapt her approach to the assignment. She takes the case to group supervision where one of the ideas is for her to encourage that team member to seek formal diagnosis.

This case study analyses the dilemmas the coach faces while doubting she is equipped to handle this assignment and assessing whether it is appropriate for her to bring up the suggestion of a diagnostic process to the team member.

Case study

Background

Steglitz is a global food manufacturing corporation. During the COVID-19 pandemic, Steglitz Brazil had to adapt its strategy, changing its focus from exports to supplying the rising domestic market demand.

Daniel was brought back from a leadership position in Europe to chair the leadership team (LT), composed of himself and six directors. Four directors had been appointed more than five years ago and two of them had been recently promoted by his predecessor. Daniel heard from the former president: "you have a dream team ready; they are all highly qualified and committed".

Six months after his arrival, Daniel felt that they needed to learn to collaborate as a team. He agreed they were individually technically excellent but lacked

DOI: 10.4324/b23351-21

cohesion. Daniel talked to a few peers from other industries, seeking ideas on how to address his concerns. Sophia was recommended by two executives consulted by Daniel to conduct a team coaching process.

The assignment

Daniel interviewed Sophia, without consulting his human resources director, outlining his challenge, and asking for a team coaching proposal. He had many questions about the process and the conversation evolved mostly around clarifying what team coaching is, roles and responsibilities, confidentiality, and other aspects of the engagement.

Sophia also explained that, prior to submitting her proposal, she would like to conduct in-depth one-to-one interviews with Daniel and all directors, to better understand their perceptions and to assess their openness to engage in team coaching. Daniel consented and formally introduced Sophia to his team and she began the individual interviews.

The coaching

There were common themes in all interviews. The team members attributed to their former president's leadership style the fact that they had gotten used to a silos culture which was no longer consistent with their strategy. They were unanimous in welcoming the idea of team coaching.

During the interviews, Sophia probed the team members on how they perceived the effectiveness of their conversations, especially when challenging was needed. She was left with the impression that the team had developed a pattern of superficial harmony in their communication.

Her last interviewee was Tom, one of the recently promoted directors. He was 41, the youngest in the team. In the beginning of their conversation, what Tom shared was mostly a repetition of what the other directors had mentioned.

Then came a surprise when Tom stated he was struggling and added: "I know I can intimidate people". When asked what he might do that can be perceived as intimidating, he was quick in replying:

from feedback in my previous jobs, I know that I am seen as arrogant, and people are afraid of questioning me. And that's because I have extraordinarily fast thinking/rational skills and it's hard for me to listen to other people's opinions that contradict data. I trust data, not opinions!

Tom continued:

I have tried to show myself vulnerable, which does not work for me. I end up being inappropriate, in 'my autistic way', because I am not good at reading social cues. I 'push' my high energy and choose the wrong language or timing.

Tom brought in examples of what he referred to as being "quite confrontational, especially in group settings", repeating the expression "in my autistic way".

Sophia noticed his choice of words and hesitated. Tom's speech contained elements that were consistent with what used to be called "high-functioning Asperger's" two decades ago, when she got her degree in clinical psychology. This term is no longer used and might be considered offensive.

Eventually, Sophia asked for Tom's permission to share what she was observing and referred to what they had agreed at the beginning of their conversation, in terms of confidentiality and transparent, non-judgemental sharing of what might emerge in the interview.

Sophia, still feeling hesitant, probed:

I am curious about your choice of words, as you referred a couple of times to "my autistic way". I'm wondering if there is anything else on this topic that you feel comfortable sharing if you think it might be relevant for our conversation.

Tom: "I have never been officially diagnosed but suspect mine is a case of Asperger's. I've read a lot about this and have not sought a diagnosis for fear of being labelled".

Sophia was puzzled by the fact that no one had made any reference to Tom. "He says he is struggling, but nobody seems to notice", she thought.

When they closed the meeting, Tom affirmed he welcomed the team coaching initiative and asked her if she could help him create a list of concrete behaviours he could practice to "earn more respect from others". He then added he was used to being the first in his class, winning awards and medals in school and college. "As an adult, I still seek constant recognition. Earning respect is my equivalent of a trophy for grown-ups".

As Sophia engaged in self-reflection after that interview, she found herself wondering if she had the required competence to serve that LT as their coach. She had never worked with clients on the autism spectrum and wondered what she should know, learn, or be aware of to adapt her team coaching approach. She was also concerned with the 'do no harm' principle.

Sophia took the case to her next group supervision session. She knew that at least one person in that supervisory space was personally quite experienced with autistic people. One of the recommendations from the group was for Sophia to discuss with Tom the value of going through a proper diagnostic process to raise his self-awareness and capacity to show up with authenticity, thereby increasing his chances of genuinely working on earning respect from his peers.

Sophia now needed to present her proposal. She pondered if and how she should suggest a formal diagnostic process to Tom. If she chose to ignore Tom's struggle, might she be paralleling the team's behaviour?

Key challenges

- Neurodiversity can be positioned as either a form of disability or a valuable form of cognitive difference. The coach and Tom have fallen into the same trap of assuming it is a problem, rather than a different strength. The team seems to be operating under the same assumption, choosing denial as a coping mechanism to deal with an evident difference. Changing perceptions means addressing the whole system, not just one individual.

• Neurodiverse people learn to cope in a neurotypical world by 'masking' – adopting learned behaviours to try to fit in, rather than being their authentic selves. The team might be paralleling Tom by also 'masking' to create superficial harmony.

EXAMPLE ETHICAL IMPLICATIONS

• **Responsibility to clients and to practice** – the coach needed to recognise her limited understanding of neurodiversity and reach out for support.
• **Creating a safe environment** – for Tom to be able to contribute at his best, there need to be accommodations to his way of thinking and being. For example, many people on the autistic spectrum struggle to cope with background noise and other forms of sensory overload.
• **Disclosure** – whose responsibility is it to bring this issue into the open, and how?

REFLECTIVE QUESTIONS FOR DISCUSSION

1. How can the coach help the team value the difference that Tom's neurodiversity brings?
2. What are the opportunities in this scenario, for both Tom and the team?
3. How can the coach surface and address her own biases?

Working with confidentiality in team coaching engagements

Colm Murphy

Overview

Team coaching focuses on helping teams collectively achieve the team's work, in terms of taskwork and teamwork, through a sustained series of conversations that raise the individual and collective level of reflection and self-awareness, and challenge the team's thinking and behaviours as they develop sustainable solutions and practices. The multi-relational aspect within team coaching means that the contracting process is more complex than in business coaching (Turner & Hawkins, 2019), especially the "knotty question of confidentiality" (Leary-Joyce & Lines, 2018, p. 41). Leary-Joyce and Lines (2018) highlight two approaches to confidentiality: the team coach commits to keeping all one-to-one conversations anonymous and confidential, but agrees to share themes with the team from the data collected; or the team coach agrees that all data and perspectives are shared and therefore can be disclosed by the team coach within the team.

This case study is about the implications of the latter approach which arose during team coaching when the diagnostic data-gathering stage uncovered the perceptions of some female team members about the behaviours of the male team leader, and the ensuing dilemma of the two team coaches (one female, one male) regarding what to share with the team.

Case study

Background

This case study is based on a six-month team coaching engagement with a team within a global financial services organisation. The team consisted of ten team members including a male team leader (Paul) and seven female team members. All team members were based in the same office. The team was focused on supporting customers with financial transactions of a manual nature. The team's stakeholders, when asked about their expectations of the team, spoke of the importance of service line agreements (SLAs) being met, and of the need for accuracy and minimal complaints or to "get it right first time, do it quickly" (a stakeholder comment).

DOI: 10.4324/b23351-22

The assignment

The purpose of the team coaching was to assist the team in working better as a team as opposed to team members concentrating just on their own roles and tasks. A secondary objective was to create a more supportive and harmonious environment within the team, as the pressure from the stakeholders often resulted in team members focusing on who was perceived as working hard or not, and who was perceived as causing errors that in turn impacted the workload of others.

The team coaching process

Separate contracting meetings were held between the two team coaches (Stephen and Sam) and the organisational sponsor (Alex), the team leader (Paul), and the full team including the team leader. A six-month engagement was agreed consisting of a diagnostic of one-to-one interviews with each team member and some team stakeholders and then a series of monthly team coaching sessions, ranging from two hours to a day, starting with a full-day session comprising the diagnostic debrief and action planning. In the contracting meeting with the team and Paul, the two team coaches explained that, to avoid the coaches being conduits for conversations that others didn't feel comfortable raising within the team or outside of the team, all comments shared in the one-to-one interviews and beyond would be anonymous but not confidential. The team coaches would support any team member with having an open conversation with the rest of the team. As part of the contracting meeting, the team members agreed that their key norms or ground rules throughout the team coaching process were to be open-minded, positive, willing to change, patient, and calm.

The diagnostic stage in the team coaching process aimed to gather enough data from the team and its stakeholders to present a picture of the current perception of the team from within and from outside the team, in order to lead a co-design of the team coaching journey.

During the one-to-one interviews between team members and one of the team coaches, four of the female team members shared their perception that Paul was tougher or more critical of them than their male colleagues when it came to errors or mistakes.

In analysing the ten team one-to-one interviews and the four one-to-one stakeholder interviews, the team coaches faced the following dilemma. To include the theme about the team leader being tougher on female members as part of the debrief to the whole team could potentially shame and shut down Paul, and indeed bring the team coaching to a sudden stop if Paul decided not to continue with it. To leave the theme out of the debrief would risk making the four team members, who separately shared the perception, feel like their voices had been edited out and the team coaches were being selective in what they shared in contradiction to what they and the team had agreed in the contracting meeting. Not sharing it would also mean that Paul might remain unaware of the impact of his behaviour on some team members.

Sam had a one-to-one with Paul about this specific theme as part of providing him with an overview of the general themes a few days before the debrief session. It was felt that having both coaches at this conversation might feel a bit overwhelming for the team leader. In sharing the specific theme about his behaviour, Sam emphasised that they wanted to support him on the day and that sharing the theme would be important to show the team that the coaching was going to be open and challenging at times.

On the day of the debrief with the whole team, Paul role-modelled receiving and working with challenging feedback. When the theme about the perception of him being too hard on female team members was shared, there was a palpable sense of discomfort in the room due to the nature of the feedback, but also because it was the only theme directed at an individual as opposed to the whole team. A few people, including some who shared the perception in their one-to-ones, made brief comments about being surprised by the feedback on the leader's behaviour. At this point, Paul spoke up and said

> that the perception was important to acknowledge as a number of people shared it in the one-to-one interviews and that it was important feedback for him to take on board, just as it was important for the collective team to take on other feedback from team members and stakeholders.

It felt like a critical moment not just for the team coaching, but for the openness in the team.

At the end of the debrief and action planning session, the team members were asked to write down their reflections on what had happened over the entire session and what the impact was. Reflections mentioned "uncomfortable conversations" and "things needed to be said." One of the younger female members commented that "Yesterday was a shock to everyone. I think that maybe people should not be identified by name (if given feedback) … but it was good that the issues were identified." The same team member said that the impact on them was the realisation that they and the team needed to be "more honest and open with each other and it is better to communicate than let things fester."

Stephen and Sam feel that they did the best they could in service of the team, the affected team members, and the team leader.

Key challenges

- Choosing if and how to share confidential feedback from some of the female team members about their perception that the team leader tended to be softer and less critical with the male team members.
- Holding the space to support the team in opening up to face courageous and honest communication amongst all members.

EXAMPLE ETHICAL IMPLICATIONS

- **Confidentiality and trust** – the team coaches had to find ways of sharing confidential information with the team leader in the best possible manner to serve the whole team and increase the perception of trust amongst them and in the team coaching process.
- **Inclusion and transparency** – respecting the voices of team members enough when there are implications to sharing the perspectives; the heart of team coaching is to open up conversations as opposed to shutting them down or off.
- **Respect and neutrality** – staying non-judgemental and treating Paul as an adult meant that he was able to hear and process some challenging feedback and to find a way of owning the feedback and leading through it.
- **Integrity** – having values is easy when the ride is smooth. When there is a challenging dilemma, that is when we get to test and grow what we stand for.

REFLECTIVE QUESTIONS FOR DISCUSSION

1. What would you have done if faced with the situation outlined above?
2. What else could the team coaches have done to prepare the team leader and the team members for the disclosure at the debrief session?
3. What might have been the options and implications if the team coaches were doing one-to-one coaching with the individual team members and/ or the team leader?

References

Leary-Joyce, J., & Lines, H. (2018). *Systemic Team Coaching*. St. Albans: Academy of Executive Coaching Ltd.
Turner, E., & Hawkins, P. (2019). Mastering contracting. In J. Passmore, B. Underhill, & M. Goldsmith (Eds.), *Mastering Executive Coaching* (pp. 10–25). New York: Routledge.

Chapter 6

External coaching

Many coaches are contracted by consulting companies to then provide coaching assignments across a number of organisations; they are providing external coaching. Concerns arising include whether the coaching client is coachable, tensions in priorities, trust and confidentiality, assignment fit, systems contracting and alignment; these are described in this chapter.

DOI: 10.4324/b23351-23

To coach or not to coach

Clients with few resources

Eva Hirsch Pontes

Overview

This case study explores the reflections of a group of coaches in supervision as they worked as external coaches in a pro-bono project. The sponsor of the project was a non-government organisation (NGO) whose leaders (the clients) did not match the coaches' experience with their corporate clients. Through collaborative reflection and discussions, the coaches in this case realised they were 'othering' their clients.

Case study

Background

A coaching organisation partnered with an NGO to provide pro-bono coaching to support their leaders. The NGO brings together thousands of shanty towns in a Latin American country and is dedicated to empowering the impoverished to become their own change agents.

The structure of the NGO relies on 27 local leaders from each state of the country. These leaders are volunteers who are, themselves, residents of the shanty towns.

The NGO and a coaching organisation agreed to provide coaching to these leaders to improve their management skills, to support them more effectively coordinate the projects under their responsibility. These are programmes in education, environment, arts, and sports, aiming at promoting the welfare of their communities as well as teaching life and professional skills to teenagers, to give them personal and professional opportunities to move away from crime.

A few of these leaders have graduate degrees, whilst some were unable to finish secondary education. Their volunteer activities for the NGO happen concurrently with their jobs, which are quite different from those usually found in the corporate world, such as, for instance, truck drivers or artists.

The assignment

The coaching organisation invited credentialed coaches to offer eight sessions of pro-bono coaching to each client. Optional group supervision was proposed to the

DOI: 10.4324/b23351-24

coaches by volunteer supervisors. This case is inspired by the reflections and discussions that took place in the group meetings with the coaches Amy, Cleo, Lory, Nora, Susan, and Taylor, who engaged in five monthly supervision sessions to support them in their work with their clients from the NGO.

The coaching

After all coaches have checked in for their second supervision session, the supervisor invites them to share a coaching case or questions on their mind for which they would like the group's support to reflect on.

Nora, feeling eager to voice her concerns, goes first:

> my client does not have enough resources; he asks me to give him tools and models. I find myself giving him more than I would normally offer to my regular corporate coaching clients who are so much more privileged in their access to resources and education. I feel I am at times entering teaching mode. What should I do?

Cleo picks up on the theme of privilege and states: "As soon as I learned about my client's life conditions, I felt guilty. I can understand this urge to give them more".

Susan adds:

> my client has limited access to the internet; they always come late for the sessions, which does cause me some irritation. And we need to remember that many clients in this project are calling us from their home after their regular working hours, and they don't have a room where they can have privacy. It is hard to hold a true coaching session when there are other people in the same room.

Lory goes on saying:

> I am wondering if coaching is suitable for everyone. I am thinking of Maslow's hierarchy of needs. For many of the clients with whom we are working, their basic needs are not met, so can we really support them with coaching only? I don't think they have the repertoire to respond to coaching. And my client doesn't show up for the sessions. I have doubts about his motivation and usefulness of this project.

Taylor states her agreement with Lory, repeating the reference to Maslow. She asks: "they don't seem to appreciate what we are offering. How can we access them?"

Amy poses a question to the group:

> what does it mean to be a good leader or manager in their reality? I have asked this question to my client, and they do not seem to have the vocabulary to give

me an answer. How can I support them in having goals if they are incapable of defining which skills they need to hone?

The supervisor invites the group to reflect on the underlying patterns that appear to connect their narrative. The group realises there seems to be a repetition of 'othering'. That is, the clients are seen as less worthy, equipped, or suitable for coaching because of a mismatch with their expectations and experience as external coaches in other kinds of organisations.

The group chooses to engage in joint reflection on their common pattern rather than selecting one specific case to work on. Their main insights are:

- When we fail to regard our clients as equals, we seem to be re-enacting (parallel process) the same reactions these clients face in their lives. No wonder we are finding it hard to coach them!
- It is up to us to open ourselves to be able to learn together with them how to best serve them as their coaches in their reality, instead of trying to access them from our own frame of reference.
- It is not about 'them'! We are the ones lacking the vocabulary, repertoire, and resources to serve these leaders in their context.

The group goes on exploring these insights and creating alternative approaches and behaviours for when they next meet their respective clients.

One last point that arose from the subsequent group sessions is that, although the coaching organisation had clarified to the NGO representative several aspects of the contract, such as the nature of coaching, roles, responsibilities, and rights of all parties involved, etc., it seemed that the sponsor had not shared with the clients that they were free to choose whether to engage in coaching. The coaches were left feeling that the NGO leadership had interpreted the coaching offer as a mandatory requirement.

Key challenges

- How experience working in the corporate coaching space influences coaches' expectations when coaching in other sectors.
- Becoming aware of and navigating unconscious biases in coaching relationships.

EXAMPLE ETHICAL IMPLICATIONS

- **Unconscious biases and potential for discrimination based on power and status difference** – feelings of superiority or inferiority, rather than partnering with clients.

- **Systemic equality** – doubting these specific clients could benefit from coaching instead of exploring and embracing differences.
- **Potential role confusion** – urge to step out of the coaching role.
- **Coaching agreement clarity** – coaches relied on the fact that the coaching organisation had a clear contract with the sponsor and did not explore some aspects of the agreement with the clients.

REFLECTIVE QUESTIONS FOR DISCUSSION

1. How would you answer the question: "Is coaching suitable for people whose basic needs aren't met?"
2. How can a coach remain aware of and monitor their verbal and non-verbal biases if these are unconscious?
3. What conditions of the coaching agreement with the sponsor does a coach need to ensure are also contracted between themselves and the client?

Case study 17

When stakeholder priorities collide in a coaching engagement

Sam Isaacson

Overview

The founder of a successful company appoints an executive coach for the new CEO due to differences emerging in terms of business strategy and approaches to organisational culture. As the coaching moves forward, conflicting agendas and priorities come to the fore, including a sense of misaligned values stemming from the coach. What was agreed in a tripartite is ignored, and the coach wrestles with their professional responsibilities to the founder as coaching sponsor, the CEO as the coaching client, and their craft. The coach commits to bringing new nondirective challenges to future coaching sessions.

Case study

Background

Twenty years ago Sarah opened a pop-up stall selling perfume, and had no idea it would grow so large. Today, with several deals with big retailers and established manufacturing and distribution processes, she decided to step back from the business, appointing a new CEO, Peter.

Peter's first few months in the role didn't go as planned. His approach was quite different from Sarah's, and he had ambitious plans for growth that she thought would take away from the culture she had fostered for so long. With Peter's agreement, Sarah brought in an executive coach, Toby, to work with him on his leadership.

In an initial conversation with Toby, Sarah explained her vision for the company, including her historic strategic priorities and carefully curated organisational culture. "I'm not precious about Peter's plans for growth," she explained, "but I'm concerned about his approach to the people. I've worked hard to foster an environment that's made it a great place to work, and it feels like he's going to damage it."

DOI: 10.4324/b23351-25

The assignment

Sarah, Peter, and Toby held a tripartite meeting. Toby was careful to state his professional commitments as a coach, highlighting his responsibilities to keep the conversations confidential, and to remain nondirective, non-judgemental, and challenging. He listened to Sarah's desired goals for the engagement, which Peter agreed with. The goals were to support Peter in developing a strategic plan that delivers growth, while maintaining the organisational culture and established leadership style.

The coaching

Toby's first warning sign came in the first ten minutes of the first coaching session, when Peter said "I've been doing some thinking, and am going to use these sessions to escape from this hell on earth."

Toby hid his surprise, asking "What other options might you have that would allow you to stay in this role?"

The conversation developed, concluding with Peter deciding that, while he would continue to explore other opportunities, he'd put some real effort into digging into the company.

The next day, Sarah called Toby with clear instructions.

I need you to convince Peter to just keep things the same. I've worked hard to make this business what it is, and I haven't done that for someone else to come along and ruin it. I like the guy, but I need him to rein his plans in a bit and focus on just keeping my employees and customers happy.

Already feeling uneasy, torn between Sarah's and Peter's priorities, Toby entered the second session trying to force himself to have an open mind despite dread settling in.

"I've been thinking about it," Peter announced, "and I've made a decision. I'm going to stick around, and I'm going to transform this business. Together, we're going to turn the company's potential into reality."

Toby did the best he felt he could to maintain his commitments to keep the conversations confidential and to remain nondirective, but was profoundly uncomfortable with the situation. He wanted to honour Sarah as the sponsor, feeling a sense of responsibility towards the agreed-upon objectives. However, Toby was feeling challenged as Peter was clearly approaching the sessions with a different agenda in mind. Toby's desire to be transparent had so far led nowhere so it appeared, with Peter hiding his true priorities from Sarah who, in turn, was trying to influence the coaching process behind the curtains.

He took the issue to his coaching supervisor and concluded that he needed to bring some strong nondirective challenge in a second tripartite session, to explore with them both the purpose of the coaching intervention and how they would collectively honour his commitments to confidentiality, nondirectiveness, and systemic awareness.

Key challenges

- The coach needed to juggle two different agendas.
- The sponsor was seeking to influence the process by calling the coach directly after the initial tripartite meeting.
- The coach had to find ways of simultaneously honouring confidentiality and helping the sponsor and coaching client engage in open and transparent conversations about their goals, for the benefit of the business.

EXAMPLE ETHICAL IMPLICATIONS

- **Conflicting values** – when the personal values of coaching client, coaching sponsor, and coach are misaligned, coaches can feel unable to remain within clear ethical boundaries in their work.
- **Conflicting priorities** – the purpose of the coaching, while clearly stated at first, can still be perceived differently by each person.
- **Meddling coaching sponsors** – those who are paying for the coaching may want to see specific outcomes from the engagement, and can try to overstep the mark.

REFLECTIVE QUESTIONS FOR DISCUSSION

1. What should a coach do when the client chooses an agenda that is contrary to what was agreed with the coaching sponsor?
2. Toby defaulted back to the tripartite meeting as a solution to the problem, which hadn't prevented the issue from emerging. What other tools or approaches could he have considered?
3. What would determine Toby's inability to continue the work due to the misaligned agendas? How would this be communicated to Sarah and Peter?

Three-way contracting

What are your legal and ethical responsibilities?

Marie Stopforth

Overview

The purpose of this case study is to present an example of the challenges that can arise when three-way contracting within an organisation leaves the coach in a vulnerable position and leads to ambiguity around confidentiality. It will highlight why this is such an important step when coaching in this context. By providing an example of what can go wrong, it will challenge the reader to consider what good three-way contracting should look like in order to protect all of the stakeholders. It will also raise a dilemma relating to safeguarding and confidentiality that will challenge the reader to consider which is most important in the context of this example.

Case study

Background

The coach, Amy, was approached by a colleague, Natalie, who had been contracted to work as a wellbeing advisor within an organisation. The organisation had identified a member of staff who they felt would benefit from coaching. Although Natalie was a coach herself, she felt that she was not the best person to undertake the coaching assignment. She knew the colleagues involved well and felt that it would be more beneficial for the coaching client to have a coach who had no prior experience of the organisational context.

Natalie asked Amy if she would be interested in coaching this client. Natalie didn't know much about the proposed nature of the coaching engagement, just that Melissa had identified to their human resources (HR) department that she was struggling at work. Amy agreed to talk to the sponsor within the organisation to scope out the work and decide whether to work with them.

The assignment

Amy met with a member of the HR team, Sarah, to discuss the coaching needs and to explore how the work would be contracted. Sarah explained that Melissa had experienced a lot of change recently through organisational restructures, and in

DOI: 10.4324/b23351-26

her personal life. Melissa reported feeling undervalued, angry and let down by the organisation. Sarah also described Melissa as having lots of "emotive stories," and said that her manager finds himself needing to spend lots of time with her. Sarah's four hopes for coaching were that Melissa would:

1. Embrace change.
2. Be able to voice concerns without emotion.
3. Experience increased confidence.
4. Be more actively invested in the future direction of the organisation.

Amy recommended the following format for the coaching assignment and quoted a price for nine sessions:

1. A four-way meeting between herself, Sarah, Melissa and her line manager to discuss and agree coaching goals that met Melissa's needs, but also aligned with the needs of the organisation.
2. Three coaching sessions.
3. A mid-way review point with Amy, Melissa and her line manager to assess progress and recontract if necessary.
4. A further three coaching sessions.
5. A final end of programme review with Amy, Sarah, Melissa and her line manager.

Sarah said that she felt that "there wasn't really a need for the initial, mid-way and final end of programme meetings." She said that they were "happy to pay for six sessions of coaching, and for Melissa to use them in any way she wished." She said that they were "just keen for Melissa to feel supported."

Amy reiterated that it was important that the line manager and organisation were fully invested in the coaching process, and that there was mutual, transparent agreement about the desired coaching outcomes. She also highlighted the importance of there being a 'feedback loop' should anything arise during coaching that needed to be fed back to the organisation. She was clear that anything discussed in coaching would remain confidential between herself and Melissa, and that the mid-way and final end of programme review were opportunities to ensure that coaching was meeting the needs of both Melissa and the organisation. It was also an important and structured way to ensure that the organisation could have access to any information that came out of the coaching that they might want to act upon.

Sarah declined, and chose to contract only for six sessions of coaching. Amy agreed to this.

On reflection, Amy felt uncomfortable with what had been agreed. She therefore went back to the organisation and offered a free initial three-way meeting with Melissa and her line manager. She felt that this was important in ensuring that there was agreement and understanding about the coaching goals.

This meeting took place. It was very productive, and it was clear that coaching goals and organisational needs were aligned. Amy therefore proceeded with the one-to-one coaching sessions.

The coaching

In their initial coaching session, Amy and Melissa agreed that anything discussed within the coaching sessions would remain confidential.

During the first session of coaching, Melissa told Amy that she understood that she had some issues with hierarchy, that she felt that she had been overlooked for promotion, and that she lacked confidence. She felt that this lack of confidence impacted on her ability to clearly articulate her ideas and needs within the workplace, and that this led her to become quite frustrated and emotional.

These were therefore prioritised as important areas of work in the initial stages of coaching.

However, as the coaching progressed, Melissa began to share more information about the behaviours of some of the senior management team in the organisation, for example, the perceived lack of consistent clarity of direction, and how sometimes communication was unprofessional and disrespectful.

Amy spent some time exploring and at times challenging Melissa's perception of the culture within the organisation. They did some reframing work together, and examined Melissa's attributions (i.e. her explanations for her own and others' behaviour). Amy became quite concerned about some of the behaviours Melissa was describing. Some of it seemed to stem from poor leadership and organisational culture, but there were also allegations of bullying. Amy was left wondering if and how this could be fed back to the organisation given the original contracting. She was also very conscious of the fact that she was only hearing about Melissa's personal experience and had no other perspectives.

Amy and Melissa continued to work on what Melissa could influence and control, identifying and building coping mechanisms for what was outside of her control. As time passed, Melissa gained confidence. She reported trying to have conversations about her experiences within the organisation but that she felt that her judgement and reality were being questioned. She was left feeling that this was all in her imagination, and that nobody else had a problem with it. Melissa doubted this as she had witnessed colleagues being spoken to in a derogatory way, but her confidence to assert herself deteriorated.

Key challenges

- Amy feels that she has a responsibility to raise her concerns with the organisation, but doesn't have the permission or the pathway to do so.
- Her initial recommendation when contracting would have provided this, but she is now left with the question of 'who is the client?'

- The organisation is paying for the coaching, but Amy feels that they are not an active or invested stakeholder. She wonders to what extent she should feed this information back, and whether she has a legal duty of care to do so.
- Confidentiality was agreed between Amy and Melissa; however, Melissa is concerned about the possibility of broken confidentiality and is anxious about the repercussions of any such feedback.

EXAMPLE ETHICAL IMPLICATIONS

- **Contracting** – the nature of the contracting leaves the coach in a vulnerable position.
- **Ethical and legal responsibilities** – the coach is faced with a decision about whether they have an ethical and/or legal responsibility to disclose some of the information shared by the client.
- **Confidentiality** – coaches need to understand when they have an ethical responsibility to disclose information.

REFLECTIVE QUESTIONS FOR DISCUSSION

1. Who is the client, and therefore with whom do Amy's ethical and legal responsibilities lie?
2. Should Amy break confidentiality and raise safeguarding concerns with the organisation? To challenge your thinking, consider whether your answer would be the same if Melissa had contracted with you as a private client, but raised the same concerns about the organisation she worked for.
3. How could Amy adapt her contracting to prevent a similar situation in the future?

Case study 19

Between a rock and a hard place
Coaching clients within the same organization

Inga Arianna Bielinska

Overview

Engaging in coaching requires a high level of trust between the partners who are about to embark on a collaborative effort. That is why confidentiality is a prerequisite to successful work. **Confidentiality** is an "agree[ment] that what is discussed and shared between parties will be confidential with agreed exceptions to that rule" (Carroll & Gilbert, 2011, p. 44). The concession is usually described as the release of information required by law. Internal coaches occasionally struggle with biases held by some coaching clients against their ability to respect confidentiality, due to their engagement in the company's system. It might seem that an external coach providing services for an organization is less prone to suffer from confidentiality challenges. However, sometimes multiple one-to-one coaching engagements by the same coach within an organization where conflicts are present may create unexpected challenges about confidentiality. This case study presents a scenario where the coach is feeling biased and wonders if it would be appropriate for her to share with her coaching clients that she is working with both.

Case study

Background

An international coaching team was selected to offer executive coaching services to a global research organization with infrastructure spanning 50 countries and offices in the Americas, Europe, and Asia. The pool of designated professionals included 15 coaches who would provide services in seven languages. The sponsor selected 32 vice presidents (VPs) and senior vice presidents (SVPs) from their global leadership team to engage in 6 months of one-on-one coaching. This was later extended to a second period of six months. Each client could preselect two coaches for introductory calls and then choose which coach to work with. Due to the role the clients held in the organization, processes were self-managed without three-way meetings to set goals with their higher-ups. The team of coaches had agreed as part of their contract to participate in monthly group supervision provided by an external coach supervisor.

DOI: 10.4324/b23351-27

Anna, a bilingual coach, was chosen by four leaders. Each leader was from a different country and working in different areas of the organization. Two of the leaders – Ian and Vikram – were both involved in the same high-profile cross-organizational project regarding the strategic transformation of their global services. The coach understood that their clients were not encouraged to share any details about their coaching engagements with peers or their superiors.

The assignment

As it turned out, Ian and Vikram knew each other well and their roles in the project were interdependent. Moreover, they often held opposite views on how to manage challenges the project team was facing. Each one brought a similar topic to a session relating to influencing stakeholders. They knew who among VPs and SVPs had a coach, yet were unaware that both of them were working with the same coach.

Vikram wanted to work on his assertiveness and ability to collaborate with more dominant colleagues. Ian, on the other hand, felt he was misunderstood by the team, and felt he spent too much time thinking. He often said, "I am a different one. They all have their PhDs and MBAs. I am pragmatic. I am a doer." Hence, he wanted to help the team move forward more quickly and improve his reputation among his peers.

The coaching

With a strengths-based approach, Anna started by supporting her clients in defining their communication "superpowers" and understanding what areas might be crucial to improve when managing high-stakes negotiations.

Anna helped Vikram identify the cultural foundations of his inability to speak up when more dominant and expressive colleagues talked. At times Vikram brought specific situations and challenges he encountered in the project team. Most of them were connected with Ian and, according to Vikram, "Ian's aggressive communication." Sometimes Vikram even said, "This man is a bully."

Simultaneously the coach worked with Ian on his ability to influence peers, improve his aggressive communication style, and improve his reputation. They worked on understanding his inner critic and the need to prove to others that he was good enough. After a few months, Anna noticed that the more she supported Vikram in learning to be assertive, the more tension showed up between him and Ian.

After some reflection, Anna started to believe that, for Ian, 'influencing' meant changing an opponent's mind. At the same time, she interpreted that, for Vikram, it meant finding the best solution possible. The coach quickly realized she was in a difficult position. She found herself mentally defending Vikram's views and judging Ian's approach as inappropriate.

Anna became uncomfortable with her preference for one client's style. She took the case to group supervision to discuss what she was thinking and experiencing in her coaching with Ian and Vikram. The supervision did not help Anna deal with her internal dilemma, and she often found herself deliberating on whether or not to share with both of her clients that she was working with them.

Key challenges

- The coach felt she knew too much about the context and the overall situation that resulted in her inability to remain impartial.
- The coach eventually developed opinions she interpreted as facts about her clients. *Ian wanted to be right. Vikram wanted to find the best solutions.* These beliefs made her biased against the person she interpreted as 'morally wrong.'
- The ultimate challenge was the aspect of confidentiality, since the coach did not know how to manage open communication with her clients. She felt guilty and took responsibility for the tension that grew between Ian and Vikram.
- Anna felt trapped because she wanted to have transparency with her clients. Yet, she feared that, after months of working together with Ian and Vikram, the revelation might make her look untrustworthy or manipulative. Leaving her clients without explanation seemed self-serving and dishonest.

EXAMPLE ETHICAL IMPLICATIONS

- **Inability to remain impartial** – most of the time the coach was unable to stay impartial and objective. She developed opinions and started to create stories about what should or should not be done in the project.
- **Coach's bias** – the coach found herself identifying with one of the client's ways of working.
- **Boundaries of coaching engagement** – confidentiality in the coaching agreement did not take into account a coach working with clients who worked in the same project.
- **The paradox of confidentiality** – the coach wanted to uphold the confidentiality of her clients, so she did not tell them both that she was working with the opponent. On the other hand, she felt she wasn't being honest by not disclosing this.

REFLECTIVE QUESTIONS FOR DISCUSSION

1. How could a coach ensure they are working without bias when supporting two clients who work on the same project?

2.   What are other potential ethical implications of working with two clients engaged in the same project?
3.   What is the best way to define confidentiality in an external coaching agreement when working with multiple clients in the same organization?

References

Carroll, M., & Gilbert, M.C. (2011). *On Being Supervisee. Creating Learning Partnerships*. Australia: PsychOz Publications.

Case study 20

Multi-layer alignment

Jo Leymarie

Overview

Working as a coach, business comes in many ways. We work with companies and individuals directly and also with partners and coaching firms who sell coaching services and then subcontract the coaching to independent coaches.

The number and variety of companies working in the coaching space have increased hugely over the last few years. Many are independent coaches, or small bespoke companies, and numerous coaching platforms are also entering this space. The changes in the way coaching is sold and purchased can lead to a multiplication of intermediaries both inside and outside the client company, which brings up questions of alignment, such as:

- What are the expectations of the company purchasing the coaching and to an even greater extent the expectations of the coaching client?
- How are the expectations of the company who is purchasing the coaching communicated to the coach?

Whether the company holding the original client contract is large or small, and however well the process is managed, this multiplication of layers in the coaching process can, in certain cases, bring to light various issues, some of which are presented in this case study.

Case study

Background

The coach (Mary) was contacted by a partner, a coaching company called Coach Partner, who had a contract to coach a dozen top executives in a financial institution. They explained to her that the company had recently appointed a new general manager (GM: Claire) and had decided to accompany the top executives during this transition. Objectives would be fixed individually by the participants during the three-way meeting at the start of the coaching.

DOI: 10.4324/b23351-28

Coach Partner offered a contract to Mary to coach one of the executives. The coaching would consist of eight to ten sessions with a three-way meeting at the start and end of the coaching, with the coaching client and the new GM. After a couple of chemistry meetings, Mary was chosen by one of the participants (Tom) to be his coach. The date of the three-way was fixed between them.

The assignment

The intention of the coaching was to get each executive to work on their leadership skills, as each of them had recently taken part in a 360° campaign. During the three-way meeting a number of objectives were discussed and decided upon. Everything seemed clear.

The coaching

Before the first session, Tom contacted Mary and said that he'd like to change some of the wording around the objectives. Mary replied, "that would be fine, as the contract hadn't yet been signed." Tom then changed the contract and it was signed by Tom, Claire and Mary.

During the first session, it became apparent that the intent and purpose of the coaching remained unclear for Tom. In spite of his senior position, Tom had never received coaching previously and questioned exactly what would be happening in the sessions.

Tom: I'm still not sure that I really need coaching. What are we going to do exactly?
Mary: Well, we'll be looking at your 360° and working on the objectives that you chose with Claire during the three-way meeting. I'm here to support and challenge you as you work towards them.
Tom: It's just that I'm still not sure if these are the right objectives. Claire has asked me to work on my communication with my team and how I motivate them, but I feel that's one of my strong points. I've never had anyone complain about it before. Do you think that she doubts my abilities?

It became apparent that things weren't as clear as they had, at first, seemed.

Tom and Mary worked on what might lie behind the objectives that Claire had proposed (and that Tom had indeed accepted at the three-way). They also worked on Tom's need to speak up and to communicate clearly to his boss when he didn't understand something, or didn't agree. As the coaching progressed, Tom also began to see how coaching could bring real value to him and help him with his professional goals.

As the coaching progressed, Tom shared with Mary an experience from a recent board meeting.

"I wasn't too sure why the coach had asked us to do this," Tom shared, "but I wanted to show Claire that I was somebody she could rely on, so I decided to go first."

"Which coach would that be?" Mary asked.

"Our team coach!" said Tom. "You know him! He works for the same company as you."

It transpired that not only was each executive receiving individual coaching, but Mary had also put in place team coaching, supplied by Coach Partner. This had not been shared with the coaches providing one-to-one coaching.

Another surprise was in store. Halfway through the coaching, Claire decided to reshuffle her board, moving each member to a new portfolio. Was this a surprise decision or was it an integral part of the strategy from the outset? Had it been communicated to Coach Partner? In any case, the impact on the coaching was evident, as Tom's focus, quite naturally, shifted to succeeding in this new role.

Key challenges

- The intention and communication were spread over a fairly wide number of people – Tom, Claire, Coach Partner, their sales lead, their coaching lead and Mary as external coach, creating a number of interactions where information could be lost or distorted.
- Coaching was introduced at a key moment in the company's history, where the personal trust between Claire and Tom was not yet strong and where the strategy may, or may not, have been decided beforehand.
- The tension for Mary, as coach, was to constantly check in to see if she was aligned with all of the stakeholders during the coaching and indeed to see if alignment between all stakeholders was possible.
- Tension was also present during the coaching process, as the transition into a very different role within the organisation caused the coaching to become naturally focused on succeeding in this new position.

EXAMPLE ETHICAL IMPLICATIONS

- **Lack of clarity on stakeholder alignment as to the intentions of the coaching** – the messages on the choice of coaching within the company didn't appear to have been communicated to all parties in a consistent manner and understood by them. There was a lack of communication between the different stakeholders.
- **Lack of transparency** – the multiple layers of contracting created a lack of transparency between both parties and this had a direct impact on the level of trust between the coach and the coaching client, and also between coaching client and boss and coach and partner.
- **Non-acceptation of contracted objectives** – the coaching client had agreed to something that he didn't want to work on or he didn't want to participate in the coaching, yet felt unable to voice that point of view with their boss.

REFLECTIVE QUESTIONS FOR DISCUSSION

1. How can the coach facilitate the alignment of clear expectations of the coaching by all parties? What are the key points that need to be high-lighted to all the stakeholders and whose responsibility is it to do this?
2. How can the coach raise their awareness so as to pick up on poten-tial indicators that there may be a misunderstanding or misalignment between two or more of the stakeholders?
3. When working for a third-party external coaching vendor, how can the subcontracted coach ensure they have all relevant information regarding the contract?

Chapter 7

Internal coaching

Internal coaching provides a plethora of nuanced tensions to explore. This chapter describes scenarios surrounding mental health, organizational change, gender, leadership styles, dual roles, diversity and inclusion.

DOI: 10.4324/b23351-29

Case study 21

Internal coach and mental health

Andrea Giraldez-Hayes

Overview

Drawing a line between what falls within the scope of coaching and what falls within the territory of therapy can be challenging, and several books, chapters and papers related to the topic (Aboujaoude, 2020; Bachkirova & Baker, 2019; Giraldez-Hayes, 2021; O'Connor & O'Donovan, 2021, among others) have addressed this topic. When attempting to explain the differences between coaching and therapy, it is often said that "coaching deals with nonclinical populations, whereas therapy is designed to address the needs of people suffering from diagnosable clinical disorders such as depression and anxiety" (Cavanagh, 2005, p. 21). Although this seems to be a clear distinction, the decisions coaches must make in their practice are not always straightforward and require knowledge, a reasonable degree of reflection and a consciousness of ethical principles. Two crucial questions every coach should ask themselves are "Do I have the skills and knowledge to hold the client's presenting issue?" and, if that is the case, "How do I discuss the way forward with the client and, if necessary, recontract our engagement?"

This case study refers to an instance in which the coach needs to make crucial decisions to deal with the boundaries between coaching and therapy and the necessary ethical considerations.

Case study

Background

Paul was a regional sales manager at a big multinational company. In response to the uncertainty surrounding the COVID-19 pandemic, the company decided to open up coaching to all managers using their internal pool of coaches. Each member was offered six months of unlimited coaching. In addition, each client received an offer that included three different coaches so that they could choose in consideration of their profiles and other criteria. The client chose Nina, a coaching psychologist in her third year of practice. During the first meeting, the client mentioned that he thought someone with a psychological background would be better prepared to understand his issues.

DOI: 10.4324/b23351-30

In the pre-coaching questionnaire, the client, who had been working in different departments, wrote:

> I am moving into a totally different role. I would welcome support on taking over a team in an unfamiliar function whilst we all work from home. I also want to work on how I can build deeper relationships with my team and stakeholders; part of this is how I come across to some people, as I tend to form deep connections with some but struggle with others.

The assignment

The difficulties Paul had experienced in his working relationships in the past were mentioned in his line manager's report, who, although invited by the client to the second session, declined the invitation. According to the client, his line manager's primary expected outcome was for Paul to become more aware of his behaviour and to learn to manage his emotions in his interactions with his direct reports.

The coaching

During the first session, Paul mentioned he had a long previous career in the army, where some decisions could be unpopular but had to be followed. He observed that his team members sometimes got frustrated because of his leadership style and how he communicated with them, which he attributed to his background in the army. Paul said,

> I do not talk to inferiors in an appropriate way, mostly with women. I am just used to do it this way, and they think I am being harsh. Men are usually fine, but women find my style intimidating and I've had some issues in the past.

He also said, "I work hard and fast, and expect others to do the same."

Paul's top strengths were empathy, problem-solving, encouraging participation, cognitive agility and authenticity, and the bottom five were resilience, growth mindset, social connection, rest and self-awareness. When the coach explored some of these strengths with the client, he explained he had lately been trying to put himself in other people's shoes and attributed the questionnaire's result to the fact that he had lost his mother a year ago, making him more empathetic. The client also focused on some lesser-developed strengths and mentioned that people thought he was an extrovert, but he was not; he had to make an effort to connect with people. Finally, regarding his self-awareness, he mentioned he could get blindsided, and he would have never expected the adverse reports he had received in the past.

Paul also explained that he could be friendly and gentle when he needed to persuade people but was ruthless when frustrated. Although Paul was aware of this, some emotional dysregulation soon became apparent, as he often had problems recognising the emotions he was experiencing when he became upset. The emotions could make him feel overwhelmed to the point that Paul could not manage some behaviours. Let us consider a scale between 1 and 10. We could say Paul's emotional dysregulation was a 4, meaning that he was not experiencing a mental health issue, but still had problems managing his emotions in specific situations.

Because of Nina's psychology background and one year of training in counselling, she thought she could help Paul work on emotional regulation. When they started exploring the agreed coaching topic, exploring Paul's trauma became inevitable and the focus of the sessions almost wholly moved to something Nina was not 100% able to handle. She had enough experience to support people to become aware and connect to their emotions, but had never worked with a client who, like Paul, has experienced trauma. Paul soon became confused and very uncomfortable during the 'coaching.' He thought to himself, "I expected to find a way to build deeper relationships with my team and stakeholders, but did not think the coaching would focus on my trauma."

Paul began to worry about what this disclosure would mean for his career. He wondered if Nina would refer him to the organisation's counsellor or if she would write about the challenges shared during the session in her report to the organisational report.

Nina, however, was lost, not knowing what to do. She was questioning everything about that particular session. She decided she would report the session and her reflections to the company counsellor.

Key challenges

*   Dealing with clients who present some degree of psychological distress or mental health issues.
*   Setting, monitoring and maintaining boundaries.

EXAMPLE ETHICAL IMPLICATIONS

*   Contracting and re-contracting when some degree of emotional distress or a mental health issue that is outside of the scope of coaching becomes apparent during the session.
*   Consider the end of the coaching engagement when the presented issue is outside of the scope of coaching and the coach's knowledge and professional capabilities.
*   Consider the ethical implications of referring a client to therapy or other kind of helping intervention.

REFLECTIVE QUESTIONS FOR DISCUSSION

1. To what extent was Nina aware of the implications of her decisions and the limits of her role?

2. What assumptions do you make about working with clients presenting trauma and/or mental health issues?
3. What other resources, besides the code of ethics, could a coach use to reflect on ethical considerations related to the boundaries between coaching and other helping interventions?

References

Aboujaoude, E. (2020). Where life coaching ends and therapy begins: Toward a less confusing treatment landscape. *Perspectives on Psychological Science*, *15*(4), 973–977. https://doi.org/10.1177/1745691620904962

Bachkirova, T., & Baker, S. (2019). Revisiting the boundaries between coaching and counselling. In S. Palmer & A. Whybrow (Eds.), *Handbook of Coaching Psychology: A Guide for Practitioners* (pp. 487–499). Routledge.

Cavanagh, M. (2005). Mental-health issues and challenging clients in executive coaching. In M. Cavanagh, A. M. Grant & T. Kemp (Eds.), *Evidence-based Coaching (Vol. 1): Contributions from the Behavioural Sciences* (pp. 21–36). Academic Press.

Giraldez-Hayes, A. (2021). Different domains or grey areas? Setting boundaries between coaching and therapy: A thematic analysis. *The Coaching Psychologist*, *17*(2), 18–29.

O'Connor, M., & O'Donovan, H. (2021). *Coaching Psychology for Mental Health: Borderline Personality Disorder and Personal Psychological Recovery*. Routledge.

Case study 22

Navigating the constantly moving pieces of organizational change

Lorraine S. Webb

Overview

In the mid-1990s, the owners of the venerable MidWestern Ltd made the decision to divest themselves of the company. This resulted in a significant loss of knowledge and talent in areas such as finance, technology, engineering, and administration. Further, the culture was so destabilized that employee morale plummeted and voluntary terminations continued to rise to unprecedented levels. 'Battlefield' promotions became commonplace with less tenured and knowledgeable employees moving into more senior technical and managerial positions. The sourcing of key talent was constrained and the organization experienced changes in leadership teams for several years.

Focus was turned to the talent of the organization, especially to those promoted into new supervisory and leadership positions. New to these positions, most were subject matter experts, with little leadership skills. Senior management decided to contract an external consultant organization in liaison with human resources to make recommendations on the training and coaching needs. It was decided by senior management to provide coaching using the internal pool of coaches they employed. The use of internal coaches exacerbated what was already a very tenuous environment within the organization. Trust and morale were at an all-time low. Resources were scarce and the willingness of departments to collaborate on organizational initiatives was tenuous at best.

Case study

Background

An organizational review was conducted by a third-party coaching and organizational development firm (Allisan's Consultancy) at the behest of the C-suite and in collaboration with HR. The vice president of the human resources department (VP of HRD) was responsible for working with the consulting organization Allisan's Consultancy as well as the management team of MidWestern Ltd.

The recommendations from the consultants at Allisan's Consultancy concluded that the organization needed to re-establish core values, develop and implement

DOI: 10.4324/b23351-31

leadership development and supervisory programmes, institute a talent management programme with a rewards and recognition programme, and provide individual coaching for the leaders of the organization. The leadership decided to engage their internal pool of employed coaches to provide coaching and mentoring rather than contracting external coaches. Most of the internal coaches were new hires and not aware of all the recent history or dynamics of the organization. The supervisor of the internal coaches was known to be in a romantic relationship with one the C-suite leaders which was causing some disquiet among the coaching team. Finally, discussions between the coaches and the coaching clients (C-suite and leaders) were deemed confidential. The only information relayed to the manager would be in update meetings in which the coach, coaching client, and manager would be present.

It was believed that the coaching would:

1. Strengthen the overall leadership team in terms of core competencies.
2. Ensure that individual leaders' values were aligned with the established core values of the business.
3. Further help in developing individual leaders so that they could become stronger performers in their present or future positions.

The assignment

Coaching consisted of chemistry sessions, meetings between the coaching client (leadership), internal coach and leader's manager to set expectations, and 360 assessments. All leaders, including the C-suite, were entitled to 12 coaching sessions, over a period of six months, plus top ups when needed or requested, and attendance of various team development workshops. Coaching plans were designed by the coaching client and their manager.

The coaching process included the following:

• Ascertaining career goals for promising leaders.
• Developing a comprehensive coaching plan in concert with the leader's manager.
• Monitoring and meeting on a quarterly basis with the leader, their manager, and the coach.
• In addition to coaching, leaders were encouraged by senior management to pursue advanced educational degrees or certifications.

The C-suite agreed to the plan and communicated it to the managing team. It was understood that this would be a long process, but it was essential to the future viability of the organization. It was the expectation that all would be engaged in the process and would be evaluated on their commitment and performance.

The coaching

As the organization moved deeper into the coaching process more senior members wanted to be privy to the coaching conversations. Some of these leaders felt that their direct reports were not performing and wanted the coaching to be focused on encouraging reassignment or termination. Others wanted to know specifics of the conversation stating a false narrative that "this information will help me manage the employee better".

The HR leader (Jack) had to have direct and clear discussions with a number of senior leaders who wanted to change the purpose of coaching. Specifically, those who were being coached were told that this was a benefit and should be viewed as a career development process.

Some senior leaders wanted to be privy to the conversations between the coach and the leader. Again, Jack redirected these queries by suggesting that if needed at the appropriate milestones the coach, coaching client, and manager could meet to discuss progress or concerns as they related to work. Further, on a monthly basis, the internal coaches provided feedback via meetings to the supervising manager along with the employee being coached. These meetings were to focus on progress towards goals, roadblocks, and other pertinent information.

As coaching continued and the request for information from senior managers did not abate, Jack met with those senior leaders who wanted access to the 360s of their subordinates or information regarding coaching conversations. The coaches were increasingly feeling pressure to disclose information. All were concerned about the potential ramifications of not sharing when asked and also of sharing.

Key challenges

Leaders felt unable to fully express themselves in the coaching. The coaches felt their work was limited due to the leaders not trusting the communication processes outside of the coaching sessions.

The coaches felt pressured and struggled to remain impartial. They were concerned about the political and personal consequences of not sharing the content of their coaching conversations.

The coaches were working with leaders who were not familiar with coaching and had a negative view of its introduction.

Leaders perceived the introduction of coaching was punitive and one move away from releasing employees from their roles if found to not be performing.

EXAMPLE ETHICAL IMPLICATIONS

- **Contracting** – exploring ethical boundaries and the range of effectiveness for internal coaches emerging from the contracting phase of a coaching engagement.
- **Confidentiality** – ethical and confidentiality challenges faced by internal coaches compared to external coaches.

- **Trust** – internal contracting dynamics have trust issues built into them. They can deepen or erode trust depending on leaders' handling of coaching engagements and contracting.
- **Respect** – personal relationships at work can impact how assignments are allocated or apportioned, and leaders may gain or lose respect with their engagements.

REFLECTIVE QUESTIONS FOR DISCUSSION

1. Given the turmoil that the organization faced, how and what would you do to ensure trust and confidence in the coaching initiative?
2. What strategies would you employ to ensure that the whole coaching team and the internal management team were aligned?
3. Coaching is an ongoing process – what steps would you take to make sure that the coaching process became part of the company's DNA?

Internal coaching

Prejudice against women leaders

Rosie Evans-Krimme

Overview

While evidence consistently demonstrates the advantage of diversity to business success, 61% of employees feel negatively about inclusivity in their workplace (McKinsey & Company, 2020). With regards to gender equality, there remains an imbalance between women and men in senior managerial positions. The scientific literature exploring the gender gap has revealed many psychological dynamics in the workplace that have a detrimental impact on women in the workplace, including working in organisations and industries that are male-dominated. Male-dominated industries present systemic challenges that internal coaches working within them need to be aware of, which may include a 'typical leader' bias. Eagly and Karau (2002) discuss how this incongruity between leadership and female gender roles creates a prejudice against female leaders. The following case study explores this prejudice within the automotive industry and the ethical implications for an internal coach.

Case study

Background

Jennifer is a first-time manager at a factory for a leading car manufacturer. She spent the last eight years working as a process engineer, designing machines and tools needed to build automobiles and processes for large-scale auto production. Now she leads her old team.

In addition to Jennifer having to navigate leading a team for the first time, the automotive industry is going through a major transformation towards achieving net-zero, which is significantly changing the way automobiles need to be manufactured and produced. Her organisation has initiated a global transformation project, which includes changing production processes to become more sustainable, and Jennifer has to guide her team through this change. The pressure is high for Jennifer's organisation to make quick progress towards net-zero and her success is being closely monitored.

DOI: 10.4324/b23351-32

A few months after launching the transformation and being in her new role, Jennifer is told by her manager, Jason, that she is underperforming and refers her to coaching. From the pool of internal coaches, Steve was identified due to his availability, and a tripartite meeting is set up between them.

The assignment

During the tripartite meeting, Jason shares his concern that, with the way Jennifer's team is progressing, they will not make the next project milestone in four months' time. He believes that Jennifer needs to improve the way she communicates the new changes to the team and work on holding them accountable to make these changes. Jennifer agrees that progress is currently slow and to work on her communication style with Steve. Jason asks for weekly updates on Jennifer's progression. Following the tripartite session, Jason pulls Steve to one side and shares that he doesn't think Jennifer is fit for the role and that she needs to learn to "talk like a man." He complains that another (male) colleague should have been promoted instead. Steve is concerned that there is a hidden agenda to Jennifer's detriment behind the coaching engagement.

The coaching

In Jennifer's first coaching session with Steve, he enquires about her motivation to take on a manager role.

Steve: What was your journey towards becoming a manager?

Jennifer: As you know, there is a lack of women leaders in the automotive industry. Ever since I started my engineering studies I've wanted to become a role model. I'm also inspired by the industry's transition towards net-zero and with teenagers at home, who are little eco-warriors, I want to show them how I am contributing towards sustainability.

Steve: I hear a strong sense of purpose and values.

Jennifer: Yes, it's what keeps me going.

Steve: Care to expand?

Jennifer: Well, I don't expect you to understand as a man in this industry. I've faced sexism throughout my career and it is exhausting.

Steve: How does this impact the reason you've been referred to me?

Jennifer: I have my own theories, but don't feel comfortable sharing them with you.

Steve: Do you agree with the feedback from Jason?

Jennifer: To be honest Steve, I know you have weekly updates with Jason and so I have to work on what he says regardless of how I feel about it.

After Steve's conversation with Jason, Steve understands why Jennifer is cautious. However, he feels conflicted. Whilst Jennifer is his primary responsibility, he also has a responsibility to Jason. Furthermore, Jason's feedback will be collected to demonstrate the impact of coaching. Steve wants to support Jennifer and decides to continue working together to improve her communication style, as agreed in the contracting.

After three sessions, Steve experiences Jennifer to have a clear and empathetic communication style that has its own strengths. However, he understands that this style of communication is what Jason believes to be ineffective and wants to see Jennifer change this style of communication. If not, there is a risk that she may lose her job.

Key challenges

- The key challenge is working with Jennifer's assumption that her manager, Jason, and the industry she is working within is sexist. When she believes this, it increases her distrust in the coaching process and willingness to be open, as observed through the above dialogue. When Steve asks open questions such as, "How does this impact the reason you've been referred to me?" and "Do you agree with the feedback from Jason?" Jennifer declines to answer. As Steve is an internal coach and a man working within the automotive industry, Jennifer also applies this assumption to Steve, which is weakening the strength of the working alliance. Based on his interaction with Jason following the tripartite meeting where he suggested Jennifer learns to "talk like a man," Steve suspects that Jason may hold some bias against women leaders. However, this is yet to be confirmed and Steve's challenge is to remain neutral.
- Amidst challenging Jennifer's assumptions is Steve's difficulty in navigating the wishes of Jennifer, her manager, and the needs of the organisation. Steve shares a potential conflict of interest as his performance as a coach is assessed by the manager's feedback, which may put him in a conflict of interest between Jason and Jennifer. This is observed in the initiation of the coaching process as Jason leveraged his position of authority to force Jennifer into coaching. Furthermore, Steve is conflicted because he disagrees with Jason's feedback about Jennifer. However, he also wants to help Jennifer perform in this role and feels compelled to help her adjust her communication style in the way Jason sees fit. Here Steve's challenge is to honestly check in with himself to assess whether his intention is blurring his judgement and potentially hindering his coaching of Jennifer.

EXAMPLE ETHICAL IMPLICATIONS

- **Confidentiality** – ability to manage expectations with stakeholders, such as manager or coach sponsor, about coach responsibility, goals, measures of success, and feedback processes that maintain confidentiality.

- **Conflicts of interest** – ensure that coach, coaching client, and stakeholders have no other stake while engaging in the coaching in order to create a psychologically safe environment.
- **Coaching competencies** – the coach went beyond the scope of his competencies and risked harming the coaching client.
- **Biases** – consistent reflection on possible internal biases that may impact the coaching engagement.

REFLECTIVE QUESTIONS FOR DISCUSSION

1. How might you improve the set-up of a coaching engagement to ensure that it best supports a coaching client from a minority employee population?
2. As an internal coach, are there any power dynamics that impact your ability to be independent?
3. How can you regularly check your biases and the way these arise in your coaching conversations?

References

Eagly, A. H., & Karau, S. J. (2002). Role congruity theory of prejudice toward female leaders. *Psychological Review*, 109(3), 573–598. https://doi.org/10.1037/0033-295X.109.3.573

McKinsey and LeanIn.org. (2022). Women in the workplace. Retrieved on 27th November 2022 from https://www.mckinsey.com/featured-insights/diversity-and-inclusion/women-in-the-workplace

Case study 24

Power challenges with autocratic leadership

F. K. Tia Moin

Overview

An internal coaching assignment is initiated by a CEO, to facilitate career planning and develop resilience in a senior leader who demonstrates problematic leadership behaviours (autocratic style, lack of accountability). Human resources recommended strengths coaching by an internal coach from their learning and development (L&D) team. Contracting commenced with a three-way meeting between the coach (internal L&D), the coaching client (senior leader) and the organisational stakeholder (CEO). The coach and coaching client perceived some problematic behaviour by the CEO, but hesitated to address it due to the power dynamics at play. This resulted in a lack of transparency with the coaching client, potentially sending the coaching client down an unrealistic pathway in the coaching. It also prevented the coach from conveying complete impartiality during the coaching. A desire for status outweighed the coaching client's focus on strengths-aligned coaching. Although confidentiality had been contracted for and agreed between all parties, there were several gaps that led to difficulties later on in the coaching.

Case study

Background

Watertech Innovations recently appointed a new chief executive officer (CEO: Gill), replacing a former CEO managed out by the board for underperformance.

Gill was experiencing difficulties with a long-standing member of their senior leadership team (SLT: Cat) and approached the organisation's human resources director (HRD: Callum) for assistance. Cat was not demonstrating the kind of leadership behaviours expected by Gill at that level, or in line with the leadership approach that Gill preferred (less autocratic).

Cat had applied for a vacancy on the executive leadership team (ELT) in which she would be working more closely alongside Gill, suggesting Cat was unaware of her performance limitations. Gill described Cat's behaviour in SLT meetings as disruptive, affecting the performance of her team.

DOI: 10.4324/b23351-33

The assignment

Callum suggested Cat be offered strengths coaching by an internal coach (Lilia) from his team to raise self-awareness and explore strengths-aligned career options.

Gill raised concerns in a pre-coaching discussion with Lilia, to ensure awareness of the full set of circumstances surrounding Cat; that Cat is a single parent and lacks the social support to manage candid feedback and the resilience to manage promotion rejection. Gill was clear that Cat was not suitable for the ELT role.

Contracting

After a 'chemistry' call between Lilia and Cat to establish the coaching relationship, a three-way goal-setting session took place including Gill, Cat and Lilia. Lilia asked both parties "What does success look like for you in terms of outcomes from the coaching?"

Gill described behaviours he would like to see from Cat: "not reacting defensively in SLT meetings, taking responsibility for decisions and outcomes" and "being prepared to support Cat in finding a suitable role within the organisation that matches Cat's skills and capability".

Cat responded: "feeling valued for the strengths she brings to the team and identifying a role that fits with her career aspirations".

Lilia asked both further clarifying questions: "What do you believe your (Cat's) strengths to be?", and "How do you observe these?" It was interesting that both Gill and Cat had different views on Cat's strengths. This increased insight for both parties on differences in their views.

Lilia also raised potential boundaries to coaching outcomes; e.g. "How would you feel, Gill, if the outcome of coaching is that Cat chooses to pursue an opportunity outside of the organisation?" Gill reiterated that they would support the best fit role for Cat, inside or outside of the organisation.

Another important question related to managing feedback about the coaching. Lilia asked, "What's the best way for Gill, as a key stakeholder, to receive feedback about coaching progress?"

Both agreed that Cat (rather than Lilia) would take accountability for updating Gill, including if coaching was not working for any reason. Should any concerns arise in relation to the quality of coaching, Cat could speak with Callum (HRD) in confidence. All agreed that would be the best way to protect trust and confidentiality between all parties but leave open pathways for feedback.

The coaching

Cat wished to explore her strengths and development areas in relation to the ELT position. Cat experienced an 'a-ha moment'; she believed working hard and ensuring rigorous quality control would earn her recognition. Yet she observed that Gill recognised and rewarded different behaviours. People with less experience, who led with influence, tended to get promoted. Empowerment was preferred over rigid control.

Cat defined her coaching goals; specifically, she wished to work on her leadership gravitas (charisma didn't come naturally to her) and empowering and coaching (rather than directing). The status of an ELT position was far more important to Cat than playing to her natural strengths (quality control) and she planned to proceed with her application. Cat worked extensively (though extra-curricular activities guided through coaching) to develop her leadership skills and planned to showcase these at future meetings with Gill to demonstrate her potential.

Lilia's supportive nature built trust with Cat, which allowed her to openly explore the demands of executive life with family responsibilities (addressing Gill's concern). Cat had solid childcare and a good social support system in place, leaving no concerns relating to Cat's capacity to manage the practical demands of an executive role.

Over time, Cat felt that, regardless of her efforts, Gill could not view her positively. Gill immediately assumed the worst in Cat and gave her little opportunity to respond to issues at work. According to Cat, there were circumstances out of her control, residual from systems the former CEO had implemented, that contributed to significant work challenges.

Whenever they attempted to discuss these, Gill saw Cat as argumentative and failing to take accountability. Cat felt she was repeatedly being shut down; "I wasn't allowed to say anything or give Gill feedback in a performance review discussion". Cat felt she had to accept all criticism without the opportunity to challenge or express her needs, because it would be viewed as shirking responsibility. Lilia felt conflicted and found herself downplaying the situation when Cat aired her concerns about Gill.

The work situation escalated to such a degree that disciplinary action had been initiated against Cat by the CEO. Cat was called into the disciplinary meeting moments before she was due to attend a coaching session, leading to a 'no-show' of the coaching session. Due to contracted confidentiality, Cat was unable to inform Lilia of what was occurring (but later apologised for the no-show explaining a significant event had occurred). Lilia had to report the 'no-show' when clocking her hours for the internal budget.

Key challenges

- The power held by the CEO over Cat and Lilia was a key challenge. Lilia was also aware that her manager, Callum (HRD), highly respected Gill. While Lilia appreciated Gill's concern that senior leaders need to demonstrate accountability, she recognised Cat's concerns about Gill as valid. The case fell into the grey category of perceived 'bullying and harassment'. Lilia was cautious of applying labels to the situation and perceived that Gill had simply lost confidence in Cat, resulting in biased behaviour (discrediting anything Cat had to say). According to Gill, the problem was entirely down to Cat's lack of accountability and not the situation. Their relationship had reached a state of disrepair.

- The contracted confidentiality between parties was another key challenge. Lilia was unaware of the reasons for Cat's 'no-show' but, in light of Gill's negative attitude towards Cat, was concerned about protecting Cat's confidentiality and managing impressions relating to Cat's engagement with coaching (which had been very high up to that point). Lilia's need to log the coaching 'no-show' for the departmental budget had not been considered during contracting. Furthermore, as Cat was bound to confidentiality regarding her disciplinary matter, it eventuated that Cat and Lilia could not speak openly with each other about the missed coaching session.

EXAMPLE ETHICAL IMPLICATIONS

- **Power dynamics** – between all involved parties affected open and impartial coaching.
- **Conflicting aims** – the CEO contracted for 'strengths coaching'; however, the client chose to take coaching in a different direction.
- **Trust** – the hiring decision was already made but was not transparent to Cat.
- **Contracting** – confidentiality became an obstruction to communication and internal reporting (clocking hours) revealed coaching attendance.
- **Partiality and power dynamics** – perceptions of unethical behaviour from an executive leader holding power over both parties were downplayed or overlooked.

REFLECTIVE QUESTIONS FOR DISCUSSION

1. How could the coach manage their lack of impartiality with the CEO and HRD?
2. Lilia was aware that Cat had little to no chance of securing the promotion she wanted. How could she have raised Cat's awareness of this?
3. What else could have been covered in the contracting to support the situation that occurred with the 'no-show' and coaching taking a different direction?

Case study 25

Where the coaching topic overlaps with the day job

Sam Isaacson

Overview

The head of diversity, equity, inclusion, and Belonging (DEIB) for a large construction company ended up coaching a white man who blamed DEIB metrics for
a recent failure to be promoted. The coach's understanding of the coaching client's
white fragility, "a state in which even a minimum amount of racial stress becomes
intolerable" (DiAngelo, 2011), made the situation challenging, leading to a decision to firmly stick with a coaching approach in an attempt to resolve the issue.

Case study

Background

Working for a big construction firm, part of Ruth's job was responsibility for
DEIB across the organisation, and she was proud of the progress they'd made.
With a workforce made up of almost 85% white men, she had led campaigns with
a particular focus on increasing the proportion of leaders identifying as female and
black. Ruth was also an internal coach, and was assigned a new coaching client,
Michael, as an outcome from his annual performance review.

The assignment

In his opening session, Michael explained that he had requested coaching because
he'd been overlooked for a promotion in the most recent round. He'd been told by
his line manager that while his performance had been good, the business case was
not strong enough for him to be considered for a promotion.

The coaching

After having reflected on the situation, Ruth asked "What strategy could you use to
build a stronger business case?"

This simple question led Michael to believe that he was capable of creating his
own, valid business case, and he left the session feeling inspired and empowered.

DOI: 10.4324/b23351-34

The first 20 minutes of the next session went quite differently. "It's not fair!" Michael complained. "The so-called 'business case' was nothing to do with business, it was to do with the colour of my skin! You'll never guess who got the job? Sandra. And the reason? To contribute to our cultural objectives. She's not as qualified for it as I am, but they're giving it to her because of her gender and ethnicity. Isn't that exactly the opposite of what's meant to happen?"

Ruth remained quiet for some time as she considered the situation. Michael didn't know about Ruth's DEIB role, and perhaps now was the time to educate him. Maybe she should explain white fragility to him, or alternatively use her understanding of it to allow him to vent more without going too deep under the surface.

"I hear," Ruth replied, "that you feel better qualified for the role than Sandra is, and that you now feel judged based on the colour of your skin." Michael nodded. "Given you'd agreed last session to build a robust business case for yourself, what do you need to do now?"

The instinctive sensation Ruth felt was one of defensiveness. Her campaign was designed to combat unconscious bias, not introduce positive discrimination. Hence the quandary she found herself in. But she stuck to the coaching principles of asking empowering, non-judgemental, non-directive, curious questions of Michael, which she knew would be challenging for both of them. As Michael wrestled with the subject over the course of the session, he came to a place of accepting that he couldn't change anything about the way things had turned out, although he didn't change his mind about feeling discriminated against. He doubled down on his original commitment to build the business case for his own promotion, and brought his line manager in for a tripartite meeting to discuss transparency around the promotions process and plot an effective strategy that would build the best case for his promotion in the next round.

Following the session, Ruth took the situation to supervision and gained new insights through her reflections on both her coaching and her own assumptions around DEIB, leading to too much emphasis on diversity, and not enough on inclusion and belonging. She ended up introducing a DEIB advisory board to better reflect the organisation's workforce, and overhauled communications around the topic to better meet the needs of the business.

Key challenges

- **The coach's role boundaries** – Ruth's role as head of DEIB led to an overlap with her role as coach. It was not immediately clear whether her day job should shape her coaching, or be ignored while she adopts this other role.
- **Beliefs and biases** – Ruth experienced the challenge of non-judgementalism head-on, as she met someone whose lived experience butted up against the agenda she got out of bed for in the morning.

EXAMPLE ETHICAL IMPLICATIONS

- **Bringing bias into the coaching conversation** – both coach and coachee cannot help but only see circumstances through their own filters at first.
- **'Wearing two hats'** – internal coaches don't drop the responsibilities of their day job when they start coaching; particularly when coaches are more senior, there's a likelihood those responsibilities may be influencing factors in a coaching client's situation.
- **Trust** – Ruth did not disclose her DEIB role in the organisation. Given the context of the coaching conversation, withholding this information might have had a negative impact on trust and safety.
- **Potential for role confusion** – particularly when a coach knows they are better informed than a coaching client on a subject, they can find it tempting to step out of a coaching role to adopt a more judgemental and directive approach.

REFLECTIVE QUESTIONS FOR DISCUSSION

1. Ruth was passionate about the topic of DEIB, so a coaching conversation around it was always going to be a challenge. What passions do you have that might trigger you in a similar way?
2. Ruth opted to stay firmly rooted in her role as coach, despite feeling like she had other options. What do you think you would have done, were you in her place?
3. Ruth took what she had learned in the conversation with Michael to adapt what she had started to do with regard to DEIB. How appropriate is it for internal coaches to make changes to their day jobs based on what comes up in a coaching session?

Reference

DiAngelo, R. (2011). White fragility, *International Journal of Critical Pedagogy*, *3*(3), 54–70.

Chapter 8

Digital and artificial intelligence (AI) coaching

The digital and AI space and the speed with which it has grown within the field of coaching have highlighted existing tensions in the coaching space, while adding to it in ways that are unknown or can only be imagined. This chapter focuses on death and bereavement, AI experts, data, team leadership and the future.

DOI: 10.4324/b23351-35

Managing digital records in the event of an unexpected death

Eve Turner and David A. Lane

Overview

In this case study, which is based on experiences from our practices, a coach dies unexpectedly with the coach having made no provision for their death. The coach did not have a supervisor but did have close friends who were experienced coaches.

One of the close friends brought this situation to their supervisor. As well as dealing with their grief at the loss of a friend, they had been contacted by the coach's partner to ask how to deal with all of the client information that was stored both in the coach's study and digitally. The family wanted to ensure confidentiality for clients, and also wondered how to deal with the coach's digital footprint on social media.

This raises questions for coaches around what needs to be in place to avoid the same situation arising in our own practices and the ensuing potential risk to confidentiality of undealt-with digital and other records. This also includes thinking about the impact a coach's unexpected death might have on our clients, our families and our friends.

The case raises issues in relation to death and grieving (Berinato, 2020; Dance, 2020), the role of coaches in preparing for unexpected events (Menaul & João, 2022; Turner, 2021) and the role of professional bodies in coaching raising awareness in this area (Lane & Turner, 2023).

Case study

Background

A coach, Antoinette, practising in Europe, has a partner Gabriel, an engineer, and two children who are teenagers. She works as an independent coach, and has a busy practice, working externally in a range of companies around the world. The sectors she coaches in are many and include defence where confidentiality is paramount, and there are many requirements such as secure digital storage with password protection.

DOI: 10.4324/b23351-36

Antoinette does not use an assistant, and her partner Gabriel does not have access to her laptop or any of her client records, paper or digital. She has always felt that this was the best way to ensure confidentiality for her clients.

Antoinette has been feeling tired and out of sorts, but continues to work, although she is not feeling on top form. She mentions this to her partner and some close friends, and eventually she is persuaded to visit her doctor. There are a series of tests and, then, a specialist tells her that she has a few months to live at most.

She does not believe this and so ignores it and declines immediate treatment, the effects of which would stop her working. While she feels increasingly tired, she decides to seek other medical opinions. However, within a fortnight Antoinette has died, unexpectedly quickly. No one was prepared for this eventuality, family, friends or clients, and this leaves both the emotional trauma, and consequences for her business.

Antoinette did not have a supervisor and had never discussed arrangements for her illness, incapacitation or unexpected death with her family or with colleagues. And because she had not wanted to believe the diagnosis was accurate, she did not put anything in place before she died.

The family has to deal with clients phoning Antoinette's mobile number wondering why she has not turned up for sessions. Clients, on hearing of her death, are very upset. Some have been working with Antoinette for years and see her as a friend; their sense of loss and, in some cases, abandonment is intense. Gabriel is dealing with this while dealing with two children who have lost their mother, his own grief and all of the challenges of sorting out other practical details as Antoinette did not have a personal will either.

After their initial upset, some clients then press Gabriel to know what is happening to their files, and to remaining sessions that were paid for but not delivered. And he takes one call from the defence sector client where they demand to know how their highly sensitive information is going to be securely destroyed.

Gabriel turns to Julie, a coach and close friend of Antoinette, for advice. He wants to ensure confidentiality is maintained but is struggling to know how to access and secure the various digital client records, her laptop files and Antoinette's social media footprint.

In discussing this with Gabriel, Julie discovers that there are no lists of what to do, who the clients were, no contact details beyond going through folders on Antoinette's laptop, and the material on the laptop is password protected. It also turns out that all of the client records are password protected online, in a safe 'vault' to which only Antoinette knew the password. This did observe the requirements of the General Data Protection Regulation (GDPR) but leaves the coach's family unable to answer client queries about what will happen to their records. They are also being pressed for where to go for help by some of the clients who seem particularly upset. And Gabriel is asking Julie if she will liaise with those clients and provide them with support.

There are also problems more generally, with no access to financial records (bank account and accountant details), their professional body and other memberships, their Zoom account, magazine subscriptions, their professional indemnity insurance and their social media accounts.

The assignment

Julie takes this situation to her supervisor, Ade, to talk it through. She is grieving herself, and struggling to deal with her friend's sudden death, which has brought some personal memories back for her. Julie also wants to ensure that the situation is handled ethically and in keeping with codes of practice, and although it is not her responsibility, she wants to support Gabriel. However, she cannot find any guidance in coaching ethical codes, though as a therapist she has access to some relevant information in other codes of practice.

The supervision

Having been brought in by Gabriel to support him, Julie is working through with Ade, her supervisor, how to deal with this situation:

- How to deal with her own grief.
- How to deal with her anger at Antoinette for the situation she'd left her family in.
- How to deal with her anger at Antoinette for being drawn into a situation she felt Antoinette could have made preparations for.
- How to deal with her guilt at her anger.
- And importantly, on a practical level, how could she help Gabriel deal with the client queries so that the profession of coaching was seen as ethical?

The coaching

When Ade, the supervisor, hears this story he is aware of the multiple facets of this situation. He sees a parallel process of unresolved grief and the possibility of traumatic grief emerging for Julie and for Gabriel and his children as well as for some of the clients. He talks this through with Julie so she feels resourced to make informed decisions and then take action, contracting appropriately.

Key challenges

- Trying to fill a hole left by someone else and acting too quickly without considering the implications.
- Dealing with significant personal grief at a time when a coach could be called on to support others with their grief.
- A coach wearing multiple hats, such as friend, coach, adviser, mourner, and how to hold these.

- Remembering what the purpose of any coaching might be, and in what circumstances it would be appropriate.
- Balancing the needs of multiple 'stakeholders' – the family, the clients, the company working with highly secret information.

EXAMPLE ETHICAL IMPLICATIONS

- **Requirements** – considering the requirements for the provision of service post-death or in the event of incapacitation.
- **Back-up** – exploring having professional systems in place, mirroring a personal will, that will ensure a smooth process in the event of death or incapacitation.
- **Continuity of care** – ensuring that client welfare is considered in planning to avoid any possibility of clients feeling 'abandoned.'
- **Confidentiality** – observing regional regulations and using systems that protect confidentiality digitally and in written form. Involving other people in having this information only with client agreement.

REFLECTIVE QUESTIONS

1. What considerations might a coach need to make in order to leave their affairs 'in order' so that if they are suddenly incapacitated or die unexpectedly, there are plans in place for their business, including dealing with clients, and dealing with stored confidential material?
2. How and to whom would a coach communicate this?
3. Where might a coach go for guidance when considering putting together a plan?

References

Berinato, S. (2020). That Discomfort You're Feeling Is Grief. An interview with David Kessler. *Harvard Business Review*, March 23rd. Available from https://hbr.org/2020/03/that-discomfort-youre-feeling-is-grief (accessed 24/07/2022).

Dance, A. (2020). Working Through the Death of a Colleague. *Harvard Business Review*. Available from https://hbr.org/2020/11/working-through-the-death-of-a-colleague (accessed 10/05/2022).

Lane, D. and Turner, E. (2023). Ethics and having an exit strategy for dealing with unexpected death, incapacity and deterioration. In W.A. Smith, J. Passmore, E. Turner, Y.-L. Lai and D. Clutterbuck (Eds.), *The Ethical Coaches' Handbook: A Guide to Developing Ethical Maturity in Practice*. Abingdon: Routledge.

Menaul, J. and João, M. (2022). *Coaching and Supervising Through Bereavement: A Practical Guide to Working with Grief and Loss*. Abingdon: Routledge.

Turner, E. (2021). Exit strategy. *Coaching at Work*, Vol. 14 (4), pp. 40–43.

The coach and the FinTech digital expert

Ramón Estrada

Overview

The CEO and co-founder of a FinTech startup celebrates with his partner the launch of their company. While reading fantastic news from the press about their revolutionary tools and services, the director of a large bank calls the CEO with an apparent demand: "change the information about our products in your comparison tool or remove them, or else we'll sue your company." The CEO calls his executive coach who promoted his coaching on the basis of his previous experience in the FinTech startup sector. However, is it coaching or consulting that the CEO wanted and needed?

Case study

Background

It's a sunny Tuesday morning with a blue sky. Michael and his business partner arrived early at their startup's office to discuss the previous day's events. The two co-founders did a press conference to share with the public the benefits of their mortgage loan price comparison platform. It was the first of its kind because its proprietary algorithm allowed the company's users not only to compare the credit conditions without cost but also to simulate the life of the mortgage.

The two partners were in the conference room drinking their morning coffee while reading newspaper articles and sharing some of the headlines and key phrases with each other. They were mesmerized by the reporters' positive opinions with comments like "potentially saving money for millions of people" and "a path to democratizing finance in Mexico."

Michael was the CEO of the startup and had more than ten years of working experience in real estate development, especially in housing. That's when he noticed the lack of transparency of the credit terms for mortgages, which made it difficult for the public to compare financial products and to make the best decision. And the difference between the best mortgage and the second-best one could impact 10% of the total payment through the credit lifetime. Not only that, the banks only provided the mortgage information in their offices after interviewing

DOI: 10.4324/b23351-37

potential clients, so if this person wanted to quote from three banks, they needed to invest half a day. This is how he came up with the idea of creating a revolutionary mortgage loan price comparison platform to bring more transparency to the system.

After lunch, Michael received a phone call from the director of mortgage credits at one of the largest banks in Mexico. The message was clear. The director demanded that the information about the mortgage in the startup's comparison tool be changed to fit what the bank shared in their advertisements, or the young startup would face a legal demand from the bank.

Michael went home feeling anxious while evaluating the potential outcomes and asked for a meeting with his coach Shauna for the next day.

The assignment

Michael hired Shauna as an executive coach. He wanted coaching to work on his leadership and communication style to better connect with his team and external stakeholders. At this critical juncture, Michael felt he needed to go deep into what was happening to him and find a solution to this problem.

The contract was for six sessions of coaching. Michael had read on Shauna's online profiles about her strong digital profile explaining her broad and deep experience working in the FinTech and startup space. However, Michael did not disclose that he also wanted advice from Shauna given her strong FinTech background.

The coaching

Shauna and Michael found their mutual interests and experiences in the FinTech startup business helped to build their working relationship. They began their coaching very quickly after the initial contracting. Some of their dialogue was as follows:

Michael: Shauna, thank you for seeing me on such short notice. But as I mentioned, my startup's survival is at risk.

Shauna: Why is your company at risk? I read the newspaper articles you sent me, and it seemed to me that everything went according to plan.

Michael: The reporters received the information with optimism, but one of the largest banks is demanding us to change the information of their products, and if we don't do it, they'll sue us. We don't have the money to defend ourselves when we're just starting!

Shauna: I see now why this is such a big deal for you and your company. I'm curious, what would happen if you change the product as the bank asks?

Michael: Their information is correct in how they present it, but when we normalize it to be able to compare it with the other mortgages in the market, their interest rates go up, so it's more expensive than what they say in their marketing. We're not going to change it because they're lying!

Shauna: Okay, so changing the information is out of the question. The bank asks you to remove their mortgage from your comparison tool. What about that?

Michael: This bank is one of the main banks in the market, and if we don't show their products, then we're not bringing transparency to the market and this is what my company is about.

Shauna: Michael, let's get clear about what you want to get out of this session.

Michael: I want you to help me to find the best way out of this mess.

Shauna: Just to clarify, how are you feeling right now?

Michael: My head is pounding, and I'm confused. I don't know what to do! I am also angry because it's unfair how this bank treats my company and me. My team joined our startup because we were making the financial markets way better for our families and us, and now I'm not sure this will happen.

Shauna had a couple of ideas to explore as a possible way out for Michael, based on a similar situation she had recently experienced and solved. Also feeling confused, she hesitated...

Key challenges

* The coaching client's escalating frustration and anger were difficult for the coach to support while maintaining focus on the coaching objectives.
* The coach had experience in the financial services industry, and the coaching client wanted answers from her; however the coach didn't want the responsibility of giving advice in this scenario.
* The coaching client was afraid that other banks could make the same demand and damage the startup's reputation for transparency. This was adding pressure to the coach to work outside of the contracted work.

EXAMPLE ETHICAL IMPLICATIONS

* **Contracting** – coaching or consulting, when does one start and the other stop?
* **Competency** – having the proper skills and experience, sharing the solution or letting the client find it?
* **Autonomy** – respecting the decision-making of a client, while feeling the urge to guide and suggest a course of action.
* **Professionalism** – staying grounded in, and focused on, staying in the coaching lane and not getting pulled into rescuing the coaching client.

REFLECTIVE QUESTIONS FOR DISCUSSION

1. When the survival of a coaching client's business is at stake, to what extent would it be acceptable for a coach to share their own business experience?
2. Is there a place for mentoring and coaching in a coaching engagement? What should the coach be mindful of?
3. How can you balance highlighting your past experiences and promoting your coaching in equal valence without confusing the purchaser of your coaching services?

Handling a data breach out of your control

Alexandra J.S. Fouracres

Overview

The exciting, evolving possibilities of digital technology and AI also mean an expansion in the ways data (both in terms of type and volume) can be exfiltrated and exploited in a cyberattack. Breaches of healthcare-related data have shown an upward trend for over a decade (HIPPA Journal, 2022). Cyberattackers do not follow the same ethical guidelines as you do as a coach; one aim they have is finding something they can sell, which they often do via commercial marketplaces on the dark web (Ball & Broadhurst, 2021).

As an example, in 2022, the Scottish Association for Mental Health (SAMH), a Scottish charity, became victim of a ransomware cyberattack (SAMH, 2022). Ransomware attacks have some variation but largely involve the immobilisation of systems, blackmail and potential data exfiltration and leakage. Whether we are individual coaches, coaching companies or digital/AI platforms, it is no longer optional that we upskill to both defend and be capable of responding to cyber threats (Fouracres, 2022). Cyberattacks put our client data at risk, and can lead to reputational damage, financial loss, legal cases and emotional and mental health impacts from being the victim of cybercrime (Jansen & Leukfeldt, 2017; Palassis, Speelman & Pooley, 2021).

Case study

Background

Morgan is proud of how she has for a year built up a number of clients on PlatformC1, a digital coaching platform. Her move to the countryside a year ago had both excited and worried her. She wanted a break from big city life, but she knew she was going to miss the excitement of working with executives who called her to their offices. PlatformC1 had offered her options to not only still work with her preferred client base but also to work with all of the data and AI it offered. Through adding information and taking some short activities, Morgan found both she and her coaching clients were able to explore and discuss some very interesting themes and topics that came up between sessions from the extra data.

DOI: 10.4324/b23351-38

It was one Tuesday morning that Morgan recoiled a little in surprise at the number of unread emails in her mailbox. Or was that apprehension she was feeling? She was used to a certain amount of email traffic each morning; however on this particular day, the number of entries in her inbox still in bold print definitely wasn't normal. Moreover, it didn't take long for her eyes to be drawn to the titles of the unread emails and pick out headings containing words such as "important", "please read".

Two emails were from John B, one of Morgan's coaching clients. By this point, Morgan had a pit in her stomach about what she was going to read. John B was a high-profile CEO, who enjoyed the flexibility of the online services of PlatformC1. Perhaps due to his visibility in the media, it had taken time for Morgan to build trust with him. After reading his emails, Morgan scrolled through to find an email from PlatformC1, sent in the middle of the night. With a mix of nervousness and adrenaline, Morgan opened it, and confirmed she was now in the middle of a scenario she had never prepared herself for.

Data breach: Important information please read
Important information from PlatformC1
Dear Sir or Madam,

We regret to inform you that we have discovered a significant data breach of data held on our platform. Currently we are still investigating the full extent of the breach which first came to light a month ago. The breach appears to be from an external cyberattack on the platform involving ransomware and we are currently investigating this.

Please rest assured that this issue will continue to have our full attention and we will inform you when we have more information.

The PlatformC1 Leadership Team

With all her clients at PlatformC1, Morgan was very active in how she used the platform itself. She used it to record notes on topics they brought up; these included work-based dilemmas, career decisions, relationships and a variety of subjects that were personal to them. These she added to each client's profile under a section for coaches to store their notes privately for their own purposes. Morgan understood from the message from PlatformC1 that all of this data was now at risk of having been breached.

The coaching

Between sessions, John B made good use of PlatformC1 to take some ad hoc questionnaires and tests via their app. Sometimes they would use the results from these in the next coaching session.

John B's conversations often revolved around his work in areas where he was responsible for classified information. Morgan was aware that PlatformC1 offered places for clients to add their own notes and that John B had made use of this as well as adding goals related to his personal life in there alongside other information which he kept out of the public eye as much as possible.

The assignment

John B and her other clients are reaching out for support from Morgan on how to handle the situation. Different clients have also now tried to call, but Morgan has put her phone on silent – she feels frozen. She knows she needs to take action, but what to do first?

Morgan starts reading links John B has sent in his last email. One of them is a discussion that started on a social media site about how sensitive data from PlatformC1 has been put for sale on the dark web. The discussion seems to have started a couple of hours before PlatformC1 had sent the email to Morgan. People responding to the post are speculating about the secrets that will be exposed if someone buys the data. Morgan starts to realise that she has no control over what has happened but one thing she can do now is work out how to respond.

Key challenges

- Morgan feels a variety of tensions. These include wondering how each of her clients might be handling this, what data could be exposed and how this might affect her. Her name is connected to all of the client records for example.
- Morgan realises that her understanding of the implications and consequences of a cyberattack – now one was happening – is limited.
- Morgan knows she needs to respond, but how?

EXAMPLE ETHICAL IMPLICATIONS

- **The client is not safe** – they have no detail on what has happened, what has been leaked, when they will be informed in more detail or who to contact if they have questions or need support.
- **Breach of trust** – the coachee/client has expected the platform to take care of their data. The platform has known about the attack and subsequent breach for a month; however, it is only disclosing it now after it was revealed on social media.
- **Boundaries of competencies** – the coach is equally not prepared for the situation, having also put trust in the platform. The coach is not sure how to deal with the situation, how they should be involved or where they should start.

REFLECTIVE QUESTIONS FOR DISCUSSION

1. Is data security on a digital platform the sole responsibility of the platform, or do coaches have an ethical role and responsibility to
   i)   Review it?
   ii) Require clear, robust, confirmed security standards from platforms they sign up to?
2. What would your first steps be, as
   i)   Morgan (the coach in the case study)?
   ii) The leadership team of the coaching platform?
3. Which actions around security topics will you, yourself, take as a coach, after reflecting on this case study?

References

Ball, M., & Broadhurst, R. (2021). Data capture and analysis of darknet markets. *SSRN*. http://dx.doi.org/10.2139/ssrn.3344936

Fouracres, A. (2022). *Cybersecurity for Coaches and Therapists: A Practical Guide for Protecting Client Data*. Routledge. https://doi.org/10.4324/9781003184805

HIPPA Journal. (2022). *Healthcare Data Breach Statistics*. HIPPA Journal. https://www.hipaajournal.com/healthcare-data-breach-statistics/

Jansen, J., & Leukfeldt, R. (2017). Coping with cybercrime victimization: An exploratory study into the impact and change. *Journal of Qualitative Criminal Justice & Criminology*. https://doi.org/10.21428/88de04a1.976bcaf6

Palassis, A., Speelman, C. P., & Pooley, J. A. (2021). An exploration of the psychological impact of hacking victimization. *SAGE Open*, 11(4), 21582440211061556.

SAMH. (2022, March 21). We regret to announce that SAMH has been the victim of a sophisticated and criminal cybersecurity attack. *SAMH*. https://www.samh.org.uk/about-us/news-and-blogs/samh-annoucenment-cybersecurity-attack

The new team leader in an AI environment

David Clutterbuck

Overview

This case study is an amalgam of several from my own experience and from cases brought to me in team coach supervision. Coaches working with individual leaders increasingly get asked to help coach the leader's team. However, team coaching requires a much wider tool kit and body of knowledge than individual coaching – to the extent that it would be unethical in many cases to take on this expanded role, on the principle of 'do no harm'. One dilemma for the coach is how to acquire the necessary skills to coach the team and the leader together. Another is how to enable the team leader to make the mental shift from individual coaching client to builder of a coaching culture, in which team coaching can take root.

Case study

Background

Alex has been transferred from another business in a publishing group, to lead a digital transformation team of eight. The aim of the team is to support a strategic shift from print to digital media in higher education and professional publications. Alex's sponsor told him early on, "Your big challenge is that they haven't got a single commercial brain cell between them". The team's creativity was both its biggest strength and its biggest weakness. It wasted time and resources pursuing ideas that were interesting, but not necessarily of much value in achieving the strategic objectives. Alex sought supervision with a supervisor coach (Drew) to support his coaching within a complex system. Supervision sessions were held virtually.

The assignment

Alex had been working with an executive coach (Pam) for a little over a year. He had learned to soften some of his directive impulses and listen more, but recognised that he had some way to go in achieving a more collaborative style of leadership. He asked Pam if she could help him "sort out" the new team, through some team coaching. For Pam, this rang several alarm bells, which she took to supervision.

DOI: 10.4324/b23351-39

The supervision: Time 1

The supervisor (Drew) introduced Pam to the concept of the 'in between con versation'. This is a bridge between individual coaching and team coaching. It helps shift the coaching client's focus from their own development to their role in developing the system – how the leader can create an environment better suited to fulfilling the team objectives. It gradually educates the leader to observe the influences at play within and around the team and to reflect upon how the leader and the team can better support each other in bringing about a higher level of supportive collaboration.

Coaching

Pam recontracted with Alex for this major shift in the relationship. She had had some exposure to constellations, but her knowledge of team systems and group dynamics was not deep. They formed a co-learning partnership, where Pam and Alex agreed to build together a deeper understanding of systems in action and use this to explore how Alex could influence the system positively. Each agreed to undertake some reading, which they shared in the coaching sessions.

An early realisation was the difference between systemic thinking, which is primarily about multiple linear relationships, and complex, adaptive systems thinking, the interdependencies and interactions between all the players in a system. Alex took from these valuable lessons about how he might engage the sponsors in his new organisation, to prepare the ground with the team. Instead of coming in to 'sort the team out', he would be there to help them resolve an issue, which they had already begun to take ownership of.

The growing systems awareness of both Pam and Alex allowed Alex to take a completely different approach when he had his first formal meeting with the team. The two of them rehearsed this approach in advance. Instead of focusing on the problem, Alec invited the team to identify the strengths they had, which could help them address the challenges they would face in the year to come. Then, he asked them to consider the strengths the key stakeholders wanted them to exhibit. "How can we work together to integrate the strengths we have with the strengths they need us to have?"

Without prompting from Alex, the team decided that they needed outside help. Alex now repeated his request to Pam to provide some team coaching.

The supervision: Time 2

In needing to explore more of the case, Pam sought supervision with Drew again. She wanted to explore the previous supervision session some more and work on what was to come. Pam explained this to Drew. She said "I have the recording of our last session to help with this". Drew was astounded. He had not known Pam had been using an online programme to record the sessions. Drew felt very uncomfortable with the idea that Pam had been recording the sessions without permission. They explored this point and possible ramifications of such behaviour before moving to the case itself, which follows.

Drew recommended several experienced team coaches, who could partner with Alex's coach, Pam, in the design and delivery of the team coaching. The selected team coach (Zoe) met with Alex and his coach Pam to contract and plan the engagement, paying particular attention to boundaries. Zoe's experience with situations involving new leaders was especially valuable. She was also able to take on the individual coaching that two of the team members requested. Pam was able to bring a deeper understanding of the organisation and its politics.

The outcome was that, instead of feeling threatened by change, the team was able to engage with it. Moreover, Alex observed:

> Once I started to understand the systems that I was part of, all the changes I knew I had to make in my behaviour and approach all made better sense – and were a lot easier to accomplish. When [his coach] shared with me the ethical dilemmas she was wrestling with, my own role became much clearer. I like to think I am a much more ethical leader now. Instead of directing or manipulating the team to behave the way I wanted, I've learned to trust them to come to the right conclusions, given time and support.

Key challenges

- The contrast between doing coaching to the team and doing coaching with the team. Alex's request invites the coach to extend the contract with him. But team coaching requires multiple contracts, with everyone in the team.
- How would the existing relationship between Pam and Alex influence the dynamics of the team coaching? The strong connection between them could lead the coach unconsciously to lean more towards Alex's perspective of reality than to that of the team.
- How much support did the coach need in making the transition to team coaching?
- Who is the client? Is it Alex, the team, the system that includes both Alex and the team, or all of these? Lack of clarity in this respect can lead the coach into ethical dilemmas relating to conflicts of interest and divided loyalties. If the client is Alex, then the team may rightly be suspicious of her motivations. If the client is the team, Alex's psychological safety may be at risk. If it is the system, where are the boundaries? Does it include key stakeholders and influencers, for example?

EXAMPLE ETHICAL IMPLICATIONS

- **The boundaries between coaching and consulting** – the clarity of the contract between the coach and the client is at risk here. Whose responsibility is it to bring about change in the team?
- **The coach's own competence as a team coach** – although Pam had long experience and multiple accreditations in coaching individuals, she had no qualifications in team coaching. This was potentially a great learning opportunity, but how ethical would it be to learn on this team, with or without their informed consent? How aware was Pam of the risks of doing harm to the team?
- **Multiple stakeholders and multiple levels of coaching engagement** – if other team members needed coaching, would it be appropriate for the same coach to work with them? If a different coach, what would be the contract between the coaches and to what extent could they ethically share information?

REFLECTIVE QUESTIONS FOR DISCUSSION

1. How should a coach balance the requirement to learn through experience against the risks of current inexperience?
2. How can the coach balance the competing interests of the team and the team leader?
3. How can the coach balance the needs of the system against the needs of those within it?

Case study 30

AI: The future of coaching?

David Clutterbuck

Case study

Background

Antoinette is coaching six managers in a digital technology company. They range in age from their late 20s to early 40s. All are highly ambitious and competitive – reputation management is a common theme alongside behavioural development.

In Antoinette's normal coaching until this time, she has conducted interviews with a selection of the client's stakeholders – typically, some direct reports, some peers and the manager's boss. She finds these invaluable in understanding the context of the assignment.

However, this time, using artificial intelligence (AI) is fundamental to the assignment and written into the contract. Antoinette was sceptical and unfamiliar with many technologies, in particular, virtual reality and an AI assistant. But because of the industry the client company is in, Antoinette has agreed to employ technologies, and attended several crash courses to become sufficiently comfortable with the technology to apply it in her coaching sessions.

The assignment

The company has taken out a licence to gather the data; hence Antoinette finds herself required to use a generic coachbot. She has doubts about the relevance of some of the questions, but the bot does allow her to add five questions of her own.

In her reflections on the situation, Antoinette identifies several ethical issues:

- The coachbot is limited by its algorithms. When Antoinette interviews, she gains much of her insights through intuition and observation of what is *not* said. Over-reliance on the limited repertoire of the bot may divert attention from or miss issues that are more significant for the client.
- Respondents tend to answer questions posed by a machine with much less reflection than when asked by a human. How reliable is the data?

DOI: 10.4324/b23351-40

- What are the implications of the cost/quality comparison? Is there a conflict of interest between the company's desire to save money and the client's need for comprehensive and tailor-made feedback?

Antoinette makes the case for an ethical compromise. She will use the bot, but sense-check the outcome data by undertaking a smaller number of interviews than she would normally. She feels this is a pragmatic compromise within the bounds of the relevant "zone of ethical acceptability."

The coaching

The next stage is the coaching session, where Antoinette is expected to partner with an AI that will be present throughout the coaching session. It will also help her with her session planning and her reflections afterwards. The AI will suggest questions and monitor the client's emotions by analysing facial expressions, body language and voice tones. It will also learn by, for example, comparing questions Antoinette asks with its observations of the impact they have on the client.

Once again, Antoinette reflects on the ethical dimensions of this interaction.

- The company has told Antoinette she must use the AI, but one of the clients insists she turn it off. "I don't trust the company not to access the data." She realises that there is a potential ethical problem relating to the conflict between privacy and transparency and contracting. The safe storage of client data is normally the responsibility of the coach, but here the data will reside on the company server. The company has given reassurances that it will not be accessible other than by the coach and the client, but Antoinette has no way of verifying that.
- The mechanics of how AIs learn means that the AI may replicate and reinforce Antoinette's existing patterns of questioning and reasoning. Similarly, it will learn what she pays attention to and make her even more aware of those things. This increased focus comes at a price – she risks being less attentive to other nuances in the coaching conversation. Consciously or unconsciously, her coaching may be driven more and more by process and routine than by her own intuitive focus on the client; on what is said at the expense of noting what is not said; on doing, rather than being. Rather than be challenged, her unconscious biases may be amplified by confirming feedback from the AI.
- Antoinette's capacity to grow as a coach, and the degree of presence she exhibits, may be diminished if she becomes dependent on the AI. She likens it to becoming reliant on virtual maps and losing the skills of map reading.

Midway through the assignment, having had at least two coaching sessions with each of the clients, Antoinette is asked by the company to provide a report on the progress of the coaching. She realises that she can ask her AI to carry out an analysis of recurrent themes and that this would be valuable information to the company in planning its leadership development curriculum. However, she does not have permission from the clients to amalgamate their data in this way.

The company has provided an accredited supervisor for all of its internal and externally resourced coaches. Antoinette has a session booked and is not surprised to find that the supervisor has an AI based on the same programme as hers. *Should the two AIs talk together to enrich the supervision conversation?* she ponders. Antoinette thinks it could provide lots of insights for her, but the ground rules are far from clear.

The supervision

She and the supervisor contract that the boundary of sharing should initially be her post-coaching session reflections. Should it be necessary to, for example, listen to specific parts of the coaching conversation, these would be the only ones examined in detail and they would be deleted from the supervisor's AI immediately after the supervision session. Almost the whole of the first supervision session was spent in four-way contracting between the coach, the supervisor and their respective AIs.

Challenges

Antoinette realises you can't contract with an AI. With a human, you can establish ground rules about how you interact. It's not possible for a human to understand the adaptive decision-making algorithms an AI uses, and the machine itself is unable to describe how it reaches a particular decision. Humans have a tendency to anthropomorphise, ascribing human motives and reasoning to animals and inanimate entities. She realises that she could easily learn to trust the AI, but that the AI has no capacity to trust her and that she has no way of identifying when she should not trust it. For example, in her first session, she recognises that she had attached greater credibility to the AI's diagnosis than to her own hypotheses, which turned out to be much closer to the truth.

EXAMPLE ETHICAL IMPLICATIONS

- **Protection of clients' data and conversations' content** – the coach cannot guarantee if and how clients' data and coaching conversations will be safeguarded. The responsibility for protecting these still remains with the coach, but there are many variables – that may impact safety, transparency, trust and confidentiality – which the coach is unable to monitor or control.

REFLECTIVE QUESTIONS

1. Can an AI be ethical?
2. What is the nature of the partnership between coach and AI?
    i) Who owns the AI's analyses?
3. How feasible is it to create a code of ethics and practice for working with AI? What would it contain?

Chapter 9

Power in coaching

Power shows itself in many forms with coaching across all contexts. This chapter highlights the challenges and tensions on the basis of culture, gender, status, race, and neurodiversity.

DOI: 10.4324/b23351-41

Cultural translations

Silvina M. Spiegel

Overview

Erin Meyer (2014) stated:

> Today success depends on the ability to navigate the wild variations in the ways people from different societies think, lead, and get things done. By sidestepping common stereotypes and learning to decode the behaviour of other cultures along all the scales [on the cultural map], we can avoid giving (and taking!) offence and better capitalise on the strengths of increased diversity.

A team coach is hired to support a recently formed multicultural team spread all over the globe. The team has numerous challenges ranging from differences in cultural perspectives to working in different time zones. As Mary interviews each member, she learns about differences in power dynamics, communication styles, and language. The team leader seems to lack understanding of the many layers that are at play and are adding to resentment amongst team members, as well as obstacles to team cohesion. It appears as if language is not a barrier, but culture doesn't translate as easily as words. Mary faces the need to make tough decisions regarding her best approach to remain true to the objectives of her role.

Case study

Background

A software solutions international company (Inc inc.) is based on the West Coast of the United States (US), with developers in the US and India. They recently acquired an Israeli startup. The manager is having some difficulties engaging the whole team, creating synergy and a predictable flow of work.

The assignment

Aware of the existence of cultural differences, the human resources (HR) director of the company hires a coach (Mary) for a team coaching engagement.

DOI: 10.4324/b23351-42

Mary is from the US and has worked as a coach for other companies in the industry. She is used to coaching multicultural teams. Since the pandemic, she developed a virtual coaching practice which allows her to work with several multicultural companies.

Mary interviews the manager (John) and his six direct reports before the beginning of the process, to understand their assessment of the situation and their expectations for the team and for the coaching process.

The coaching

During the interview process, Mary realises there are many and very different important topics that vary for each individual in the team.

John, the manager, is an engineer from the US who has worked for the company for five years. He likes his job and is a conscious and loyal employee. He is concerned that the incorporation of the Israeli startup might turn out to be more of a burden than a gain.

During the initial interview with Mary, John states "They are resisting the incorporation, trying to continue working their old way, as if nothing had happened. They don't have any respect for me or anybody".

John, in his role as manager, wants to get everyone on board before every decision, because he thinks that his work is not to tell his team members what to do. He claims: "I aspire to be their leader, not only their boss".

John is also concerned with the team in India. He says:

with their previous manager, they used to send the codes for assessment without hardly participating in any meetings. Now that they are included, instead of actively discussing the problems and proposing solutions, they just sit quietly and write down what's being discussed.

About the US part of the team, he says: "The American team is no problem".

John acknowledges that "since the team as a whole is not working at its best, the meetings are becoming longer and less productive".

Ajay and Lakshmi, two members of the team in India, state they "are waiting for clear parameters and deadlines which should be defined by John".

Their meetings with John and other team members begin at 10:30 p.m. in India, which they both consider "normal" when working for a company on the other side of the world.

Ajay joined the company before the pandemic. He was used to doing his job in regular office hours and sending the results to headquarters. His former manager would give him the parameters and deadlines and they would meet every two or three weeks to align details. John now calls for weekly team meetings.

Ajay says, "Although I do not see the need, I know my manager (John) is doing so for some reason, so my job is to respectfully attend".

Lakshmi, a systems engineer who joined the company in 2021, acknowledges that "her family life and obligations happen at more normal hours, and – after putting her two sons to bed – she attends work meetings, while trying not to disturb anyone at home". Between her family life and her work, she is busy from 6 a.m. to midnight. She thinks that John is probably unaware of these facts, for, in her words, "he spends time on apparently non-relevant things during the meetings, and this leads to sometimes longer and non-objective meetings".

Lakshmi goes on:

I understand the Israelis are not happy with the process of incorporation of their startup to the company, but I feel they overreact and are overall quite rude, especially when it comes to setting dates for meetings and deadlines. They are definitely very loud and have no respect for the boss or other people in the meeting: they just cut them through and scream their ideas.

Peter and Gabe entered the company almost at the same time, almost two years ago. They are both from the US, and they attend the meetings expecting to gain more insights about the company's goals and possibilities of growth for themselves while working towards the company's goals.

Both voice similar perceptions about the team in India: that Lakshmi and Ajay are too quiet and reserved, acting as if their job is not really that important to them. The impression is that they don't contribute anything to the meetings and that they are only waiting to see what falls onto their desks. They don't discuss their opinions and never bring new ideas to the meetings.

Pete and Gabe also think that the company shouldn't have brought the Israeli startup's team to the company, because they feel they are really difficult and rude. They speak over the other people, and they always disagree, exhibiting the worst possible attitude. They think that a firm hand is needed to lead this team and that John is losing opportunities to give feedback and assert some order.

Dorit and Moshe are Israeli programmers. The startup where they used to work, and believed that they built from scratch with others, was sold. The next day they became employees of a huge company based in the US because of the 'merger'. Suddenly they have a boss and coworkers from other countries who are used to different organisational structures. When working in the startup, Dorit and Moshe did everything: they were the developers, engineers, and quality assessors. They both believe they are now expected to wait until everyone is on the 'same page', give their codes to other people, and wait for instructions. Dorit and Moshe are not used to that type of structure, they don't like it, and in particular they don't like the 7 p.m. meetings. They consider this to be inconvenient and disruptive to their personal lives. Dorit complains for both herself and Moshe,

> we must hear, over and over again, that the best day for everyone else to join or to meet deadlines is on Fridays – which is a day that in Israel we don't work. For us, Fridays are the same as Sundays for the other team members. When we start our week, it's their weekend and we respect their right to it. It shouldn't be that hard to understand that we want the same; but no one seems to get it.

Dorit and Moshe think John is "slow and full of useless formalities", and that the "people in India are too quiet". They don't understand "why nobody pays attention to the time difference or any difference at all". Moshe says, "It is as if the Americans are blind to differences. When we try to explain, contribute, and speak our mind in the meetings, no matter how loud we tell our truth, no one seems to listen".

Mary understands that to work as planned on the contract would not be productive for the company at this stage. A different type of work would have to be done in order to better serve her client.

Key challenges

- There is a clear issue with communication happening inside of the team, and although all of the members of the group speak fluent English, it seems that culture is not translating well into their interaction. Some form of mediation could be useful.
- Since Mary has experience in multicultural companies, the cultural difference is something that she is fully aware of. In this case, however, the cultural background of Mary could hinder some of her possibilities to fully explore the matter. Mary reflects on her own cultural biases that could make her 'agree more' with some parts of the team.
- This group of people work for the same company under the same leader, but is not functioning as a team yet, so before thinking about team coaching, there would probably be a need for team building.
- The leader is experiencing a clash of expectations, so he'll need some individual coaching conversations.
- To better serve the client, Mary would have to 'change hats' between team building facilitator, trainer, conflict mediator, and coach. Some of those are not her best suit, so she would need to call in another colleague. HR would probably allow her to exchange 'hats' and even grant her permission to bring

in another professional, but surely they'll tell her to do what's needed for the same rate.
- For the project to work, it would take more time than what was estimated, would cause her to pay from her rate to at least one other person, and would end up being more complicated than it seemed. She doesn't want to lose the client, for this is her first job at this particular company.

EXAMPLE ETHICAL IMPLICATIONS

- **Conflict of interest** – the work that would really serve the needs of the client would take more time – and also more expenses – consequently reducing Mary's income.
- **Trust issues** – if she were coaching the manager and the team, it could arrive at a point where she is unable to maintain confidentiality with either the team or the manager, compromising trust.
- **Boundaries of the coaching engagement** – bringing in another professional, performing from different roles. All of this is not clearly stated within her contract and could lead to a misunderstanding of the boundaries or results of this engagement.

REFLECTIVE QUESTIONS FOR DISCUSSION

1. What are the different perceptions of power that each part of the team displays and how do they pose a challenge for the coach?
2. What steps should the coach take in order to better serve her clients?
3. What steps should the coach take in order to avoid or minimise her ethical challenges?

Reference

Meyer, Erin. (05/2014). Navigating the Cultural Minefield, *Harvard Business Review*.

Case study 32

When a woman's power is weaponized against her

Caroline Adams Miller and Wendy-Ann Smith

Overview

This case study is about a coaching engagement for the CEO of an international financial institution who wanted to burnish her leadership skills and use her power as a glass-ceiling-breaking woman to succeed, as well as help other women rise and thrive in her traditionally male-dominated industry. After a number of very successful projects an internally assigned coach was assigned to the CEO as part of a 'performance improvement plan'. During the coaching engagement, many forces emerged in the organization to undermine the coaching client's effectiveness and diminish her leadership role, leading to the assignment of a mandatory coach from within the organization to 'help' her address her deficiencies. The CEO became aware that the woman board members intended power games and so the CEO began challenging the assigned coach to tell her what was really happening behind the scenes in the organization as she felt there were attempts to discredit her. It became apparent that the outsized power wielded by several women and men was openly blocking another woman from sitting in a seat at the most powerful table at the top of the organization.

Case study

Background

The coaching client, Elizabeth, is a prominent and successful woman in global finance who ranks frequently in the top ten list of the 'most powerful' women in her region. After decades of rising through the ranks of her organization and breaking barriers for women with each successive position, she got to the very top of her region's leadership positions and broke the glass ceiling, by not only being the first woman to hold the role of CEO, but also the first woman of her culture to ascend to that role.

As part of her new job, Elizabeth would have to master the nuances of negotiation and differing political and financial outlooks across a varied region of the world, and lead a bigger team spread out across ten countries. Her new role was featured on many news broadcasts, on the front of magazines, and in a number of

DOI: 10.4324/b23351-43

gender-specific financial outlets that celebrated her success. Elizabeth felt like she had to prove that a woman could handle the varied challenges that came with so much visibility and power at a fraught time in global financial markets.

Francine, an internal coach, was mandated by the organization to coach Elizabeth. This mission was a surprise to Elizabeth. Francine had worked with several of Elizabeth's peers, and in spite of never having worked with an internal coach before, Elizabeth realized that all eyes were on her to succeed.

Elizabeth continued to participate in coaching with her long-standing trusted executive coach (Stephen), whom she privately contracted.

The assignment

Francine and Elizabeth agreed to a coaching contract that consisted of ten hour-long virtual sessions over six months, with the agreement to extend the agreement after six months if they both felt the arrangement was mutually rewarding and successful.

In the early stages of coaching, the engagement was a success in terms of creating clear metrics for progress on goals, seeing around the corners, and working on establishing a more powerful leadership presence in meetings with peers from other organizations and in her frequent media appearances and conference keynotes. Employee engagement surveys showed that Elizabeth's inspirational interactions with her team, her ability to lead a distributed workforce through the pandemic, and her promotion of women throughout every part of the organization created a positive environment. Her first performance review after the coaching engagement began was among the most positive she had ever received.

However, there was an undercurrent of disquiet that Elizabeth couldn't put her finger on and wanted to explore this with her private coach Stephen and also her mandated coach Francine. She was hoping to learn about the background dynamics and happenings that seemingly were impeding her accession to a seat at the most powerful table – the boardroom – within the organization.

Elizabeth eventually filed a complaint with HR, around a sexist culture. Several months later Elizabeth was given an ultimatum to leave the organization. Elizabeth then hired lawyers to sue for gender discrimination, age discrimination, unfair pay policies, and libel.

The coaching with Francine

Francine was assigned to act on the organization's behalf to find ways to discredit Elizabeth, essentially acting as an organization spy. However, it was clear to Francine she was coaching someone of immense integrity and talent.

Elizabeth struggled to fully trust the relationship with Francine. There was something nagging her that she couldn't put her finger on.

As the coaching continued Francine and Elizabeth generally worked well together in the coaching, even with the initial mistrust. They realized they were strongly aligned on core values, such as equality for women. Francine was increasingly finding it difficult to remain neutral as Elizabeth's stories were intensifying and their relationship was changing. Additionally, Francine would hear stories in her other coaching engagements with high-power stakeholders that troubled her, as she could see how their motives may harm Elizabeth.

Suddenly, the original coaching engagement shifted abruptly. As the organization's stance towards Elizabeth changed, so too the lines between a professional relationship and what eventually became a friendship with Francine were blurred at times.

To complicate Francine's role as a coach further, she learnt through her other coaching assignments how high-status women, and one in particular – Anne – did not want Elizabeth to succeed in her role as CEO. She was extraordinarily jealous of Elizabeth's successes and often hinted at blocking her proposed initiatives. Anne – a board member – spoke in ways that informed Francine that she was very threatened by Elizabeth's outstanding accomplishments and reputation.

Elizabeth believed Anne was deliberately behaving in ways to block Elizabeth's ascendancy to the board, something she and a couple of men on the board had always thought was a possibility when Elizabeth was hired as CEO.

So, when Francine was put in an awkward position of seeing sensitive information from the top of the financial organization that proved Elizabeth's legal charges of gender pay inequality, as well as the outsized power wielded by several women who openly blocked another woman from sitting in a seat at the most powerful table at the top of the organization, she was unsure of what action to take.

Coaching with Stephen

During one coaching session Elizabeth, feeling fed up, decided to share with Stephen audio recordings she made during 'performance reviews' and sessions with the head of human resources. They made known the times and how she was accused of being a bully and poor leader without any supporting documentation. Elizabeth wanted Stephen to believe her, to be on her side as Elizabeth filed a formal complaint. Stephen, a long-standing advocate for women's rights, equality, and inclusion at the top positions of the workplace, was appalled at the behaviour of the board members. He worked hard to remain neutral in supporting Elizabeth but struggled to do so. He wasn't sure what he should do about his struggles or Elizabeth's plight.

Challenges

* Francine was concerned about her coaching contract and potential future contracts when she became embroiled in organizational power play by women with significant status and influence on organizational practices. She had "real" concerns about losing her own opportunities to move up the hierarchy of the organization, but also wanted to remain a coaching presence and retain her relationship with Elizabeth.

- Stephen found himself deeply affected by the events outside of the coaching and struggled to maintain impartiality to best support Elizabeth.
- With a lawsuit pending, both Francine and Elizabeth found their relationship changing from coach and coaching client to comrades fighting the good fight for the rights of women to be successful and were not sure how they should proceed with their coaching relationship.

EXAMPLE ETHICAL IMPLICATIONS

- **Gender-based power of both genders** – women using their power to halt the growth of other women and men using misogynistic language.
- **Values clash** – variability in values between internal coach, external coach, coaching client, and organization.
- **Breaking confidentiality** – the breaking of confidentiality has implications for the organisation (the paying client) and the coach–coaching client relationship as collusion is disrupted.
- **Contracting irregularities** – who is the client/s when circumstances change dramatically?
- **Impartiality** – coach worked within the same organization and was personally impacted by the events. She had also formed bonds and an alliance with her coaching client.

REFLECTIVE QUESTIONS FOR DISCUSSION

1. How can women who have attained status support other women who equally perform well to grow and break the glass ceiling of power determined and protected by some? What role does the coach have in this scenario?
2. What should the coach be mindful of when they realize their values and work contracts are clashing?
3. Should coaches be taking action when faced with gender bias, sexist language, and power plays along and across gender lines? What might have been at stake for Francine, if she chose to act, considering she worked for that same organization?

Case study 33

Under one condition

A case of identity-based aggression

Pamela A. Larde

Overview

Women leaders experience a wide range of identity-based challenges while pursuing professional advancement and growth. As women, aggressions such as harassment, silencing, and minimizing are common forms of oppressive barriers that hinder career and economic advancement. When these leaders are entrepreneurs who lead their own companies, the recourse for seeking support and advocacy is limited, as there is typically no human resources department to report to. This case study presents an instance of identity-based aggression while negotiating a contract with a potential corporate client. In addition to the emotional implications this experience presents, the coach is positioned to sort through a set of decisions that require her to consider financial gain/loss, her own levels of physical and psychological safety as it pertains to the pros and cons of taking legal action, and the ethics around proceeding or declining the partnership offer.

Case study

Background

Melinda, founder and CEO of Cyburn Executive Coaches, Inc., started her company with the vision of integrating values of human dignity, diversity, and whole person approaches into her executive coaching techniques. Her firm, which began with just herself and a colleague who was a certified coach, primarily focused on local business leaders and entrepreneurs in the Chicago metropolitan area. After a healthy amount of networking and strategic marketing, she managed to grow her company to a team of 50 coaches that served a roster of 20 small businesses.

After her fifth year of attending an international coaching conference, she became a recognizable face in the industry. It was at this conference that she was introduced by a friend to Chad – the vice president (VP) of organizational development for a well-known Fortune 500 company. His intention at the conference was to vet and hire a coach to address a major change that his company was undergoing. After the introduction, Chad and Melinda had a robust conversation about his company's needs and her company's unique approach to coaching.

DOI: 10.4324/b23351-44

Chad's company recently brought in a new leader and the response throughout was a mix of fear, curiosity, uncertainty, and optimism. Most people in his company were fearful of the types of changes that may occur, including stability of employment and whether or not work from home arrangements could continue. Additionally, changes to benefits, paid time off, and salary were among the concerns being discussed. Melinda assured him that the approach utilized by her team was designed to address exactly the types of challenges he described, highlighting the whole person approach in particular. It was just what Chad stated he needed for his leaders.

Chad: Our biggest struggle is getting the leaders to trust the plan and to communicate it well to their divisions. We suspect that some employees may want to leave, but these changes can actually create a better place to work. Our divisional leaders will be a critical part of getting the buy-in we need. The coaching your company provides is really spot on for us. Can you come to our headquarters to share your company's coaching program?

Twenty-four hours later, the following Wednesday was confirmed for the in-person proposal meeting, which Melinda agreed to attend at her company's expense.

It seemed to be the chance of a lifetime. This was the first big opportunity for her company. Chad was a highly visible leader who often made media appearances and received accolades for his work. Melinda was excited about the opportunity and was eager to bring her company's approach to meet his company's needs. After what proved to be a well-received presentation to the leadership team and an on-the-spot unanimous recommendation from other VPs to move forward, Chad asked Melinda to debrief the presentation in his office. Still on a victory high and oblivious to his underlying intentions, she joined him to discuss next steps.

He began with great excitement and amazement over how well the VPs received the coaching program she presented. "We can really do a lot with this program. I see beginning with our division leaders and then branching out to the members of their teams." After about a 20-minute debrief, and being mindful of her impending flight schedule, Chad wrapped up, concluding that after he had a chance to meet with the leaders to gather their thoughts, he would be in touch with details about next steps.

As she was about to say her goodbyes and head for the door, his tone suddenly changed. "But I have another offer." To her absolute shock, the offer he presented was a sexual advance – a compliment of her body and an offer to sleep with him to seal the deal. "Remember, I can shut down this entire operation at any time." Melinda did *not* see this coming. She was angry that all of her hard work and the quality of her product came down to what she would allow her body to do for this stranger. She saw a life-changing opportunity. He saw a body that he could control.

Suddenly, she found herself faced with a series of decisions that she had to make in an instant.

What do I say? How do I safely get out of this situation? Do I report this? And to whom? Is this opportunity suddenly gone? Is there no one else to work with to close this deal? If I expose him, will all of the media attention destroy me?

The assignment

The intent of the assignment was to hire Melinda's coaching firm, Clyburn Executive Coaches, Inc., to provide coaching for the 32 divisional leaders of the Fortune 500 company.

The coaching

Chad's vision was that the leaders he oversaw would receive the coach training. He would be the primary point of contact over the next year as the coaching program was implemented across the divisions.

Key challenges

- After her dynamic presentation, the leadership team wanted to work with Melinda's company, but Chad's misconduct made her feel unsafe.
- Chad's threat of being able to shut down the entire operation if Melinda didn't accept his offer was one that would merit reporting, but who would she report to? What would be the consequences of reporting? What would be the consequences of not reporting?
- Melinda was deeply embarrassed by this experience and wasn't sure who to speak to, but knew she needed some emotional support to process this situation.
- Considerations of blame in this situation can bring up some difficult and deeply enlightening observations around our own biases and worldviews about cases such as these.

EXAMPLE ETHICAL IMPLICATIONS

- **Identity-based power dynamics** – the power dynamics in this situation had a profound impact on Melinda, positioning her to endure levels of trauma while processing ways to protect herself.
- **Boundaries** – the boundaries of the working relationship were challenged before the agreement was established.
- **Trust** – the sponsor broke trust by making a sexual advance to finalize a partnership between his company and the coaching company.
- **Care for self after micro/macroaggression occurs** – coaches should recognize the need for self-care and an opportunity to process this situation, but should also consider who to trust with vulnerable experiences such as these.

- **Examination of one's own values** – Melinda's decision-making process requires an acknowledgment and examination of her own values around justice, safety, peace of mind, self-advocacy, privacy, professionalism, and harassment. Ideally, her decision would be grounded in her value system.
- **Considerations for action** – there are a number of options that exist for taking action. This would require considering the pros and cons of those options. Speaking up, selectively speaking up, or remaining silent all have benefits and consequences. The key is finding peace with your decision.

REFLECTIVE QUESTIONS FOR DISCUSSION

1. What course of action most resonates with you while in the situation?
2. What course of action most resonates with you after the situation?
3. How might this situation inform your approach with future partnership opportunities?

Power play

Shifting roles and the ripple effects of legacy leaders

Monica Murray

Overview

An executive coach has been engaged by a CEO of a privately held business to work one-to-one with members of the executive team. The CEO has just taken over from her father and there is tension with legacy leaders and new members of the team (including the new CEO). The CEO and the coach have been acquaintances for several years and have gotten to know each other quite well following each other's careers. As the engagement continues, the coach sees significant dysfunction with the team and wonders if team coaching would be a better fit for the group. However, she has limited formal experience with this sort of work, even though she has 15 years' experience as a CEO of her own organization where she worked through team conflict on a regular basis. Originally, the CEO stated to her executive team that she would not be coached by the same coach, but as her team culture starts to deteriorate, the CEO approaches the coach to be coached.

The case study

Background

The company, HiRise Inc., a 35-year-old privately held real estate development company, is growing quickly. The organization was founded by 70-year-old Geoff Leibermann who is retiring this year. His daughter, Lena Leibermann, has been with the company for the last ten years and took over as the new CEO. Headcount has gone from 100 to 300 people in the last four years and is expected to grow another 20% as they expand into new locations.

Lena, the new CEO, is six months into her role as head of the organization. Although she is not new to the company, some on the executive team think she's not ready for the responsibility. She has a very different style from her father and is working to integrate her ethos into the company's long-established values of quality, safety, and respect.

The dynamic of the six leaders on the executive team is shaky as people figure out their new boss. Four members of the executive team are legacy leaders, having moved up through the ranks under the former CEO. The two other leaders are

DOI: 10.4324/b23351-45

relatively new and are dealing with their own leadership roles, as well as navigating the very fast growth of the company whilst managing their teams. Lena is aware that there are different personalities on the team and already sees some underlying friction in the executive meetings.

Hannah Yang is a seasoned CEO and executive coach working with leaders within organizations. Based on Hannah's own successful leadership experience, her coaching clients often look for guidance from her and occasionally ask for advice. Her practice is primarily focused on one-to-one coaching with limited team coaching engagement experience.

Hannah and Lena met at a business event five years ago and they have stayed in close touch as colleagues.

The assignment

Lena is an advocate of coaching and has hired Hannah to work with members of the executive team on a one-to-one basis. The executive coaching is not mandatory. Lena wants to support her team as they work through the CEO transition, company growth, and personal career development. Lena makes it clear that she will not be coached by Hannah.

The program is set for 12 sessions: six sessions every two weeks, followed by six monthly sessions after that. The coaching sessions are confidential, and nothing discussed in the coaching meetings is shared with Lena. There are quarterly 'triangulation meetings' with the coaching client, the coach, and Lena to discuss observable shifts Lena has noticed and any insights the coaching client is willing to share.

Lena and Hannah have monthly administrative update sessions where Hannah shares how many sessions have been completed and with whom.

The coaching

For the last three months, Hannah has been working with one of the legacy leaders, Phil Sands, and one of the newer members, Jake Albury. The other four members of the executive team have not yet expressed an interest in coaching. Through her discussions with these two members, she can see there is a dynamic in the group that has a 'legacy' vs. 'newbie' mentality. In addition, this rift in the team is showing up as a serious conflict with breakdown in collaboration and communication in the meetings, undermining Lena and threatening the growth of the company.

Lena approaches Hannah for a private meeting and asks to be coached to help her through these challenges.

Hannah is conflicted.

Although the coaching engagement is still fairly new, she can see there are underlying team issues. She wonders, "Is one-to-one the best approach or should I suggest complementing it with team coaching?" As she considers this, she also self-assesses her skill set and thinks, "I've got several years as a CEO managing my teams, and I've seen a lot of conflict, but is this the same as formal team coaching? Perhaps I should suggest bringing in another team coach."

Additionally, Hannah has been working to build trust with the team. At the onset, it was made clear to the team that Lena would not be coached by Hannah. Based on her long-term relationships with Lena, Hannah is worried that the team will not see her as independent and objective if she is also coaching the 'boss.'

Key challenges

* Hannah's awareness that one-to-one coaching may not be the only approach that will help the organization. Her limited experience providing team coaching makes her consider if she has the right skill set to truly help the team find some cohesion and common ground.
* Hannah needs to consider whether to take on individual coaching with Lena the CEO. First, this was not agreed on at the beginning of the coaching engagement, and secondly, there is a pre-existing relationship with Lena and Hannah.
* The above challenges must be faced while Hannah detects a culture of mistrust in the executive team with 'newbie' vs. 'legacy' leaders along with a new CEO navigating the trust waters.

EXAMPLE ETHICAL IMPLICATIONS

* **Transparency** – Hannah and Lena have become close acquaintances. They have helped each other through various pivot points in their careers and each knows the inner details. How might this be a blind spot for Hannah as she takes on coaching Lena's team members?
* **Trust** – if Hannah accepts Lena as a client, this might affect the trust she's built with the team members she coaches, as this would constitute a breach of their initial agreement.
* **Professionalism** – Hannah must decide whether this is the right coaching engagement (one-to-one vs. team coaching) and also factor in her inexperience as an external team coach.

REFLECTIVE QUESTIONS FOR DISCUSSION

1. Is Hannah's previous experience managing conflicts in her own team enough for her to conduct an external team coaching assignment with paying clients? What would be her best alternatives to approach the decision?

2. What are the risks involved if Hannah agrees to take on Lena as her coaching client, having in mind their long-standing relationship? (Consider risks for the coach, the coaching client, and the team.)

3. How can a coach hold one-to-one conversations with her coaching clients without bringing previous knowledge and assumptions to the table?

Coaching in the neurodivergent landscape

Jonathan Drury

Overview

Early in the coach's career, during training, they were offering pro-bono work to gain experience. The female client, in her early 40s, approached privately via email after hearing from one of her colleagues about the trainee coach's speciality in coaching neurodivergent and autistic adults. "Autistic people have the skills to share information well with one another and experience good rapport" and "when there are mixed groups of autistic and non-autistic people, much less information is shared" (Crompton et al., 2020, p. 1). The client self-identified to the coach as "high-functioning autistic" (a now outdated term) and was a newly qualified self-employed therapist, working with executive and corporate clients.

This case explores a critical moment in the coaching, where the coach felt insufficiently trained and didn't feel comfortable in themselves, yet also identified with the client as a neurodivergent peer. Support weakened as the pair became disconnected and a level of relational tension arose.

Case study

Background

The coach (Ziggy) was an early career coach still in coach training. He decided to offer pro-bono coaching to build his coaching hours.

The coaching client (Julie), a therapist looking to expand into the corporate environment, saw the offer for pro-bono coaching advertised on LinkedIn and decided she would like a series of coaching sessions. She did not disclose her neurodivergent status.

At the first meeting, Ziggy noticed Julie was punctual, spoke rather quickly and presented on screen as highly organised, and had a range of unusual ornaments and books lined up according to their colour behind her. Julie described her aim of wanting to "minimise stress, ensure sustainability, and achieve success during and beyond a looming change" where she saw "much higher levels of self-awareness and self-mastery would be required."

DOI: 10.4324/b23351-46

Upon further enquiry, Julie stated a deeper intention to explore her identity as an autistic person, as she was struggling with social communication and being understood by others both personally and in her therapist role, which was holding her back. She reported having increasing meltdowns where, after a few weeks of intense work and training, she would "self-medicate with alcohol and cry myself to sleep." Ziggy sensed distraction and a quickness about Julie's manner and, when asked if she had ADHD (commonly accompanied with autism), she said she didn't know, but at times struggled with attention.

Ziggy took this information to his coach training tutor/supervisor, and they felt confident to go ahead with coaching.

The assignment

Ziggy and Julie agreed that a period of online coaching might help Julie foster the ability to connect with her deeper identity and who she is behind the role, to relate to herself more creatively and productively and mitigate some of the impact of her role. Ziggy was careful that contracting was done slowly and carefully with a written version sent via email.

The coaching

In the first session as the relationship was built, there was a mutual sense of aligned values. Similar neurological profiles, ages, backgrounds, and interests all supported Julie's trust in the relationship. Ziggy recalled to mind studies showing that autistic people are more comfortable communicating with each other, than with non-autistic people, backing up some of his own experience.

During the initial relationship building and exploration, Julie was reasonably open and Ziggy shared snippets of his personal life. Ziggy felt the need to be aware of over-identifying with another neurodivergent person. Ziggy held the space well in focusing on current experiences.

During session three the coaching focused on Julie framing her current concerns around identity. Ziggy found it difficult to fully understand how Julie saw herself. Whenever he tried to reflect back to Julie his understanding in the coaching frame, Julie would reply "no, that isn't what I mean."

It was increasingly obvious there were significant barriers for Ziggy to assess and understand how Julie saw herself. Also, Ziggy felt they occasionally jumped too quickly to a deeper space: the spiritual level.

There were occasional tears from Julie, a repeated sense of anger, and further irritation with herself for being upset. Ziggy reserved the question of referral in case her mental health got out of hand, at one point needing to remind Julie that coaching isn't therapy. They also explored Julie's history and what possible links there could be to some of her limiting assumptions. Some of the dialogue that ensued is as follows:

Julie: It goes back to my childhood. I always liked to rock or sway, from side to side and my mum encouraged me to. But at school I just totally got the piss ripped out of me for that.

Ziggy: That sounds hard.

Julie: Yeah! It's really hard, and I'm angry about it but also I'm [sigh] OK with it in the sense that something I can point to, to say well this is probably one of the reasons why I'm like that. I always have not fitted in so that has a bearing on who I am now, but that's the way it is and I've done processing with it. I've dealt with it. [pause] I obviously haven't dealt with it completely or I would be out there, fitting in [laughter].

Ziggy paused to reflect, sensing how this landed in the room. Whilst Julie showed her usual acute self-observation and openness, there was a contradiction, accompanied with loud but nervous laughter. Ziggy recalled the deep implications of autistic masking or camouflaging in autistic females.

Ziggy was increasingly feeling disempowered as a coach in the relationship. He felt a dark cloud around them both and boundaries flexed. He was reminded of Julie using the phrase "looming change" and saw that pursuing the corporate environment could be potentially damaging and that she may have not yet realised how much was at stake. It seemed there was suddenly a lot of data to process.

Ziggy had to make a choice about the type of intervention and started second-guessing the potential impact on Julie. There was an underlying existential dilemma between the pair. As he tried to reflect and form hypotheses about what was occurring and how to manage it, he became anxious and no longer felt he had an active supporting role.

He also became more aware of the neighbour's power tool and the sun landing on his screen. It was distracting and as time passed he became irritated and vacant, feeling the connection ebb and flow. Ziggy remained silent, which allowed Julie to take some of the weight of responsibility. Julie's attention had waned, evidenced by her looking around her room. Ziggy felt responsible yet detached while processing his experience of the situation and was increasingly concerned about the possibility of a widening gap between them.

Key challenges

- As a coach in training, Ziggy lacked the experience to take on an assignment with the potential of over-identification, which is always challenging and requires maturity and more experience (and engaging in coaching supervision).
- As Ziggy over-identified with Julie, he was unable to see her as a unique individual, failing to explore her strengths and distinctive coping mechanisms.
- Ziggy engaged in an abundance of self-blame for how he presented, reacted, and coped with his heightened sensory input in certain coaching scenarios, which diverted the focus from the client to himself and affected his ability to be fully present.

EXAMPLE ETHICAL IMPLICATIONS

- **Safety** – the coach's available tools were not sufficient for a neurodivergent (autistic) client, Julie, resulting in a lack of competence and reduced sense of safety.
- **Responsibility to professional practice** – the coach was aware of his limited experience as a coach and asked for his tutor's guidance.
- **Boundaries** – the coach was aware of and monitored the risk of stepping out of role, reminding the client about the boundaries of their work together. The shifting values of typical and atypical neurology and society were played out in the setting.

REFLECTIVE QUESTIONS FOR DISCUSSION

1. What do you think the "looming change" mentioned by Julie at the clarity session was or may have been pointing to?
2. Considering Julie's potential for mental fragility and the coach's minimal experience, what could have been done (or avoided) to improve ethical attunement and create a safe environment for Julie?
3. How could the educational setting and supervision have been more ethically attuned to the coach's individual experience?

Reference

Crompton, C. J., Ropar, D., Evans-Williams, C. V., Flynn, E. G., & Fletcher-Watson, S. (2020). Autistic peer-to-peer information transfer is highly effective. *Autism*, 24(7), 1704–1712. https://doi.org/10.1177/1362361320919286

Chapter 10

Promotion in coaching

The business of coaching has within itself a myriad of complex ethical challenges. These include challenges for the owner of a coach consulting organization. This chapter highlights concerns about how a coach or coaching business promotes themselves, contracting with multiple stakeholders, and changing careers – becoming a coach.

DOI: 10.4324/b23351-47

Case study 36

Ethical challenges of sub-contracting the delivery of coaching work to associate coaches

Kim Morgan

Overview

Companies which provide coaching services will often engage with a network of self-employed associates to deliver coaching on the ground to employees of their corporate or organisational clients. This means that the associate will often develop close working relationships with individuals and managers within the sponsor organisation. Requests for further or different work will often arise and may be made directly to the associate. These situations raise issues of contracting, lines of communication, and legal and ethical issues regarding the roles and responsibilities of the coaching company and the associate coach.

Case study

Background

Peter is the owner of an executive coaching business. He trained as a coach ten years ago, having become disillusioned with his corporate role. Soon after starting his business, Peter was in high demand, largely because of his 'little black book' of connections from his previous career. Peter's clients are mostly senior executives working in banking and insurance. Peter offers a six-session one-to-one executive coaching programme which he follows to the letter with all his clients. Prospective and current clients know in advance what to expect, and what each session will cover.

A year ago, Peter took stock of his work/life balance. He was in demand as a coach but had found himself working more hours than ever. Peter decided to recruit some trusted coaches who would work on an associate basis for him, delivering his coaching programme to his clients.

He had associate contracts drawn up, which set out the fees which would be paid to the associate and defined the services to be provided by the associate broadly as 'coaching services.'

Associates contract with Peter's company and fees are split 60/40 in Peter's favour. Peter's company procures the work, contracts with the client organisation about the scope of the work, and invoices the client organisation directly.

DOI: 10.4324/b23351-48

Peter sub-contracts delivery of the coaching to associates. Peter gives each associate full training in his standard six-session coaching programme and provides them with the workbooks which accompany the programme.

Jane is one of Peter's associate coaches. She has a banking and accountancy background and was delighted to be offered regular associate work with Peter. She has had good feedback from Peter's clients for the nine months she has been working as an associate.

The assignment

Peter recently introduced Jane into a new client organisation to coach a senior manager in the business. Peter had worked hard to win this client. The CEO of the company, Anita, had not used coaching in the business before and had concerns about coaching not being sufficiently focussed on business results. Peter had confidently reassured Anita that his programme was focused on the coaching client in respect of their role in the business.

In accordance with Peter's usual practice, Jane was required to take part in an initial three-way meeting, involving Anita, Jane, and the coaching client, Rina. Jane had agreed with Anita that the primary goal of the coaching was to increase Rina's assertiveness at work and to improve her ability to prioritise tasks.

Peter stressed to Jane that this coaching assignment was an important opportunity for his company to make an impact. It was the sponsor organisation's first experience of coaching and if they had a good experience, there was potential for a lot more work there.

The coaching

When Jane and Rina met for their initial coaching session, Jane followed Peter's prescribed process and began by asking Rina to complete a 'Wheel of Work' coaching tool. Rina ignored the coaching tool and instead spoke at length about her childhood, her cultural conditioning, the difficulties of being a woman in a male-dominated environment, and how she felt the 'glass ceiling' was well and truly immovable. She really wanted to believe in herself more and felt that her lack of assertiveness was hampering her career prospects.

Jane was conflicted. She ran a women's development programme in her own right when she wasn't working for Peter. She was torn between the terms of her contract with Peter and where she instinctively wanted to take the coaching conversation. However, Jane had made a commitment to deliver Peter's coaching programme. She attempted to follow the process, asking Rina, "What actions are you prepared to commit to between now and the next session?"

Rina replied, "I'm not ready for setting actions yet. The most valuable work for me would be exploring my role as a woman in the workplace."

Without thinking, Jane said, "Actually, that's what I do most of the time. I offer women's development coaching and courses … but our agreement with your organisation is to follow the Executive Coaching programme."

"Can't we renegotiate?" Rina asked, excitedly.

Jane ignored Rina's question but instead suggested, "Well, maybe we can work some of the exercises from my women's development course into our next session."

A couple of weeks later, Rina made an online booking for Jane's forthcoming women's development course. Jane realised that Rina must have googled her.

Before Jane had time to speak to Peter, Peter called Jane to say that Anita had phoned to cancel the coaching sessions. She was disappointed that the organisation's first attempt to offer executive coaching to their employees had not been a success.

Anita said that Rina had been very clear that the best development solution for her would be a women's development course. It had the added value for Rina of being in a group of like-minded women, and networking opportunities within the group.

Anita had agreed to fund Rina's place on Jane's course. Anita explained to Peter, "we had no current requirements for one-to-one coaching but would 'bear him in mind' in future."

She felt it was only appropriate to let Peter know that they were also considering running Jane's women's development course in-house at a future date, and that whilst Rina was on the course, she would assess its suitability for their organisation.

Peter has lost a large corporate client.

Jane has a new delegate on her programme and the potential for more work from the organisation.

Key challenges

Lines of communication – what more could the parties have done to agree in advance clear lines of communication about the coaching contract? Where do the responsibilities for this lie?

Dealing with changes in client requirements – how to conduct any re-contracting in a transparent and ethical manner.

Who is contracting with whom? Can Rina agree things with Jane? Does Jane have authority to terminate or re-contract an agreement between Peter's company and the sponsor?

EXAMPLE ETHICAL IMPLICATIONS

- **Contract breach** – the coaching consultant operating outside of their contract. Breaching terms of contracted assignment.
- **Conflicts of interest** – personal, financial, legal, commercial.
- **Contracting** – open and transparent contracting with a systemic view and setting out the roles, responsibilities, and rights of all parties involved.

REFLECTIVE QUESTIONS

1. How might Jane balance her responsibilities towards Peter, the sponsor, and the coaching client against her own personal interests?
2. What might Peter and Jane do to seek to resolve the situation on an agreed commercial basis, always bearing in mind ethical principles and values, and the importance of each continuing to 'craft their reputations' in the coaching space?
3. What terms could Peter set out in his associate contracts to ensure that he gets what he needs from his associates and that his associates have clarity as to what is required and expected of them when dealing with sponsor organisations?

The best business coach

Francine Campone

Overview

Like physicians, ethical coaches intend to 'do no harm.' Coaches must consider the potential impact of their choices and actions on clients, colleagues and the profession, as well as compliance with codes of conduct and relevant laws. In creating promotional materials and activities, ethical coaches consider the expectations they are creating with words and images. Prospects form a mental image of the coach they expect to meet based on that coach's promises and self-presentation. Exaggerated claims of competence, skill and knowledge, and uncritical belief in the magic of one's own process are contrary to ethical principles of truthfulness, integrity and responsibility to the profession. Such explicit and implicit claims can cause individual harm as well as harm the credibility of the field. In the case offered here, the coach promotes an idealized self, creating unrealistic expectations. Consequently, the trust essential to effective coaching does not exist. Further, the coach's focus on his presented self fails to meet the ethical principles of respect for the client's autonomy and dignity, as well as demonstrating the coach's lack of integrity and respect for the work of others.

The case study

Background

Lucre Coaching Associates is a website offering coaches who specialize in business and entrepreneurial coaching. The coaches listed as associates on the website are not required to hold a coaching credential from a professional coach accreditation organization. They are, however, required to prove their own success in for-profit organizations and they pay a fee to be included in the site's directory. The website's branding promotes the business credentials of the coaches and states that coaches will "share their expertise to ensure the client's business success." The site includes an unattributed quote: "Lucre is the top site for world-class business coaches," and the logos of several Fortune 500 companies.

One of the associates, Joshua, built a small grocery business into a global specialty food-importing company. He recently retired as president and CEO to start a

DOI: 10.4324/b23351-49

career as a coach. He completed a three-day intensive coach training offered by an author whose successful trade book promises to give coaches a "proven process" for coaching leaders to be successful. Joshua has created an e-book that draws heavily from the workbook provided in the coach training and with examples from his own business experience as illustrations. The book consists of leadership tips and practices that Joshua has paraphrased without attribution from books and articles written by other leaders and leadership coaches.

In building his associate webpage for Lucre, Joshua emphasizes his business success, stating he is "highly skilled" in strategic financial management, interpersonal communication and international networking. He offers potential clients a free copy of his e-book as an "invitation to step into a more powerful and dynamic self." He considers the language and images that will present his idealized coach persona. Joshua promises to "transform followers into leaders" and "create incredible breakthroughs for my clients." He posts a photo that shows him receiving an award in front of an applauding audience.

Derrick is the founder of an innovative technology business that he wants to grow. He recognizes that part of his challenge is his natural reticence and inclination to avoid risks and conflict. He and his two partners have very different ways of working and communicating and they argue about the direction the business should take. He notices Lucre's emphasis on business expertise, and the variety of global company logos suggest that the coach he chooses will be able to help him break into a wider market. Derrick reaches out to Joshua, seeing someone who seems to have the dynamic and confident leadership style he wants to cultivate for himself.

The assignment

Derrick reaches out to Joshua to set up a chemistry meeting. Joshua responds, confirming the appointment and attaching his e-book, thanks Derrick and encourages him to "think of this book as your new bible."

In the chemistry meeting, Derrick is both attracted to and somewhat overwhelmed by Joshua's confidence, self-belief and high-energy presentation. Nonetheless, he and Joshua agree that they will work together for a specific number of sessions to coach Derrick in two areas: developing his own voice as a business leader and being more assertive in interactions with his business partners.

The coaching

(Example 1) Derrick presents a recent conversation with one of his partners and states he'd like to find a more convincing and confident way of responding.

Joshua: Great! Let's look at that little book, the page titled 'Making a Strong Response'.
Derrick: I read those but none of them feel right for me. Something holds me back and I think I need one of those incredible breakthroughs that you promised to help me figure it out.

Joshua: I'm asking here for your trust. I've used every one of those statements and they work every time. Would you be willing to try out a few here?

(Example 2) Derrick tells Joshua he'd like to work on developing a strategy to bring his technology products to global companies.

Derrick: I noticed that the Lucre coaches seem to have worked with major global corporations and I'm hoping you can provide some insight as to how I might find an entry into that market for my products.
Joshua: Let me tell you what I did to create partnerships with food manufacturers.

(Example 3) Derrick mentions the award photo on Joshua's webpage and asks: "What was the occasion?"

Joshua: It was recognition for something I had done for a local small business group.
Derrick: Did the group recognize you for some coaching or for a leadership role?
Joshua: I made a substantial donation to the scholarship fund.

Key challenges

- Failure to respect and honor client autonomy. Derrick feels manipulated by Joshua in their conversations as Joshua's 'coaching' seems to consist primarily of returning attention to his process, his materials, his business experience and his definitions of success.
- The coaching client has increasing doubts about the accuracy of the coach's statements and finds he does not trust him.

EXAMPLE ETHICAL IMPLICATIONS

- **Honesty and accuracy in representing coach qualifications** – the coach claims to be highly skilled in interpersonal communications and states he can create breakthroughs for his clients. His brief coach training, however, teaches a specific and unsubstantiated method of business coaching and is not directed at cultivating a broad range of coaching skills. The use of global corporate logos on the consultancy website and the photo of an award on the coach's page are misleading and suggest experience the coach does not have.
- **Respecting the intellectual property of others** – the coach represents the material in his e-book as his own, despite borrowing heavily from the work of others without attribution. Respect for and acknowledgment of source materials are required by professional codes of ethics as well as legal standards in most countries.

- **Promising unrealistic outcomes and creating false expectations** – language such as "step into a more dynamic and powerful self" and "create incredible breakthroughs" is emotionally manipulative and implies coaching outcomes that are non-specific, not measurable. Such promises imply the coach can produce 'magic' and omit reference to addressing the client's specific needs and the client's role in the coaching partnership.

REFLECTIVE QUESTIONS FOR DISCUSSION

1. Joshua makes claims to several kinds of expertise. How ethical are these claims, considering Joshua's background and training?
2. The language of Joshua's webpage and that of Lucre emphasizes business acumen and expertise. What does that language imply with respect to how Joshua and Lucre see the role of coach in the coach–client relationship? What's the potential impact on a client's perspective of coaches and the coaching profession?
3. Joshua's e-book draws heavily on the work of others. To what extent does adaptation and paraphrasing release a coach from responsibility to respect the intellectual property of others? How much 'originality' can a coach claim ethically?

Case study 38

Coaching is your dream career

Francine Campone

Overview

Moral sensitivity requires an individual to be attuned to social situations and the potential interpretations of words and actions (Narvaez & Rest, 1995). Bauman (2017) suggests that in a postmodern age, we are all consumers in a consumer society. Online and digitized media offer an environment for promoting a commodity devoid of interpersonal engagement or social context.

In this case, we see how a coach training organization has manipulated language and image to appeal to a prospective buyer's self-esteem and self-interest. The use of an automated response system provides a seemingly personalized series of promotional offerings. Consistent with the postmodern framework of consumer and commodity, the practice of coaching is presented as a means of personal gain, and coach training is offered as a means of income and lifestyle. Quality and qualifications are addressed in vague terms and a potential client is unable to access specific details useful to make an informed choice. Ethical issues include concerns about accuracy and transparency, respecting the field and profession of coaching, and assurance of quality and qualifications.

Case study

Background

(Note: This case is constructed from statements taken from a variety of coach training program sites and does not represent any individual organization. URcoach is a fictional entity.)

Janet is planning to retire from a 30-year career in human resources and is considering coaching as a next career. A colleague forwards a link to the URcoach Training Institute website, a for-profit company offering short-term coach training and certification programs. The founder and CEO of URcoach is an entrepreneur in the media technology sector and holds a coaching certificate from an unaccredited and unaffiliated coaching school.

The opening page for URcoach Training Institute begins with a headline:

DOI: 10.4324/b23351-50

Become a certified coach and start your ideal career! Certified coaches earn high incomes and help others to grow. If you are a professional in any field who wants to have a positive impact on others while setting your own pace and work life, coaching is for you.

Following this paragraph, the site offers three photos of professional-looking pairs of people in conversation. The photos are followed by more text.

Do others come to you for advice and support? If so, you are a natural coach. All URcoach Institute programs use transformative learning processes and give you the tools and techniques you need to coach others with confidence. All programs are on-line, combining recorded webinars, readings and discussion. In the eight weeks of each certificate program you will learn: how to conduct a coaching session, questions and tools guaranteed to transform your clients, and the business side of establishing and operating a financially rewarding coaching practice that includes services and products for multiple revenue streams.

We offer specialized coaching certificates in Business, Life or Health coaching. Our graduates attract clients even before completing the program and you can too. Our instructors are certified coaches and provide individualized attention to support your success. Program graduates form a community of like-minded colleagues and have access to resources to continue your learning and growth. To find out more and hear from successful graduates, **click here** and sign up for a free webinar: *You ARE a coach.*

These paragraphs are followed by the company logos of five major global corporations.

The assignment

After looking through the website, Janet signs up for the free webinar, scheduled for the following week. Through her HR experience, she is somewhat familiar with the coaching field but is not sure what kind of training and investment are needed to become competent herself. She is hoping to gain a better understanding of the training offerings: content, faculty qualifications, methods of delivery. Janet also wants to get a feel for the organization and how it compares with other training options.

The coaching

Janet receives an email acknowledgment for the webinar and the Zoom link. Along with the acknowledgment, Janet receives a self-assessment questionnaire inviting her to "uncover your hidden coach now!" Curious, Janet completes the questionnaire and returns it. The next day, Janet receives a personalized note from URcoach's director that begins

Dear Janet,

Thank you for returning the questionnaire. It's clear you have a powerful inner coach just waiting to be set free.

The email goes on to say that program graduates who have completed all three certifications from URcoach earn six-figure incomes working only three days a week. The director gives Janet a special offer: if she signs up for all three certificate programs at once, she can complete them in six months and be on her way to marketing herself to a wide audience. In closing, the letter offers a "bonus for enrolling," an e-book detailing three strategies for attracting clients.

The following week, Janet attends the free webinar.

Janet notes that the program graduates who share their success stories on the webinar are much younger people who have built big profiles on social media. The speakers are highly energetic and enthusiastic and speak with passion about how the program was life-changing. While it's a 'feel good' experience, the webinar provides little in the way of additional information about the program content or faculty content. Janet does not find the kind of professional substance she expects in a training program.

Following the webinar, Janet begins to receive weekly emails from URCoach Training Institute inviting her to take a taster course for a small fee. Despite choosing the opt out link on the bottom of the page, the emails continue to arrive weekly, each containing an offering of a taster course for a small fee. Janet emails the address on the institute's web page asking to have her information removed from the email list.

Key challenges

From a buyer's perspective, the information is incomplete and does not offer sufficient detail for Janet to make an informed decision about the truthfulness or accuracy of the program's claims of program quality and career prospects. Her inability to be removed from the mailing list and the continued offer of 'taster courses' make her suspect that the program itself is a scam and the original offer a means to identify prospective sources of income rather than a legitimate educational program.

EXAMPLE ETHICAL IMPLICATIONS

- **Accuracy and transparency in promotional materials** – the language of the website relies heavily on implicit, emotion-oriented, and vague language. The use of "certificate" and "certification" implies a credential which would be recognized in the marketplace.
- **Presenting coaching and coach training as financial commodities** – the profession of coaching and ethical codes in the field center priority on client and client service, coach competency, and qualifications.

> • **Competencies and standards are not identified** – the self-assessment appears to be one element of a marketing pipeline, not a legitimate evaluation tool.

REFLECTIVE QUESTIONS FOR DISCUSSION

1. Are there people who are natural coaches? If so, what training, if any, will ensure their competency as practicing professionals?
2. What laws, policies, or regulations might govern the use of corporate images and logos by unaffiliated companies?
3. What are the ethical considerations in offering enticements such as a free webinar or e-book in exchange for contact information and contact permission?

References

Bauman, Z. (2017). Tourists and vagabonds: Or, living in postmodern times. In Joseph E. Davis (ed.), *Identity and Social Change*. Routledge. Ch. 1, pp. 23–41.

Narvaez, D., & Rest, J. (1995). Four components of acting morally. In William M. Kurtines & Jacob L. Gurwitz (eds.), *Moral Development: An Introduction*. Allyn & Bacon, pp. 385–400.

Case study 39

Ethical challenges in contracting with organisations and their stakeholders

Rob Kemp

Overview

When seeking to work as an external coach providing coaching into organisations, coaches often find themselves meeting with organisational stakeholders and commissioners of coaching. These commissioners can come from a variety of places within an organisation: coaching specialists, learning and development professionals, human resources professionals and senior managers (as well as often line managers). In addition, professional buyers may also be part of the process at times. This is a role with which coaches have differing degrees of familiarity, comfort and discomfort. Coaches describe themselves in the position of "business owner" or salesperson at this moment, and some of the skills and approaches which coaches use may be at odds with how they work as coaches, which leads to a tension. This scenario can lead to several dynamics being present which are important for the coach and the organisation. When paid work is at stake there are potentially influences at play which require deeper thought and examination. This case study is a composite of many of my own personal experiences, as well as those described to me during my research which also closely resemble this scenario (Kemp, 2022).

Case study

Background

Alice is a professional coach of long standing. She is well educated in general terms and has excellent credentials in her coaching training, having successfully completed several postgraduate programmes at good universities. She is a credible and well-practised coach having worked with senior executives in the City of London for over five years. Her early corporate career generated a good network within big firms, and she uses these relationships to gain access to corporate 'buyers' of coaching.

On just such an occasion Alice met with several key stakeholders within a London-based multinational financial services firm. Alice knew the culture and tone of the firm and dressed to meet expectations for their meeting. She presented

DOI: 10.4324/b23351-51

her credentials to them in a 'one-pager' and knew that her educational background would appeal, as would her testimonials which she selected carefully.

Present at the meeting were the human resources lead, Dominic, who also has responsibility for learning and development within the organisation; Naomi, the line manager of the potential coaching client; and, for a short time the head of the UK business, Kurt, who was also Naomi's manager.

After the usual preamble the discussion started around the intent for coaching with Simon, the potential coaching client.

The assignment

Dominic lays out the scenario of why they are looking for a coach by describing some issues with Simon's performance. "He just doesn't seem to get the urgency and is often delaying projects because of his late input" – says Dominic. Kurt, the most senior person in the room, says that he notices a very different style of operating with Simon – and that he is unlike the rest of the team (who he says are "on it"). Naomi, Simon's manager, then inputs with what she wants from the coaching assignment:

"I just need you to get him with the programme, up to speed, and operating at the level of his peers – because if we can't get to that place, then we are in a whole different ball game!"

The internal team agreed that the problem is Simon's performance, and that the role of the coach was to address the lack of urgency, lateness of work submission and differences in operational style compared with his colleagues. There is a unity of critical voices about Simon, but the thought occurs to Alice that there are no voices representing Simon or his perspective at the meeting.

The senior leader, Kurt, then left having made his observations about Simon – his 'difference' – and the discussion continued with Alice, Dominic and Naomi.

Alice, the coach, asked for specific examples where Simon's behaviour was seen to be causing problems, and Naomi provided some examples of where she feels his performance has been under par, at times openly showing frustration. One example was raised in which Naomi explained that Simon had not completed a piece of work in time for a face-to-face client proposal – which she felt left her exposed in front of the potential new client. She said that she "covered for him" but was "less than pleased". Alice wondered whether she was covering for Simon, or saving face for herself.

Alice asked what had happened because of that example – to which Naomi said, "That's why we're having this meeting".

Throughout their time together thoughts had been running around in Alice's mind. She was worried about much of what had been said, and the setup of the assignment: it was remedial, the problem was seen in sitting fully with the coaching client, as the role she had was "to get him up to speed". Coaching was seen as a "fix to the problem". Alice also was mindful of the senior people in the room and their roles – and she was concerned about the state of the relationship between

Naomi and Simon. She wondered about the potential future for Simon – was this just a step in his exit from the organisation? Alice had significant concerns as these thoughts occurred to her during the meeting.

However, rather than voicing any of these areas, apart from probing for clarity and examples, Alice gave no fundamental challenge back to the business. She nodded, took notes and listened intently. She maintained a professional demeanour and allowed things to unfold.

This *way of being* seemed to satisfy Domonic and Naomi that she was the coach for the job and that she understood what needed to be done.

Alice believed that she didn't really challenge anything about the situation, and she felt uneasy about that. She felt annoyed with herself that she didn't raise any questions which might have positioned the work more helpfully. On reflection after the meeting, she was left with a feeling that took some time to subside – that she hadn't been the best version of herself.

The coaching

Alice consoled herself with the idea that challenging at this point in the process probably would have lost her the work and that she could do so later if the need arose, once she had found out some more about the situation from her new coaching client.

At least she got the work, she thought, and she would be able to go and connect with Simon to go and do "the real work of coaching". It's a prestigious client too, and there may be further work for her there – she had *a foot in the door* at least – even if she had to go through some discomfort to win it.

Key challenges

- Alice is conflicted between keeping the paying client satisfied that she is the right coach for the job (*getting the work*), and expressing her concerns and observations about the assignment. She has not expressed or spoken about her thinking with the client, and they are not aware that she is feeling any tension around the assignment.
- Alice is starting the assignment with a remit given to her around organisational intentions for coaching (directive) and feels a conflict with her belief that coaching should be led and directed by the coaching client (non-directive).
- Alice is unsure about the relational dynamics and system dynamics which may be playing out in this assignment; she feels these have a potential to compromise her ability to leave all stakeholders satisfied with her work. She is doubtful that it is possible to meet everyone's needs in the scenario.
- Power is highly present in this situation: the power to award paid work, the power to define and state the problem and the power to direct action and define outcomes. Conversely, there is a lack of power and voice for Simon, the coaching client, at the outset of this work.

EXAMPLE ETHICAL IMPLICATIONS

- **Contracting** – the initial agreement failed to address the roles, responsibilities and rights of all parties involved, including those of the coaching client, who was excluded from the conversation.
- **Value of coaching** – the coach did not explore with the sponsor what coaching is, and is for, leaving differing views unaddressed, and implicitly accepted their expectation that she was being hired 'remedially' or to 'fix the problem'.
- **Conflict of interest** – the coach was led by her reputational concerns (personal and professional), leading her to prioritise her own intentions and behaving in a seemingly deferential way to those in a position of power to award her the paid work.

REFLECTIVE QUESTIONS FOR DISCUSSION

1. How can coaches be open and honest in contracting discussions with stakeholders?
2. How might money distort in organisational coaching assignments?
3. How might we serve ourselves, our clients, organisations and the profession more fully when we contract with organisations?

Reference

Kemp, R. (2022). The emotional labour of the coach – In and out of the coaching 'room'. *International Journal of Evidence Based Coaching and Mentoring*, S16: 185–195.

Case study 40

Head of Learning and Development hangs her coaching practice plaque

*Wendy-Ann Smith, Eva Hirsch Pontes,
and Dumisani Magadlela*

Overview

Career change is as old as career development itself. Changing careers, especially among practitioners such as human resource professionals, has seen many become coaches. While integrity of the field of coaching struggles to find a strong footing, the entry into the field by lightly educated practitioners puts at risk the field of practice as a whole. Experience and research suggest that unqualified or poorly trained practitioners are among the biggest risks and threats to the field of coaching practice (ICF Global Study, 2020). This case presents a professional's transition from a senior role as a human resource executive to becoming a coach. The choices and privileges of some who transition have the potential to harm the reputation of the field of coaching due to how they represent themselves, their work and their capabilities and services. It illustrates the ethical challenges and the minefield of changing professions, from training to acquiring business. Coaching is a helping profession where effective working relationships are reliant on a foundation of trust in competency and knowledge and it requires patience to build practitioner experience. Deep or solid professional wisdom, knowledge and practitioner know-how, alongside good connections and professional networks, do not guarantee success in a new career or role.

Case study

Background

Judy had a long-distinguished career as head of a human resources learning and development department in a multinational organisation. She felt she needed a career sea change. During her career, she participated in leadership development workshops and executive coaching provided by the organisation. She had long felt this would be a new direction for her to transition to after her corporate leadership career. She gave her notice and left work just as she completed a number of courses.

While completing the courses, Judy employed a web-tech person to set up a website. The website stated she was trained in coaching, wellbeing and the neuropsychology of coaching. It also stated she had a long history of supporting C-suite

DOI: 10.4324/b23351-52

and global talent. She also employed a personal assistant who had significant competencies in coach promotion across all social media channels.

Given her long history receiving coaching and working in learning and development for over 20 years, plus the completion of the three courses, Judy felt these together would be sufficient for her to hang her coaching practice plaque and get to work.

In her last months in her role as head of learning and development, she had quietly arranged with her employer to return as an independent coaching contractor to coach the global leadership talent and the C-suite team. Given she had pre-established positive relationships within the organisation, Judy's business took off. They were all very happy to be supported by her leadership experience as they were heading where she had been – leader of a department of a multinational corporation.

The sea change

Judy began researching coaching courses. She was attracted to short, quick courses. This fit her personality and pragmatic approach to change. There were a number of interests in the sea of potential found. Judy decided to apply for a short course in the fundamentals of coaching skills, that consisted of four half days of self-learning online. The completion of each of the course elements meant an automatically generated certification of completion would be emailed to her the following day.

A second course she applied for was a little longer – two weeks of half days. Some content was self-learning online, with a number of virtual groups for mentoring. This course was promoted as learning about wellbeing for leadership. Judy thought this would be a great complement to her first course, since wellbeing is a hot topic post-COVID. A certificate of completion was provided by the training company.

Judy also completed a course that was promoted as teaching the neuropsychology of coaching. This was a course consisting of three-hour sessions, for one day per week for six weeks, that promised to transform her coaching acumen and enable her to stand out in the crowded coaching space. She was provided with a certificate of completion after passing a final exam and receiving appropriate peer feedback from the course content mentoring programme.

Eight months after hanging her coaching plaque, Judy decided to expand her business. She had high-level contacts in other multinational organisations that she had had relationships with during her 30-year career, and she decided to offer manager-as-coach training programmes. She won three contracts and began training coaching skills to the corporate leadership and new global talent.

Her website was updated to include a range of short coach training programmes for multinational organisations, that included as standard practice three one-to-one coaching sessions for all attendees.

Judy had contemplated undertaking coaching accreditation but decided against it at this time. She did not see this as a priority, and thought "I should invest my money and energy in what really matters now."

Her business was flourishing.

The coaching

During one of Judy's trainings of the manager to coach workshops for a global leadership talent group, one attendee (Fabrizio), who had previously studied neuropsychology as part of his undergraduate degree, expressed concern about the validity of the assertions Judy was presenting. Fabrizio understood enough from his limited studies to know that the assertions were not valid. This had Fabrizio questioning much of Judy's course material. He wanted to provide feedback to the organisation's human resources department but was concerned as he knew Judy had close ties to the department still, with a number of powerful people very loyal to her and her new professional endeavours.

When it was time for Fabrizio to commence his one-to-one coaching with Judy, he was reluctant. In fact he rescheduled twice before finally relenting and attending the first session. The session was scheduled to take place in the lobby of a swanky hotel in the city. Fabrizio had trouble feeling well connected and trusting of the relationship with Judy. He was also uncomfortable with the choice of location. He questioned her capacity and skills to provide coaching as he understood it. It seemed to him Judy wanted to spend much of her time imparting her 'self'-determined professional wisdom.

Judy was unaware of this growing distance and mistrust, of the disconnect in the relationship. She decided to have the next session along the coastal boardwalk. They would walk and talk and meander through the various rugged pathways. Judy had read that walking in nature while coaching eased tensions and so helped to enhance the coaching. However, Fabrizio again was very uncomfortable talking in public, even if there were only a few people in the vicinity. He subsequently informed Judy he didn't wish to complete the available coaching sessions. She began to question what the problem was and was worried about possible consequences. She contacted her long-standing friends from her former employment in the human resources department to try to ensure that this wouldn't impact her contract.

Key challenges

- Judy had previously had a very successful career in the company. Her reputation and personal relationships were at risk while she re-entered that environment as a supplier.
- Judy needed to start somewhere, as all coaches do. She relied on her relationships with her former peers to gain access to new business and grow her practice; however these same relationships became a source of potential lack of trust from her coaching client.
- Judy was compensating for her lack of coaching experience, skills and capacity for creating and holding a coaching space. Building a partnership was difficult, due to it requiring a different mindset to what was needed when she was leading a department within a multinational company. Her self-confidence in her professional capacity was being depleted.

- Judy's usual approach was over-assertive, and this was evident in her way of being when in the coaching space. It impacted her confidence in her coaching capacity and the trusting and confident relationships with her coaching clients. They questioned her competency, skills and capacity. A vicious circle was created. The more the students/coaching clients challenged her, the more insecure, assertive and directive she became.

EXAMPLE ETHICAL IMPLICATIONS

- **Professionalism** – the coach over-relied on short courses and certificates to guide her practice. Her beginner's level of coaching competency and experience should have been acknowledged by her. Further training, mentoring and supervision would also have been necessary for her to flourish in her coaching practice, not only the business side of it.
- **Conflict of interest** – the coach was more concerned with her relationship with the sponsor, rather than with the coaching client, as her goal was to guarantee future business opportunities with her former employer.
- **Trust** – it was a well-known fact that the coach had long-standing personal relationships with people in the human resources department. The coach did not make a point of clarifying aspects such as confidentiality and roles to provide the coaching client with a safe enough space for the coaching relationship to evolve.

REFLECTIVE QUESTIONS FOR DISCUSSION

1. How can a coach draw on their previous work and business connections and maintain trust and safety in their coaching engagements resulting from such relationships?
2. What are the pathways for clients to right a perceived wrong in scenarios such as the above?
3. How can a coach in their early stages of practice guarantee they are representing themselves with integrity?

Reference

International Coaching Federation (ICF) (2020), Global Coaching Study: Executive Summary. Source: https://coachingfederation.org/app/uploads/2020/09/FINAL_ICF _GCS2020_ExecutiveSummary.pdf

Appendix A

Coaching and psychology bodies

Association of Coach Training Organizations (ACTO)
https://actoonline.org

Graduate School Alliance of Education in Coaching (GSAEC)
https://gsaec.org

International Society for Coaching Psychology
https://www.isfcp.info/

The Africa Board for Coaching, Consulting and Coaching Psychology
(ABCCCP)
https://www.abcccp.com

The Association for Coaching (AC)
https://www.associationforcoaching.com

The Association for Professional Executive Coaching and Supervision (APECS)
https://www.apecs.org

The Center for Credentialing and Education (CCE)
https://www.cce-global.org

The European Mentoring and Coaching Council (EMCC)
https://www.emccglobal.org

The Institute of Coaching at McLean, Harvard Medical School Affiliate (IOC)
https://instituteofcoaching.org/

The International Association of Coaching (IAC)
https://certifiedcoach.org

The International Coaching Community (ICC)
https://internationalcoachingcommunity.com

The International Coaching Federation (ICF)
https://coachingfederation.org

The Worldwide Association of Business Coaches (WABC)
https://wabccoaches.com

Psychology (coaching)

Australian Psychological Society (APS)
https://psychology.org.au

British Association for Counseling and Psychotherapy (BACP)
https://www.bacp.co.uk

Psychology Board Australia (AHPRA)
https://www.psychologyboard.gov.au

The American Psychological Association (APA)
https://www.apa.org

The British Psychological Society (BPS)
https://www.bps.org.uk

Coaching supervision

Association of Coaching Supervisors
https://www.associationofcoachingsupervisors.com

Appendix B
Associations and forums

Australian Association for Professional and Applied Ethics (AAPAE)
http://aapae.org.au/

Coaching Ethics Forum (CEF)
www.coachingethicsforum.com

Foundation for Professional Development
https://www.foundation.co.za/

Globethics: Global Ethics Forum
https://www.globethics.net/web/gef

Graduate School Alliance for Education in Coaching (GSAEC)
https://gsaec.org/

International Ethics Organizations: Centers and Organizations Working in
Business Ethics
https://www.bentley.edu/centers/center-for-business-ethics/resources/interna-
tional-ethics-organizations

Markkula Center for Applied Ethics
https://www.scu.edu/ethics/

Appendix C
Coaching codes of ethics

Association of Coach Training Organizations (ACTO)
https://actoonline.org/global-voice/ethics-news/

International Society for Coaching Psychology
https://www.isfcp.info/ethics/

The Africa Board for Coaching, Consulting and Coaching Psychology
(ABCCCP)
https://www.abcccp.com/services/#standards

The Association for Coaching (AC)
https://www.associationforcoaching.com/page/AboutCodeEthics

The Association for Professional Executive Coaching and Supervision (APECS)
https://www.apecs.org/apecs-ethical-stance

The Center for Credentialing and Education (CCE)
https://www.cce-global.org/credentialing/ethics/bcc

The European Mentoring and Coaching Council (EMCC)
https://www.emccglobal.org/leadership-development/ethics/

The International Association of Coaching (IAC)
https://certifiedcoach.org/about/ethics/

The International Coaching Community (ICC)
https://internationalcoachingcommunity.com/standards-and-ethics/

The International Coaching Federation (ICF)
https://coachingfederation.org/ethics/code-of-ethics

The Worldwide Association of Business Coaches (WABC)
https://wabccoaches.com/wabc-advantage/global-standards-and-ethics/

Index

Page numbers in **bold** refer to tables.

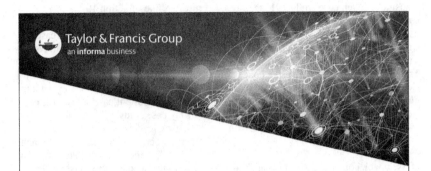

Printed in the United States
by Baker & Taylor Publisher Services